Windows® XP Media Center Edition 2004 PC For Dummies®

Cheat Sheet

P9-AGT-053

Unless otherwise noted, all commands are on the remote control.

Remote Control Commands in My TV

To do this	Press this
Play selected show	Play
Watch full screen	Live TV
Shrink viewing window from full screen	Esc on the keyboard
Freeze live TV (activate pause buffer recording)	Pause
To move from buffered TV to live	Live TV
Open the Onscreen Guide	Guide
Skip ahead or behind 12 hours in the Guide	Skip or Replay
Move up or down 7 channels in the Guide	CH/PG up or down
Jump back to last channel viewed	OK
To record the show you're watching	REC
To stop a recording	Stop or CH/PG
Select a channel	CH/PG or numeric buttons
View program information	More Info (or Details)
Adjust aspect ratio (16:9 monitors only)	More Info
Watch TV in a inset window	In an MCE window, select the Minimize button in the upper-right corner, then press Live TV on the remote
Display closed captioning	In an MCE window, select Settings, then TV, then Audio, then Captioning: option to select
Adjust volume	VOL

Remote Control Commands in Recorded TV

To do this	Press this
Stop a recorded program	Stop
Resume paused TV	Play
Fast forward (or rewind) movie 3 times normal speed	FWD (or REW). Press Play to resume at normal speed
Fast forward (or rewind) movie 40 times normal speed	FWD, FWD (or REW, REW). Press Play to resume at normal speed
Fast forward (or rewind) movie 250 times normal speed	FWD, FWD, FWD (or REW, REW, REW). Press Play to resume at normal speed
Replay 7 seconds back	Replay
Skip 29 seconds forward	Skip

For Dummies: Bestselling Book Series for Beginners

Windows® XP Media Center Edition 2004 PC For Dummies®

Cheat Sheet

Remote Control Commands in My Music

To do this	Press this
Play selected track	Play
Go to next song	Skip
Go to previous song	Replay
Fast forward 1.4 times normal speed	FWD. Press Play to resume at normal speed
Fast forward 5 times normal speed	FWD, FWD. Press play to resume at normal speed
Pause track	Pause. Press PAUSE again to resume
Stop playback	Stop
Turn off sound	MUTE
Adjust volume	VOL

Remote Control Commands in My Pictures

To do this	Press this
Go to next picture	Right arrow
Go to previous picture	Left arrow
Fast forward	FWD
Pause slide show and music (if playing)	Pause. Press Pause again to resume
Stop slide show	Stop
Enter selected menu item or show selected picture	OK

Remote Control Commands in My Video and Play DVD

To do this	Press this
Play a video or DVD	Play
Pause a video or DVD	Pause
Resume a paused video or DVD	Pause or Play
Fast forward (or rewind) 3 times normal speed	FWD (or REW). Press Play to resume at normal speed
Fast forward (or rewind) 40 times normal speed	FWD, FWD (or REW, REW). Press Play to resume at normal speed
Fast forward (or rewind) 250 times normal speed	FWD, FWD, FWD (or REW, REW, REW). Press Play to resume at normal speed
Skip 29 seconds forward	Skip*
Replay 7 seconds back	Replay
Stop video	Stop
Frame-by-frame advance (or rewind)	Pause, FWD (or Pause, REW)

*Because some video file formats do not support fast forward and rewind, Skip and Replay are often the best controls to use. Press Skip to skip ahead 29 seconds. Note that some videos will skip to the end if you use this control.

For Dummies: Bestselling Book Series for Beginners

Windows® XP Media Center Edition 2004 PC

FOR DUMMIES®

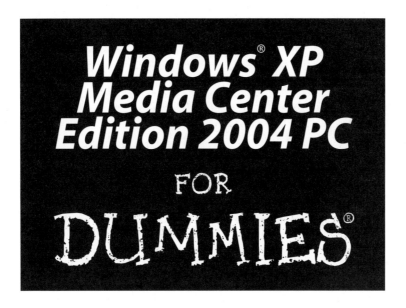

Windows® XP Media Center Edition 2004 PC FOR DUMMIES®

by Danny Briere and Pat Hurley

WILEY

Wiley Publishing, Inc.

Windows® XP Media Center Edition 2004 PC For Dummies®
Published by
Wiley Publishing, Inc.
111 River Street
Hoboken, NJ 07030-5774

www.wiley.com

Copyright © 2004 by Wiley Publishing, Inc., Indianapolis, Indiana

Published by Wiley Publishing, Inc., Indianapolis, Indiana

Published simultaneously in Canada

For general information on our other products and services or to obtain technical support, please contact our Customer Care Department within the U.S. at 800-762-2974, outside the U.S. at 317-572-3993, or fax 317-572-4002.

Wiley also publishes its books in a variety of electronic formats. Some content that appears in print may not be available in electronic books.

Library of Congress Control Number: 2003114375

ISBN: 0-7645-4357-1

Manufactured in the United States of America

10 9 8 7 6 5 4 3 2 1

1B/QW/RR/QT/IN

 WILEY is a trademark of Wiley Publishing, Inc.

About the Authors

Danny Briere founded TeleChoice, Inc., a telecommunications consulting company, in 1985 and now serves as CEO of the company. Widely known throughout the telecommunications and networking industry, Danny has written more than one thousand articles about telecommunications topics and has authored or edited nine books, including *Internet Telephony For Dummies*, *Smart Homes For Dummies* (now in its second edition), *Wireless Home Networking For Dummies,* and *Home Theater For Dummies*. He is frequently quoted by leading publications on telecommunications and technology topics and can often be seen on major TV networks providing analysis on the latest communications news and breakthroughs. Danny lives in Mansfield Center, Connecticut, with his wife and four children.

Pat Hurley is a consultant with TeleChoice, Inc., who specializes in emerging telecommunications technologies, particularly all the latest access and home technologies, including wireless LANs, DSL, cable modems, satellite services, and home-networking services. Pat frequently consults with the leading telecommunications carriers, equipment vendors, consumer goods manufacturers, and other players in the telecommunications and consumer electronics industries. Pat is the coauthor of *Internet Telephony For Dummies*, *Smart Homes For Dummies*, *Wireless Home Networking For Dummies,* and *Home Theater For Dummies.* He lives in San Diego, California, with his wife and two smelly dogs.

Dedication

In the past few years, Danny has thanked his wife for being so understanding, his kids for helping Dad with his projects, his parents for investing in his education, his sister for her daily support at work, and a host of other friends, relatives, and business associates who make each book a success. One person whom Danny wants to thank in particular this time is Tom Redford, known to me as Mr. Redford when I was growing up in Richmond, Virginia. Tom was my scoutmaster, my employer, and many years later, my friend. He took me under his wing and introduced me to the way things really work in life. "Briere, how can someone so smart have so little common sense," he used to tell me all the time, and unfortunately, he was right. Tom didn't put up with my slick book smarts but rather challenged my lack of street smarts, whether I was navigating the furnaces and rats at his brick yard during a summer job or carrying the dutch oven to the top of a mountain on a camping trip. All of us need someone like Tom to whip the wimp out of us and challenge us to be something we would not otherwise become. To Tom, I owe my larger (yet still small) amount of common sense, the knowledge that sucking blood out of a snake bite really does not work, and the ability to describe how bricks are made. Oh yeah, and a much stronger and more thoughtful character. We all need a Tom Redford when we're growing up, and I hope I can have such an effect on some smart yet stupid young kid someday.

Pat thanks — well, *thanks* is insufficient but the best that can be offered in this venue — his wife, Christine. She put up with four books in ten months, rooms full of gadgets and gizmos, cables strewn across the floor, espresso stains everywhere, missed Padres games, terrorized dogs, working vacations (oxymoron anyone?) — plus a house move. And she had to deal with all that while (in the words of Loretta Lynn) "One's on the way." Pat dedicates this book to her and to the schmoos (they know who they are). And he promises a real vacation, and soon!

Authors' Acknowledgments

You can't write a book alone. At least not a good one. You need help from all sorts of people — and we were lucky enough to find people who were generous with both their time and their knowledge.

We'd like to thank Tom Laemmel at Microsoft most of all. Tom is one of Microsoft's Product Managers, and he gave us unprecedented access to Microsoft's work on the latest version of Media Center, answered innumerable questions, introduced us to many Microsoft partners, and generally gave us what we needed. Thanks Tom.

Continuing the Microsoft theme, we'd also like to thank Ed Rich — he did the technical review of the book (right in the middle of finishing up the launch of Media Center's newest version) and kept us honest. Mark Pendergrast at Microsoft got us "in the door" and introduced us to a bunch of other helpful folks at Microsoft.

The folks at Gateway and Viewsonic outfitted us on the equipment end — thanks to Jason Martineck at Gateway and Trevor Bratton at Viewsonic. We've got nothing but good things to say about the Media Center PCs from these two companies and their technical support.

We'd also like the thank Paul Lefebvre at Sonic, Larry Fischer and Doug Barrett at Show & Tell, Deborah Hamilton at UEI, Ann Finnie at HP, Glen Chiswell at Mind Computers, Andy Marken and Linda Herd at InterVideo, Larry McDonnell Director of Public Relations at Sprint, Michael Scott at D-Link, Kelly Poffenberger at Toshiba, Roger VanOosten at InFocus, Lisa Hawes and Tracy Yen at NETGEAR, and Duval Hopkins (Shutterfly's PR representative).

Ed Ferris, TeleChoice's IT Director, deserves special thanks for supporting us and our numerous PCs (MCE and otherwise). Everybody should have their own Ed — someone they can run to when the latest PC experiment goes awry.

Finally, we'd like to thank Susan Pink, our project editor, and Melody Layne, our acquisitions editor at Wiley. They supported this project from the first "Here's an idea" stage right on through to completion, and gave us a needed kick in the rear end on occasion. Thanks for the support.

Publisher's Acknowledgments

We're proud of this book; please send us your comments through our online registration form located at www.dummies.com/register/.

Some of the people who helped bring this book to market include the following:

Acquisitions, Editorial, and Media Development

Project Editor: Susan Pink

Acquisitions Editor: Melody Layne

Technical Editor: Ed Rich

Editorial Manager: Carol Sheehan

Media Development Supervisor: Richard Graves

Editorial Assistant: Amanda Foxworth

Cartoons: Rich Tennant (www.the5thwave.com)

Production

Project Coordinator: Maridee Ennis

Layout and Graphics: Joyce Haughey, Stephanie D. Jumper, Heather Ryan, Janet Seib, Melanie Wolven

Proofreaders: Laura Albert, Andy Hollandbeck, Brian Walls, TECHBOOKS Production Services

Indexer: TECHBOOKS Production Services

Publishing and Editorial for Technology Dummies

    Richard Swadley, Vice President and Executive Group Publisher

    Andy Cummings, Vice President and Publisher

    Mary C. Corder, Editorial Director

Publishing for Consumer Dummies

    Diane Graves Steele, Vice President and Publisher

    Joyce Pepple, Acquisitions Director

Composition Services

    Gerry Fahey, Vice President of Production Services

    Debbie Stailey, Director of Composition Services

Contents at a Glance

Table of Contents

Introduction

*W*elcome to *Windows XP Media Center Edition 2004 PC For Dummies.* What a mouthful! But each word is important, nay, critical! This book is about Microsoft's next generation of operating system, Windows XP. But this is not an ordinary piece of software — Media Center 2004 is Microsoft's major push to merge the computing and entertainment domains in your home. In other words, Microsoft is getting involved in something called *convergence* — where two previously separate worlds (computing and entertainment) become one.

But wait, there's more — it's not just about the software, because this software comes matched with purpose-built PC hardware platforms: souped-up, totally-wired (and wireless), processor-rich computers that can drive your television and stereo as easily as they can download your e-mail.

This book tells you everything you want to know about these Media Center PCs. We're truly on the verge of a new revolution in the home, in which the power of your stereo, home theater, TV, VCR, CD/DVD player, radio receiver, satellite/cable receiver, and other entertainment devices are sucked into a powerful computing platform that can sit beside your TV.

About This Book

If you're thinking of purchasing a Media Center Edition (MCE) PC and installing it in your home, this is the book for you. Even if you've already purchased an MCE PC, this book will help you install and configure your entertainment system. What's more, we help you get the most out of your investment after it's up and running by connecting it to the Internet and your home network, if you have one.

With this book in hand, you'll have all the information you need about the following topics:

 ✔ Planning your home computing and entertainment system

 ✔ Evaluating and selecting a Media Center PC

 ✔ Installing and configuring Windows XP Media Center Edition in your home

 ✔ Watching and recording live TV

 ✔ Recording and playing DVDs and CDs

- ✔ Surfing the Internet connection on your TV
- ✔ Playing computer games over your home network
- ✔ Viewing photos in Media Center's slide-show mode
- ✔ Watching home videos (and videos downloaded from the Internet too)
- ✔ Archiving your home camcorder videos
- ✔ Connecting your PC to your home network

Conventions Used in This Book

Pat and Danny don't like to think of *anything* as conventional, but, alas, when your publisher asks for conventions, you must have conventions.

All Web site addresses have this type of font:

`www.microsoft.com`

When we introduce a new term for the first time, we put it in *italics*. We also remember to define what that term means, or refer you to a section of the book that describes it in greater detail.

We've also created a bit of a shorthand terminology to describe how you use your remote control to perform actions on the screen in Media Center. You'll notice that we use the term *select* a lot. When we say select, we mean that you should use the arrow buttons on the remote to move the cursor to that item and then press the OK button on the remote. This is a basic action that you'll perform almost every time you use Media Center, so we figured we'd give you some quick and easy instructions up front.

Keep in mind that you can also use the mouse and keyboard in Media Center, just like you would on any Windows XP PC.

If you're stumped by normal Windows XP operations, don't worry, lots of people are. Check out Andy Rathbone's *Windows XP For Dummies* (published by Wilcy Publishing, Inc.). It will help you get up-to-speed on all aspects of the Windows XP experience. Just e-mail Andy if Windows XP doesn't work — it's all his fault. (Just kidding, we don't know Andy but we hear he has a sense of humor.)

What You're Not to Read

If you already have a Media Center PC and are looking for help with the new features in the 2004 version, you can skip Parts I and II and go straight to Part III.

If you've cheated and already assembled your new MCE PC, but are having some problems finding your way around, go straight to Chapter 7 and 8, where we discuss how to customize and navigate MCE.

Other than that, feel free to move around the book at your desire. The *For Dummies* style enables you to dip in and out of the book as your attention span permits.

Foolish Assumptions

Unlike other operating systems — which you can install on your existing PC, as long as they meet some basic requirements — Windows XP Media Center Edition requires a specific hardware setup. At the time of this writing, the hardware was available from only 12 PC vendors (listed in Chapter 3). These PCs meet strict system specifications that Microsoft provides only to the PC vendors who build MCE PCs.

Microsoft has put a lot of effort into refining Windows XP Media Center Edition so that it can run on less powerful and therefore lower-priced machines. So we expect to see many more inexpensive MCE PCs hit the market soon. (As of this writing, HP just announced the first MCE PC under $1,000.)

You can't buy XP Media Center Edition software in a store without the hardware, so you can't load it on an existing PC. You have to buy a new system — at least now.

You don't need a separate TV set to run MCE. Instead, you can display it on a monitor. You also don't need a receiver or other stereo components except speakers. However, MCE is compatible with most standard entertainment gear, connecting to them through RCA composite, S-video, coaxial cable, and other interfaces.

How This Book Is Organized

This book is organized into five parts. The chapters are presented in a logical order — from buying and installing your Media Center Edition PC to using it. You should feel free to also use the book as a reference, reading the chapters in any order you want.

Part I: Introducing the Media Center Edition PC

The first part of the book is a primer on evaluating, buying, and installing your Media Center PC. If you've never seen an MCE computer in action — much less attempted to configure one — this part of the book provides all the background information and techno-geek lingo that you need to feel comfortable. Chapter 1 presents the general concepts surrounding Microsoft's software; Chapter 2 looks under the hood of your customized PC and discusses key PC technology that will drive your decision about which MCE PC to buy from the available vendors. Chapter 3 walks you through that purchase process and makes sure you get the best bang for the buck!

Part II: Integrating Your Media Center PC

The second part of the book helps you set up your Media Center PC and connect it to all your home audio, video, and networking components. You get help in deciding what to connect to the PC and where to put what in your home. By the end of Part II, you'll have connected your PC to all your entertainment gear as well as to the Internet — laying the foundation to serious fun ahead.

Part III: Using XP Media Center Edition

Part III discusses how to use your MCE PC. Whether you want to watch TV or play your home movies, this part of the book explains how to access, play and record all types of audio, video, and photographic content. We cover each of the major media capabilities of Windows XP MCE: MCE-driven TV, audio, photos, DVDs, and home videos, as well as some third-party applications.

Part IV: Connecting to the Rest of Your House

The first chapter in this part introduces you to the concept of whole-home networking. The next chapter looks at ways to extend your PC around the house wirelessly, including the latest in low-cost wireless access points.

Part V: The Part of Tens

Part V provides three top-ten lists that we think you'll find interesting We describe ten neat things you can add to your Windows XP MCE PC to give extra oomph to your entertainment dollar. In the next chapter, we don our sooth-sayer's hat and list ten things to expect from Windows XP Media Center Edition in the near future. We close out the part with ten neat places to go on the Internet to show off your newfound capabilities.

Appendix

In the appendix, we help you tackle the sometimes difficult task of connecting your Windows XP MCE PC to all the home-entertainment equipment it's been designed to work with: TV, cable and satellite set-top box, home-theater receiver, surround-sound speakers, and more. We use lots of clear before-and-after pictures to show you how you can get an MCE PC into almost any kind of home-entertainment setup — whether you have a simple antenna and TV or a compli-cated digital surround-sound home-theater system.

Icons Used in This Book

These days, everyone is hyper-busy, with no time to waste. To help you find especially useful nuggets of information in this book, we've marked the infor-mation with little icons in the margin. The following icons are used in this book:

This icon is your clue that you should take special note of the advice that you find there — this is essential information. Bottom line: You'll accomplish the task more effectively if you remember this information.

Computers are high-tech toys that make use of some pretty complicated technology. For the most part, however, you don't need to know how it all works. The Technical Stuff icon identifies the paragraphs that you can skip if you're in a hurry or just don't care to know. If you're a bit geeky like us, however, you may *want* to read this stuff.

As you can probably guess, the Tip icon calls your attention to information that will save you time and maybe money. You might want to skim through the book, reading the tips.

The little bomb in the margin should alert you to pay close attention and tread softly. You don't want to waste time or money correcting a problem that you could have avoided in the first place. Definitely pay attention to warnings.

We're almost entirely devoted to using the remote control and the special 10-foot interface that Media Center provides. (It's called a 10-foot interface because it's designed to let you sit on the sofa, 10 feet away from the screen, while using your MCE PC.) But some features and functions of the MCE PC require you to get off the couch and sit in front of your computer with the mouse and keyboard. To reduce confusion, we use this special XP icon to tell you when you need to leave Media Center's interface and perform an action in the traditional XP interface.

Where to Go from Here

Where you should go next in this book depends on where you are in the process of buying, installing, configuring, and using your Windows XP Media Center Edition PC. If computers and the Media Center Edition of XP in particular are new to you, we recommend that you start at the beginning with Part I. When you feel comfortable with computing terminology, or you just get bored with the discussion, move on to the chapters in Part II about connecting the PC to all your home-entertainment and networking gear. When you have your system installed and interconnected, Part III will help you start using it straightaway. Part IV gives you the most useful and whole-home ways to use your MCE PC — something we highly recommend to get the most bang for your buck.

To begin, just point your remote control to this part of the page and press the Play button. (And if you really did that just now, make sure your kids help you with each step of the installation!)

If you find that you just don't get the answer you want in this book, drop us an e-mail at dummies@telechoice.com. Everyone in TeleChoice knows who the dummies are in the company, so the message will find its way to us.

Part I
Introducing the Media Center Edition PC

The 5th Wave By Rich Tennant

"Philip come quick! David just used Media Center PC to connect the amp and speakers to his air-guitar."

In this part . . .

Microsoft (and its partners in the PC business) looked hard at what home PC users want to do with their computers, and came up with an entirely new way of looking at the PC: the Windows XP Media Center Edition 2004 PC. The MCE PC does all the stuff that any old Windows XP PC can do — send and receive e-mail, surf the Web, word processing, spreadsheets, games, and so on — but it adds to the equation a unique new way of using the PC as a home-entertainment device. With an MCE PC, you'll find that dealing with digital media — whether it be music, TV, movies, radio, photographs, and even home movies — is easier, faster, and just plain better.

In this part of the book, we walk you through the basics of the Media Center Edition interface. Although MCE is easy to use, it's also quite a bit different than anything you've ever seen on your PC. Then we talk about the pieces and parts that make an MCE PC different than the garden-variety PCs that you're probably used to. Finally, we provide detail about the different MCE PCs on the market today, giving you some guidance on how to choose the one that's right for you.

Chapter 1

All about Windows XP Media Center Edition

• •

• •

*W*indows *XP Media Center Edition 2004.* It's a long name, so we're going to call it just *MCE* most of the time. But it's also a descriptive name. Let's break it down into its constituent parts, shall we?

✔ **Windows:** Yep, it's a Microsoft Operating System (OS), so it works on PCs using Intel or similar AMD chips and motherboards, the main components of a PC. But (and this is an important *but*), not all standard Windows PCs can run MCE. You need a special PC that meets the rigorous requirements of MCE — you can't just install MCE on your existing PC.

✔ **XP:** This is the latest version of Windows (released in 2002), with an improved user interface (it's a lot more colorful), greater performance (it goes faster), and increased reliability.

✔ **Media Center Edition:** Not only can MCE computers do all the normal computing stuff that any version of Windows XP can do — Web surfing, e-mail, report writing, and so on — but Microsoft has added enhanced functionality for managing, editing, and playing back various forms of electronic media such as TV, movies, music, home video, and digital photographs.

✔ **2004:** This is the most recent edition of the Windows XP MCE platform, and this book contains all the latest and greatest info about what you need to know. We're part of the beta team for the MCE platform, so you're getting the straight scoop here!

What's new in 2004?

Before Windows XP MCE 2004, there was one prior version, the original XP MCE 2002 program. Some of the improvements in the 2004 version follow:

✔ New online capabilities with the Online Spotlight module, so you can access online media without leaving the Media Center interface

✔ A new radio tuner interface (and related hardware) that lets you listen to FM radio stations on your MCE PC and buffer up to 30 minutes of live radio for playback later

✔ The capability to record CDs to your hard drive directly in the Media Center interface instead of using Windows Media Player

✔ Enhanced 16:9 support to take advantage of the new TV screen acreage provided by today's latest wide-screen TVs

✔ The capability to prioritize your scheduled TV recordings, in case of a conflict

✔ Advanced photo management that enables you to view slide shows as well as reduce red-eye, adjust contrast, rotate, and zoom your favorite pictures in MCE

Beyond these changes, the folks at Microsoft have spent a lot of time making general improvements and upgrades so that MCE works faster and more reliably. They've also completed some serious work on the TV capabilities of MCE PCs, with a bunch of new software upgrades that make the MCE experience look even better when you hook up your MCE PC to your big-screen TV.

This is just the tip of the iceberg. There'll be so many ooohs and ahhhhs emanating from your living room, you'd swear the Temptations joined the party.

Media management and display are at the heart of MCE. Its full-screen interface and handheld remote control enable you to sit across the room and use the MCE PC like a piece of gear from your home theater. MCE takes the PC to a whole new realm — and may very well take the PC to a whole new *room* — in your house.

Everything about Windows XP Media Center Edition is special, advanced, enhanced, entranced, romanced . . . geez we can get carried away! It's that neat.

What's Special about XP Media Center Edition?

An MCE PC is a high-end machine, with more features and faster processors than regular Windows PCs, as well as some specialized parts for media functionality. The only big differences you might notice, however, are the screen (which is usually larger), the larger and more powerful speakers, and perhaps the general speediness of the machine. (MCE PCs have the fastest Pentium processors and the biggest, baddest graphics chips in existence — we talk about these in Chapter 2.)

You can't add MCE software (the MCE OS, in other words) to just any old PC. In fact, *you* can't add it to any PC you own, even if the PC meets all the equipment and performance criteria we're about to discuss. Microsoft doesn't sell MCE this way. Primarily for reasons of reliability and performance, Microsoft has decided that MCE will be available only preinstalled on PCs that meet its minimum specifications. This requirement creates a known environment in which Microsoft can do its operating system magic, without trying to make MCE compatible with the millions of equipment permutations that more general versions of Windows must deal with.

The first time you fire up an MCE PC, it will probably look like any other Windows XP PC. You'll see the standard XP desktop interface, with the big green Start menu at the bottom left.

You can ignore the MCE features and use your MCE PC as a high-powered PC. You can surf the Web using Internet Explorer or your Web browser of choice. You can check e-mail with Outlook Express. If you have Microsoft Office installed, you can work on that spreadsheet of widgets or write that overdue paper (or, in our case, book).

But if you look on the desktop or between the sofa cushions, you'll see a shiny new remote control, as shown in Figure 1-1. If you've already installed your MCE PC, go ahead and press the start button. (It's the green button in the middle of the remote.) The start button launches the Media Center interface, which is designed to let you sit away from your computer and use it as an entertainment device, not a data terminal.

We can't guarantee that your remote will look exactly like the one in Figure 1-1. But somewhere on your remote you *will* find the arrow buttons, the OK button, and the Start button.

The first time you open Media Center on your MCE PC, it prompts you to go through a 10- to 15-minute process of setting preferences. If you want to do this now, skip ahead to Chapter 7, where we describe this process.

You might be tempted to cancel out of this process and go straight into the Media Center Start menu with the factory default settings in place. We *do not* recommend skipping the Media Center Set-up Wizard. Your TV programming guide will not be installed, your remote control may not work to change channels on your set-top box, and other features may simply not function. Complete the wizard. (Patience, patience.)

Figure 1-1:
Sit on the
sofa and
control your
MCE PC.

The Media Center Interface

The Media Center interface, shown in Figure 1-2, is the key to using MCE — it's what differentiates MCE from plain Windows XP. The Media Center interface is designed for "lean back" computer use. The text on the screen is big and can be read easily while you sit in your comfy chair across the room.

The Media Center interface does away with many of the normal Windows interface systems that require a mouse. For example, you won't find the pull-down menus that normal Windows XP (and XP applications) use in its menu bar. In fact, you won't find a menu bar (or a Start button) at all. Everything is laid out in a linear and hierarchical manner for ease of use with a remote control (though you can use your mouse as well, if you want).

Pretty much everything you'll ever want to do with MCE can be accomplished with the four arrow, or directional, buttons on the remote (up, down, left, and right) and the OK button. The MCE was designed for the remote control, not the keyboard. In fact, some things are downright hard to do without the remote control, such as access the More Info data about a movie.

To select a menu item, use the arrow buttons to reach the menu item (it becomes highlighted in green), and then press the OK button.

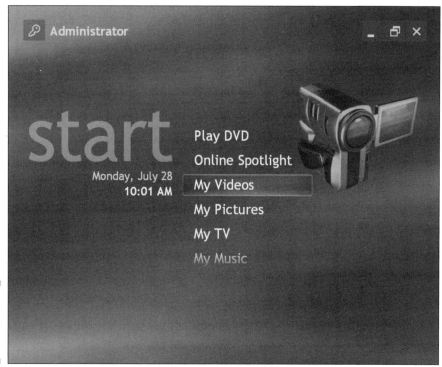

Figure 1-2:
Everything
in MCE
starts here.

If a menu item has choices below it, they appear when you select the main menu item. To select one of the subitems, simply use the arrow buttons to reach it, and press the OK button.

Want to look at that neat TV image in the little window to the side? No problem. Use the arrow buttons to reach the image (it becomes highlighted in green) and press OK. Now you're watching TV. Cool.

The Media Center interface is a lot like the interface you might see when digging around in the setup menus on a TV or a home-theater receiver attached to a TV, except that MCE is a lot more user friendly. We will now boldly predict that it will take you all of two minutes of messing around with the arrow buttons and the OK button to get the hang of making choices in MCE.

If you ever get lost in the Media Center interface, start pressing the Back button on the remote. You'll eventually return to the top of the menu hierarchy — the interface shown in Figure 1-2.

In the remainder of this section, we talk in general terms about what each choice — we call them *modules* — on the main MCE page is all about. In Part III, we describe each one in detail, telling you how it works and how you can get the most out of it.

What Media Center can't do today — but will do soon!

Microsoft is in the second iteration of Media Center Edition, and it's adding features as fast as it can. Here are a few that we hope it adds soon:

✔ Devices that let you remotely display your MCE interface on TVs and other displays, so you can control and use your MCE PC from anywhere in the home

✔ Devices that let you use the MCE wirelessly, without making Ethernet or other connections

✔ More support for online gaming

✔ The capability to create (burn) CDs and DVDs directly from the Media Center interface

✔ More options for purchasing and downloading online content (such as music) in the Media Center interface

Read Chapter 18 to find out more about the future functions and features of MCE.

My TV module

One of the coolest things that every MCE PC can do is help you watch television. And we're not just talking about watching TV the old-fashioned way — sitting in front of that glowing box, waiting like a sheep for a show to come on. Nope, MCE lets you move into the future and take control of your TV habit. (Admit it, you have a TV habit — everyone does!) All you have to do is select the My TV module in MCE.

With MCE, you can do the following TV stuff:

✔ Watch live TV (the old-fashioned way) on your computer monitor or on a TV hooked up to your MCE PC

✔ Keep track of what's on, and what *will* be on, with an on-screen program guide

✔ Record and play back broadcast TV programs at your convenience

This last feature is perhaps the most compelling. After all, you can watch TV on any old $199 box from the warehouse store. And if you have a satellite dish or digital cable, you probably have an on-screen program guide. But MCE includes a full-featured *PVR* (personal video recorder) with just about all the functions of the TiVo or ReplayTV device that a small number of TV-crazy folks have in their homes.

Like those other PVRs, MCE dispenses with the bulky and inconvenient tapes that VCRs use and instead records TV digitally on a computer hard drive. The advantages over a regular VCR are immense. In addition to storing a ton of TV shows, you can use the PVR function of MCE to pause, rewind, and fast forward live TV while you're watching it.

No longer do you have to rely on broadcasters for timing your snack and bathroom breaks. Press a button and walk away — when you come back, catch up where you left off. Or watch that last-second three-pointer again, right now, without waiting for Dickie V. and the boys in the ESPN truck to cue up the replay.

Figure 1-3 shows the main My TV interface. We talk about how to use it in much more detail in Chapter 9.

Radio module

Newer MCE PCs have begun to ship with an FM radio tuner that does for radio what My TV does for TV: gives you control over what you listen to and when. With the MCE Radio module, shown in Figure 1-4, you can use the MCE interface and the remote control to tune in to your favorite stations, and pause and record live radio broadcasts.

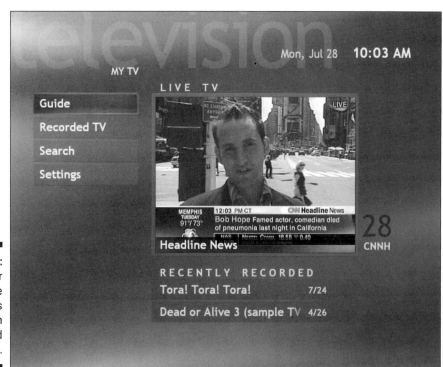

Figure 1-3:
Find your favorite shows and watch or record them here.

Figure 1-4:
Tune in
to Rush
Limbaugh or
Limp Bizkit
with your
MCE Radio
module.

You can run to the kitchen for some more mineral water (or whatever your beverage preference) while your favorite talk show drones on. On your return, you can pick up listening where you left off. The Radio module can record up to 30 minutes of live radio. Like any digital radio, the Radio module lets you scan for stations or directly enter the frequency of the station you want to tune to. You can also set up presets, so you can quickly find and tune to your favorite stations.

My Music module

Because you're interested in buying an MCE PC or have already bought one, we bet you're already into the PC music world. If you're not, are you in for a treat. People have been recording their favorite music on their PCs for years now — and online music download systems such as Napster (now dead and gone) and Kazaa (www.kazaa.com) have received tons of press (and lawsuits) as people share music online (illegally). Now legal downloading options such as a new version of Napster and the Rhapsody Music Service (www.listen.com) are taking off as well.

In other words, computer-based music is an official BIG DEAL. And the MCE My Music module makes handling music easy, no matter how many albums and songs you have on your computer. Figure 1-5 shows My Music's main menu.

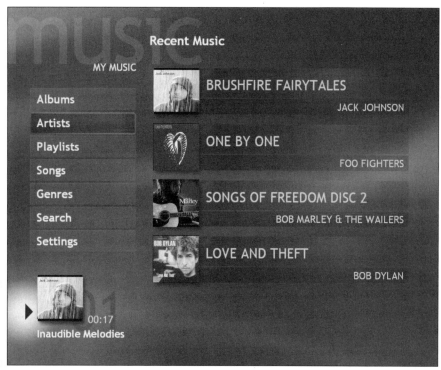

Figure 1-5:
Access
all your
music here.

My Music lets you do several things:

✔ **Organize your music:** You can navigate your music collection by sorting your MP3 files, Windows Media files, and CDs by song title, album title, and artist. You can categorize your music by genre (such as rock, punk, and blues) and create playlists of favorite songs.

✔ **Search for music:** If you have a *ton* of music on your MCE PC (we do!), you can easily search for a song, an artist, or an album name using the remote control or the keyboard.

✔ **Copy CDs to the MCE PC hard drive:** Adding your favorite CDs to your music collection is dead simple with your MCE PC — just a few presses on the remote, and your CD's audio tracks are downloaded to your MCE hard drive. In addition, the song titles, album title, and even the CD cover art are downloaded automatically from databases on the Internet. Not bad.

✔ **Buy music online:** Pressing a button on your remote automatically sends you to a Web page (outside the MCE interface) that lets you buy more music from a particular artist.

And, of course, you can use My Music to play back music through the speakers attached to your MCE PC or through your stereo or home-theater system, if you have one attached to your MCE PC.

Windows XP Media Center Edition makes use of Microsoft's powerful Media Player 9 functionality — Microsoft's standalone music software. Windows Media Player 9 is one of the few examples of something you *can't* access from the Media Center interface. Sorry, but you'll have to grab your wireless keyboard and mouse and tap away in the normal Windows XP interface to load your music onto your MCE PC. Then you can jump back into Media Center to organize and play your music. We tell you more about Media Player 9 and how to hook up your stereo to your MCE PC in Chapter 5 and how to take advantage of your My Music module in Chapter 10.

My Pictures module

Digital cameras have revolutionized the world of picture taking. No longer do you have to wait for your pictures — not even the One Hour Photo shop is fast enough compared to digital photography. Snap a picture, plug your camera into your MCE PC, and instant gratification. Can't beat that, huh?

Although you can download digital pictures to just about any PC, MCE's My Pictures module makes it even easier to deal with your photographic art (or poorly composed snapshots). With My Pictures, you can

- ✔ View any pictures you've downloaded from your camera to your MCE PC's My Pictures folder (the default folder for downloaded pictures). Pictures can be viewed in full-screen mode, zoomed, and *panned* (meaning you can zoom in on certain segments of the picture and then move your view around to other zoomed parts of the picture).

- ✔ View pictures stored on removable media such as Compact Flash or SmartMedia cards, the "digital film" used by many digital cameras. Many MCE PCs have built-in readers for this type of media; you can also add media readers through your USB port.

- ✔ Watch slide shows of your favorite pictures on the MCE PC monitor or your TV. You can even add your favorite background music from My Music.

- ✔ Correct pictures, so that those poorly composed and lit snapshots look like something your megabuck wedding photographer took. My Pictures can automatically analyze and optimize your photos.

- ✔ Print your pictures with just a few presses of the remote.

- ✔ Adjust brightness (resuscitate those dark pictures) and remove red-eye (so long, Terminator).

Figure 1-6 shows the My Pictures main menu. We delve into the digital darkroom and your MCE PC in Chapter 11.

My Videos module

If you have kids — Danny's got four, so he's speaking from experience here — you have a video camera. Or three video cameras. And if you're like most amateur videographers, you have three good minutes buried in a ten-minute tape that also includes footage of your feet, the back of your spouse's head, and one blinding close-up of the sun. MCE comes to your rescue with the My Videos module, shown in Figure 1-7.

My Videos lets you store your videos on your MCE PC's hard drive just like any other kind of media file. All MCE PCs come with USB, USB 2.0, and FireWire 1394 (we explain these systems in Chapter 3), which enable you to connect your digital camcorder to your MCE PC and import your video.

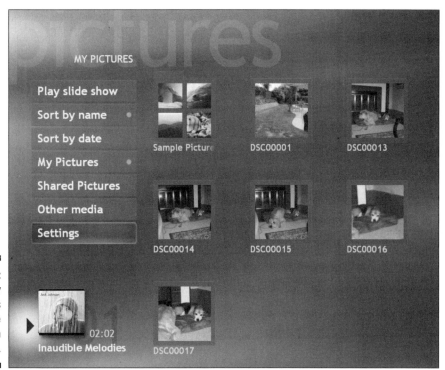

Figure 1-6:
Display photos and slide shows in My Pictures.

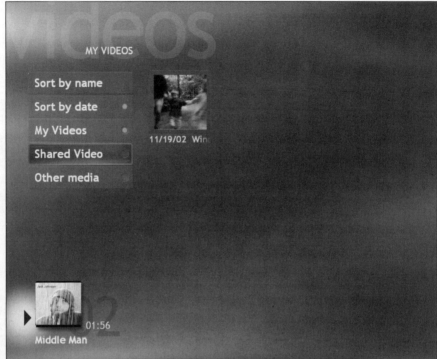

Figure 1-7:
Break out
the wine
and cheese,
we're
watching
home
videos in
My Videos.

Media Center PCs include a cool Microsoft program called Windows Movie Maker 2 that lets you edit and combine video clips into finished videos for playback later. My Videos then lets you organize and watch these videos on your computer monitor or TV.

To use Windows Movie Maker 2, you need to exit the Media Center interface and work in the regular Windows XP interface. After you've saved your masterpiece, you can jump back into Media Center to organize and play your movies.

Play DVD module

Just as PVRs (mentioned in the "My TV" section) have pretty much made the VCR obsolete for recording TV programming, DVDs (digital video discs) have made the old VCR into the video equivalent of a buggy whip for playing back prerecorded movies. And now that many people have begun to buy their own DVD recorders, DVDs can even be created at home.

Well, MCE didn't miss the boat when it comes to the DVD — all MCE PCs have a DVD player, and MCE itself includes the Play DVD module.

Play DVD lets you do the following:

- ✔ Play DVDs on your MCE's monitor or your TV

- ✔ Play DVDs in a window while you're doing other things with your MCE PC

- ✔ Access detailed information about a DVD (title, length, rating, and so on)

- ✔ Turn on parental controls to keep the kids from watching *Memento* when they should be watching *SpongeBob SquarePants.*

- ✔ Stretch, zoom, and letterbox your DVD to best fit the size and shape of your TV

Play DVD also unleashes the powerful video graphics chip in your MCE PC to provide a high-resolution, non-interlaced display of your DVDs. (If that makes no sense and you have a DVD in hand, candles lit, and a date on the way over, hurry up and skip ahead to Chapter 12!)

Online Spotlight module

Perhaps the biggest leap forward in Windows XP Media Center Edition 2004 is the addition of `Mediacenter.com` online content into the Media Center interface. The Online Spotlight module of the Media Center interface lets you use your Internet connection to do the following:

- ✔ Keep up with the latest in Media Center news, tips, and tricks

- ✔ Watch movie trailers and keep up to date on movie news

- ✔ Listen to hundreds of Internet radio stations

- ✔ Download music, movies, and photographs

In previous versions of MCE, you had to do all online activities in the regular XP interface (up close and personal to your PC, using your mouse). Online Spotlight uses a special interface designed — like the rest of the Media Center interface — for viewing and remote control from across the room. This means you can sit back and use your remote control to browse and use online content.

We can't show you a picture of Online Spotlight because Microsoft and its partners were still putting the finishing touches on this module when we sent the book to the printers. But we've used beta versions of Online Spotlight, and trust us — it's really cool.

Online Spotlight content — like any online content — is best experienced when using a broadband Internet connection such as DSL or a cable modem. We talk about these connections more in Chapter 6. Trust us on this. If you're shelling out more than a thousand bucks on an MCE PC, it's worthwhile to spend a few extra bucks a month on a fast Internet connection.

Big Screen and Big Sound, All over the House

For many users, MCE PC is the primary means of viewing and listening to content. In other words, many people use the MCE PC's computer monitor and computer speakers to watch and listen to digital media. This works great if your MCE PC is in your dorm room or home office.

But if you're like us and have your MCE PC installed in your family room or home theater or media room, you might want to branch out to a bigger display. Well, MCE has you covered, because one key attribute of all MCE PCs is that you can connect them to a big-screen TV and a home audio system for a bigger, faster, and louder media experience. All MCE PCs have video outputs and analog or digital audio outputs that can drive your TV and audio system to new heights! We talk about the hardware specifics in Chapter 2.

We highly recommend that you connect your MCE PC to your TV and audio system. (Danny has his MCE PC hooked up to his InFocus projector TV system, so he can watch MCE videos and DVDs on a really, really big screen.)

Media Center PCs also come with built-in Ethernet cards, so you can connect the MCE PC to a home network. We talk about the basics of wired home-networking options in Chapter 15 and wireless options in Chapter 16. For the details on installing a home network, see our books *Smart Homes For Dummies* or *Wireless Home Networking For Dummies* (both published by Wiley Publishing, Inc.).

In the future, we expect Microsoft to announce a lot of cool new products that will take advantage of home networks. In particular, we think that MCE PC will soon be used as the *media server,* enabling you to access MCE PC-stored media from all sorts of devices and places in your home.

Where to Get Your Media Center PC

Buying a *Media Center PC* (that's what PC makers call them) is easy. Microsoft and its partners have taken the guesswork out of the process by creating PCs that meet all MCE requirements.

More cool MCE 2004 features

As they say on TV, "But wait — there's more!" Microsoft squeezed a lot of cool little new features in the 2004 release of Media Center Edition. We discussed a few of the big ones previously in this chapter, in the "What's new in 2004?" sidebar. Some of the other features that we think make the upgrade to 2004 worthwhile include the following:

✔ **Active Accessibility 2.0:** Improved accessibility for folks who need help with reading, hearing, or physically accessing their MCE PC.

✔ **Display Calibration Wizard:** Provides an improved experience for setting up your TV to work with MCE.

✔ **Set-top box learning mode:** Makes it easier to connect different TV set-top boxes to the MCE PC.

✔ **Automatic digital media library synchronization:** MCE automatically searches for media on your MCE PC or network.

✔ **Phone call notification:** On MCE PCs with the right hardware (modem), caller ID information appears on your TV or MCE PC display.

✔ **High-contrast schemes:** The colors on the screen have been redesigned for easier reading from across the room.

✔ **Automatic Guide updates:** MCE can automatically download program guide information, whenever your computer is connected to the Internet.

✔ **Record on or around:** For programs that infuriatingly start a minute or two early (or end late), you can adjust MCE to start or stop recording early or late.

✔ **Enhanced record history:** Media Center keeps track of all recorded TV and lets you know what happened if there was a mistake — so you don't make it again

✔ **Now Playing (music):** No matter what function of Media Center you're using, you'll always see an on-screen display of the music you're listening to

✔ **Guide filtering:** MCE lets you filter the TV program guide by categories — so you can show, for example, all movies or all sporting events

✔ **Silent Personal Video Recording (PVR) functionality:** Media Center will wake your MCE PC from standby to record schedule shows and will leave the audio and video displays off so that recording doesn't interfere with other work you're doing on the MCE PC

✔ **Auto-playlists:** MCE automatically creates music playlists based on your listening habits

✔ **Full-screen visualizations:** MCE visualizations (the cool screen effects that correspond to music you are listening to) are now full-screen.

✔ **Print pictures:** You can print pictures directly in Media Center, without going into the traditional Windows XP interface.

You can get a Media Center PC from the following vendors:

- ✔ ABS Computer Technologies (www.abspc.com)
- ✔ Cyberpower System (www.cyberpowersystem.com)
- ✔ Dell (www.dell.com)
- ✔ Gateway (www.gateway.com)
- ✔ HP (www.shopping.hp.com)
- ✔ iBuypower (www.ibuypower.com)
- ✔ MIND Computer Products (www.mind.ca)
- ✔ Northgate (www.northgate.com)
- ✔ Sony (www.sony.com)
- ✔ Tagar Systems (www.tagarsystems.com)
- ✔ Toshiba (csd.toshiba.com)
- ✔ Touch Systems (www.touch-systems.ca)
- ✔ Viewsonic (www.viewsonic.com)
- ✔ ZT Group (www.ztgroup.com)

Microsoft works with a lot of different computer vendors, so this list will change (mainly with the addition of other manufacturers). For an update on who's making Media Center PCs, go to Microsoft's MCE home page, where you'll find links to all current vendors:

```
www.microsoft.com/windowsxp/mediacenter/default.asp
```

For more on where to get MCE PCs and how to buy them, see Chapter 3.

Chapter 2

A Look Inside a Media Center PC

. . . .

In This Chapter

▶ Dissecting your Media Center PC

▶ Looking at the connections

▶ Revving up with a fast processor

▶ Enhancing video

▶ Augmenting audio

▶ Rounding up the spare parts

. . . .

*I*n this chapter, you find out about the key elements that make up your Media Center PC — in other words, the hardware itself. (We talk about the software side of things in Chapter 1.) We talk about how the MCE PC is outfitted with input and output jacks compatible with your stereo, TV, VCR, and other home-entertainment gear. We explain how super-fast processors make sure your DVDs are not jerky and your real-time TV records high-quality images.

You then look at the capabilities added to enhance your video and audio experience. We wrap up with a discussion of other notable improvements that super-size your PC for media use. By the end of the chapter, you'll have a solid understanding of the key components in any Media Center PC — background necessary for Chapter 3, where we talk about how to decide which MCE PC is the best for you.

A PC as an Entertainment Device?

A Media Center PC embodies the evolution of the home PC from a powerful computing platform to a full-fledged digital media *hub* — a central gateway that consolidates your entertainment choices and allows you to access those choices with a single remote control. Through your MCE PC, you can control audio and video signals, DVDs and CDs, TVs and computer monitors, keyboards and remote controls. Anything you can do with your home-entertainment system, you can now do through your MCE PC. Way cool!

Media Center PCs are entertainment PCs because they're outfitted with the following:

- **Mid- to high-end processor:** Media Center PCs sport the faster processors — at this writing, HP is shipping its Media Center PC with a 3.06-GHz Intel Pentium 4 processor. Wow!

- **Tons of memory:** MCE PCs have a minimum 256MB RAM (*random access memory*); most have 512MB or more.

- **High-capacity drives:** All MCE PCs ship with at least an 80GB hard drive. Viewsonic's M2000 PC ships with a 160GB drive — enough space for 140 hours of video or thousands upon thousands of audio tracks. In Chapter 3, we discuss just how large your hard drive should be.

- **CD and DVD drives:** All MCE PCs have an optical drive that can play back CDs and DVDs. Many can record CDs, and a few can even record DVDs.

- **Advanced audio/video and graphics interfaces:** MCE PCs have high-end audio and video cards that can handle digital audio and video — just like the chips inside a fancy home-theater receiver or a high-end digital television. The graphics card in an MCE PC can be used with both computer displays and televisions — at the same time. In MCE 2002 PCs, these graphics cards were typically members of the NVIDIA GeForce4 family of processors. MCE 2004 PCs will ship with either NVIDIA or ATI Radeon cards.

- **Surround sound speakers:** To fully enjoy your movie soundtracks, you're going to need surround sound, just like you get in the theater. Surround sound 5.1, its official designation, consists of five speakers — front left, front right, front center, rear left, and rear right — plus a subwoofer for those deep booms when something gets blown to bits. Various computer manufacturers have teamed with the leading speaker vendors, such as HP and Klipsch, and Gateway and SoundBlaster.

- **Expansion slots:** PCs are designed to grow up — they're like kids that way. So most desktop PCs have a bunch of expansion slots that enable you to add capabilities to the PC as your needs dictate. Laptop PCs, for reasons of space, have much less in the way of expansion. Most MCE PCs have the following types of expansion slots:

  - **Optical drive expansion slot:** This is a slot for a second optical drive, so you could, for example, have a CD recorder in one slot and a DVD recorder in the other.

  - **Hard drive expansion slot:** Many tower-style MCE PCs have a slot for a second hard drive for extra data storage.

  - **PCI expansion slots:** Most MCE PC internal cards connect to a PCI bus, which interconnects any internal cards and sends data between them and the CPU. Extra PCI expansion slots leave room for additional cards, such as wireless network cards.

- **Memory slots:** You can expand the RAM in the MCE PC by simply inserting a memory card. The number of open memory slots depends on what was installed when your MCE PC was built. Unless you bought 1GB RAM or more, you should have slots available for adding addition al RAM.

✔ **Networking connectivity:** All MCE PCs have at least an Ethernet port for connecting to a wired home network. Many have built-in wireless networking systems as well, so you can hook up to a standard 802.11 wireless network (more on this topic in Chapters 15 and 16).

In addition to these features, which are shared by many other computers, MCE PCs have a few unique requirements that Microsoft imposes on its MCE partner PC makers. These items are *not* found on your typical off-the-shelf PC. When you open your Media Center PC box, you're likely to find most or all of the following components to facilitate your entertainment experience:

✔ **A Media-Center-compatible remote control:** All MCE PCs come with an infrared (IR) remote control that lets you sit across the room and control your MCE PC's audio, video, and digital photography functions without using the keyboard or mouse. You can even record live TV with a single press of a button.

✔ **A remote infrared sensor:** All MCE PCs come with an IR sensor (usually connected to a USB port on the computer) that works with your remote control — the sensor picks up the IR (light) signals from the remote and sends them to the computer as commands. Many MCE PCs also include a capability for the IR sensor and remote control to pass standard commands (such as channel up or down) to your cable set-top box or digital satellite system (DSS) satellite receiver.

✔ **A TV tuner:** All MCE PCs connect to a TV antenna, a cable TV feed, or the output of a cable set-top box or satellite receiver for TV viewing. The TV tuner is used with some other elements of the MCE PC (such as the hardware encoder) for recording live TV.

✔ **A hardware or software encoder:** MCE PCs can record television programming onto your computer's hard drive for later playback and for neat features such as pausing live TV. A hardware encoder takes some of the load off the main CPU (the Pentium 4 or Athlon XP chip), making the recording and playback process work better and faster. The hardware encoder is a computer chip that converts video to and from a digital format known as MPEG. Some cards, like the ATI cards, use software encoding with a faster processor, instead of a hardware encoder.

✔ **A TV output:** Although you can watch TV on the standard PC monitor attached to your MCE PC, all MCE PCs can also be connected directly to a TV — both traditional analog TVs and newer digital (or *HDTV)* TVs — so you can enjoy your MCE content on the big screen.

✓ **A radio tuner card:** Some of the newest MCE PCs include an FM radio tuner that lets you pick up standard over-the-air FM broadcasts that you can listen to and record with your computer.

✓ **A digital audio output:** If you have a home-theater system and an A/V (audio/video) receiver with digital connections (like the ones you use with many DVD players), you can interconnect these entertainment devices to the audio outputs of most MCE PCs. This type of digital connection gives you higher-fidelity (better-sounding) audio, and lets you listen to digital surround-sound content in all its multichannel glory.

This 5.1 channel digital audio will work only during DVD playback. Media Center doesn't support 5.1 digital surround sound for TV, even if your TV provider (digital cable or satellite) offers it.

In Chapter 3, we describe in greater detail the bells and whistles — the speeds and feeds as they're called in the data-networking industry — of the MCE PCs on the market today.

Connections Galore on Your MCE PC

Assuming that you've purchased an MCE PC that includes a monitor and speakers, you can connect your MCE PC components together and start watching TV, recording CDs to your hard drive, and listening to those CDs. But your enjoyment options really multiply when you start using all the connections on your MCE PC to get more of your media into and off your computer.

Following is a list of just some of the hookups we think you might be interested in making. Don't worry if you don't understand some of these terms; we define them all shortly. You can do the following with a Media Center PC:

✓ Use a USB connection to connect a digital camera or scanner to your MCE PC to store, edit, and display digital pictures.

✓ Use that USB connection again to connect a color inkjet printer and make prints of photographs.

✓ Use the IEEE 1394, or FireWire, connection to download video from your digital video camera. Now you can finally do something with those home movies!

✓ Use the Line Out or Digital Out connections from your computer's audio system (the sound card) to connect your MCE PC to your home-theater or stereo system.

✓ Use the composite video, S-video, or VGA connections from your MCE PC's video card to hook up your TV.

✔ Use a 6-in-1 card reader to directly grab digital pictures from your digital camera, without having to tether the camera to the computer.

✔ Use the USB or FireWire ports to connect extra external hard drives to your MCE PC for even more storage space

✔ Use the Ethernet port to connect your MCE PC to your cable or DSL modem or to your home-computer network or LAN.

Those are only some of the connections you can make. We haven't mentioned all the inputs, such as the microphone input for recording your voice and the Audio In port for connecting audio sources such as cassette decks.

We've also not talked about the standard PC connection interfaces, such as parallel ports (for some older printers), serial ports (for some older mice and keyboards) and PS/2 ports (also for older mice and keyboards). Really, when you get right down to it, you can plug a lot of stuff into an MCE PC.

✔ **USB and USB 2.0:** *USB,* or *Universal Serial Bus,* is a connection technology that takes its name seriously. USB is used for just about every computer peripheral device you can buy these days: digital cameras, keyboards, mice, scanners, handheld PDAs, printers, audio speakers, pocket-sized USB storage devices, joysticks, and controllers for games. Heck, we've even seen USB-powered fans and night lights. Two kinds of USB systems are available:

  • USB is the older, slower version and can transmit data at a maximum speed of 12 Mbps (megabits per second), which is good enough for almost all uses except video.

  • The new-fangled *USB 2.0* rockets along at 480 Mbps — 40 times faster than USB — and is great for video cameras and portable and removable hard drives.

 USB 2.0 is fully *backward compatible* with regular USB, so you can plug either kind of device into either connection, and it will work. However, if you plug a USB 2.0 device into a regular USB port, it will transfer data only at the slower speed. Most MCE PCs have only USB 2.0 ports these days, but some have a few of each kind (the ports are labeled as such).

 An *external USB hub* adds extra USB interface ports to your PC. A four-port hub can connect four devices to a single USB port on the PC. You can get a USB hub from your local computer store. These are relatively inexpensive, with a four-port unit costing $20 to $30. You can stack (daisy-chain) these too, if you get a stackable hub.

✔ **IEEE 1394 (FireWire):** The IEEE (Institute of Electrical and Electronic Engineers) standards body approved *IEEE 1394* as an international standard, so all IEEE 1394 devices work together, regardless of which company made them. Apple Computer, which was a primary developer of this technology, named it *FireWire*. FireWire is a fast system (about 400 Mbps) that supports applications such as audio and video. You'll most likely see FireWire connections on digital camcorders and Apple's iPod music player. You might see FireWire also on a handful of devices such as CD burners and portable hard drives, though most vendors use USB 2.0 instead (because it's a bit cheaper for them to manufacture). All MCE PCs should have at least one FireWire port to support video cameras.

✔ **Line Out and Digital Out:** *Line Out* connections are basically identical to the connections on the back of a CD player — they're used with standard audio cables to carry audio signals (or *line-level* signals) to a receiver or an amplifier. Line-level audio connections are analog, so they plug right into the CD In or Aux In connectors on the back of your receiver.

Digital Out connections carry audio signals digitally — surprise! — and are connected to Digital In connectors on the back of a home-theater receiver. Using Digital Out provides you with the highest audio quality and best surround sound when listening to DVDs.

With some MCE PCs, the Digital Out connection may do double duty as a Line Out connection. You select which mode the connection uses by making a software adjustment. (We describe this process in Chapter 5.)

✔ **Composite video and S-video:** Televisions have several types of connections. An antenna or cable TV connection is the most common. The majority of newer TVs also have composite video and S-video connections.

- *Composite video* connections look just like audio Line Out connections and use a similar-looking composite video cable.

- *S-video* connections use a funky-looking multipin connector (shaped sort of like a house) to carry video signals.

- *VGA* connections, for the highest quality outputs, and higher resolutions. Higher end TVs and projectors generally have this option. You will need to use VGA for output to 16:9 TVs, 1280 x 720 resolution.

When you have a choice, use S-video because it almost always gives you a superior picture on your TV screen. The S-video cable uses separate wires to carry different parts of the TV picture, so it provides a crisper, clearer picture than composite video.

✔ **6-in-1 card reader:** Found on some MCE PCs, this device can accept all the different types of media cards (or digital "film") used by digital cameras. (We discuss these readers in more detail in Chapter 11.) This feature an be a real time saver, because instead of finding the cable and hooking up your camera to the computer, you just pop the card out and stick it in the reader. You can even stick your spare card in the camera and keep taking pictures while the others download to your MCE PC.

✔ **Ethernet:** *Ethernet* is the standard system used by nearly all computer networks (or LANs) for carrying data between and among computers. Ethernet is used also for connecting high-speed Internet modems to the computer — it's a useful system! An Ethernet jack looks like a phone jack on steroids. And basically it's just that: a phone jack that uses not four wires but eight.

Figure 2-1 shows the back of a typical MCE PC. On the back of the PC, you'll find that all these fancy connectors are nicely labeled for your perusal.

MCE PC vendors want to make it easy for you to hook up your gizmos, so some connections may be on the front of your MCE PC instead of the back.

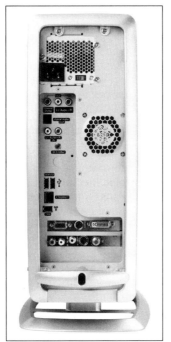

Figure 2-1:
Connections galore on an MCE PC.

Speeding Up with Fancy Processors

A crucial attribute of any Media Center Edition PC is a simple but vitally important one: raw power. An MCE PC must be capable of playing fast-moving DVD video, converting strings of 1s and 0s and playing them back in hi-fi sound, and browsing through huge digital photograph files at hyperspeed. An MCE PC needs some serious power.

One of the keys to any computer's speed or power is the CPU, or central processing unit. MCE PCs are without exception loaded with some of the fastest CPUs available to mere civilians. Two brands of processors are available in MCE PCs:

- **Pentium 4:** Intel's latest and greatest, at least until the Pentium 5 comes out
- **Athlon XP:** AMD's equivalent to the Pentium 4 — the great contender in the battle of CPU heavyweights

We're not going to debate which processor is better because we think both work equally well. Also, there are no compatibility issues with an Athlon XP versus a Pentium 4. Some folks are leery about buying a PC with a processor that's not made by Intel, but we don't share that point of view.

When you're choosing an MCE PC (as we discuss in Chapter 3), you'll probably be faced with a choice of processor clock speeds. These speeds were once measured in MHz (megahertz, or millions of hertz) but are now measured in GHz (gigahertz, or billions of hertz), due to the rapid pace of CPU development. The processor clock speed is basically the number of CPU tasks, or instructions, that can be performed per second. Although clock speed is not the only measure of CPU speed, it's a good guideline. The higher the clock speed, the faster the processor.

Intel adds the clock speed to the name of the chip, such as Pentium 4 2.80 GHz. AMD uses a number that represents the performance of the chip compared to a Pentium 4. For example, AMD's Athlon XP 3200+ is competitive with the Pentium 4 3.20 GHz, even though the Athlon's clock speed is lower.

Okay, we know you want an answer to the question, "Which chip is better?" The fastest Pentium 4 chips seem to do a bit better — but not a lot better — than the fastest Athlon XP chips. However, Athlon XP chips tend to be a bit cheaper. We leave the decision of which to buy in your hands. Whatever you decide, you can't go wrong.

Video Capabilities

The CPU is often the largest determinant in the speed of a PC, MCE or otherwise. The second largest factor is often the video card — the subsystem in the computer that does a lot of the work of displaying text, graphics, and video on your computer's monitor or your TV.

In an MCE PC, the video card is vitally important because so much of what Media Center brings to the table revolves around fast moving, brightly colored, cooler-than-heck images on the display. As such, all MCE PCs have video cards that fit somewhere between great and awesome on the official geek scale.

The two major makers of video cards for MCE PCs are

- ✔ NVIDIA (www.nvidia.com), which makes the GeForce4 family of cards
- ✔ ATI (www.ati.com), which makes Radeon cards

Both companies make excellent video cards. NVIDIA's are the most common on the early MCE PCs, but you'll see the ATI cards in the MCE 2004 PCs too.

Microsoft has strict rules about which video cards are required for MCE PCs, taking the guesswork out of choosing video cards. Many PC makers offer upgrades to the standard video card, which consist of either more video RAM (or memory for the video card to perform its calculations) or a faster *graphics engine* (the CPU, which is the specialized computer chip that's the heart of the video card). However, these upgrades aren't necessary because Microsoft already specifies a nearly top-of-the line video card for *all* MCE PCs.

Some MCE PCs include a video card with a *DVI* (Digital Video Interconnect) connection. DVI is an all-digital connection for monitors and displays and is used mainly for connecting a very large, flat-panel LCD or plasma display to a computer. If you have a display unit in your home theater that can use DVI, you should buy an MCE PC with a DVI connection because you'll get a much higher-quality picture on your big screen.

Audio Features

Except for the laptop versions, most MCE PCs have no internal speakers. Instead, for high-quality audio reproduction, MCE PCs are designed to be hooked up to external speaker systems.

To feed these external speakers with the best quality audio, MCE PCs have high-performance audio cards. Just as the video card is a subsystem of the PC for reproducing video and graphics, audio cards are a subsystem for reproducing audio. The audio card has some specialized chips that turn the digital data in the MCE PC into analog audio that your ears can hear.

And again like the video card, Microsoft has set a high bar for its PC partners when it comes to audio cards. Audio cards in Media Center PCs must be able to support 5.1 surround-sound audio, which means they must support front, center, and rear speakers and a bass-notes-only subwoofer, just like the speakers in a home-theater system.

The biggest difference between MCE PC audio cards is whether they support digital audio signals coming *out of* the MCE PC. Some audio cards, such as SoundBlaster Audigy2 from Creative Labs, can send digital audio signals out to your home-theater receiver when playing your DVDs or other digital content; other cards have only analog (line-level) outputs.

If you want to connect your MCE PC to your home theater, digital output is the way to go. Digital signals are much less prone to interference and degradation as they make their way into your home-theater receiver, so you'll end up with a sweeter-sounding listening experience.

If you look at the specifications of the audio cards used in MCE PCs, you might see *24 bit* or *96 kHz*. Music is stored digitally using a process called *sampling*, which basically slices analog sound waves into lots of little pieces that can be stored as 1s and 0s. The bigger the sample (the number of bits) and the higher the sampling rate (kHz, or number of samples per second), the better the sound. Windows Media 9.0, the program behind MCE's audio system, can handle audio with up to 24 bits and 96 kHz sampling. (In comparison, CDs are sampled at 16 bits and 44.1 kHz.)

Chapter 3

Evaluating and Buying a Media Center PC

*M*CE-powered PCs vary widely in the extra features and capabilities they offer. It can be downright confusing when you try to compare these systems. In this chapter, we make sure you get your money's worth by describing what you should look for when buying a Media Center PC.

Overview of Media Center PCs on the Market

Not just anyone can build a Media Center PC. The following manufacturers have licensed the rights for the XP MCE operating from Microsoft and offer Windows XP Media Center PCs:

- ✔ ABS Computer Technologies (www.abspc.com)
- ✔ Cyberpower System (www.cyberpowersystem.com)
- ✔ Dell (www.dell.com)
- ✔ Gateway (www.gateway.com)
- ✔ HP (www.shopping.hp.com)
- ✔ iBuypower (www.ibuypower.com)
- ✔ MIND Computer Products (www.mind.ca)

- ✔ Northgate (www.northgate.com)
- ✔ Sony (www.sony.com)
- ✔ Tagar Systems (www.tagarsystems.com)
- ✔ Toshiba (csd.toshiba.com)
- ✔ Touch Systems (www.touch-systems.ca)
- ✔ Viewsonic (www.viewsonic.com)
- ✔ ZT Group (www.ztgroup.com)

As shown in Figure 3-1, Microsoft maintains a current list of MCE PC manufacturers. Check out the Microsoft Web site (www.microsoft.com/WindowsXP/mediacenter/) to see which new PC vendors have smartened up and added a Media Center PC to their product lines.

One of the big improvements in the latest version of Windows XP MCE is a reduction in the need for computer resources such as processing power, memory, and storage space. As a result, the 2004 version can ship with some lower-end PCs — bringing MCE to the masses. Whether you buy a lower-end or higher-end PC depends a lot on what you intend to do with it now and in the near future.

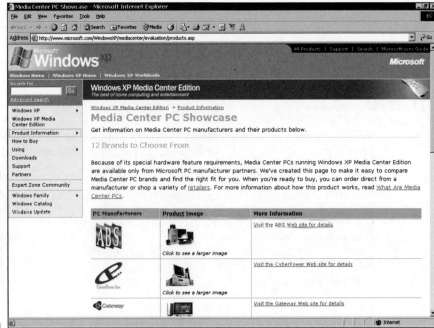

Figure 3-1: The Windows XP Media Center Edition PC Showcase at Microsoft.com.

Your MCE PC will be doing double-duty as an entertainment server in addition to its regular computer processing tasks. This places extra stress on computer resources. As we discuss in Chapter 18, Microsoft is working on future versions of MCE to make it easy for you to extend your MCE experience throughout the home. That means you could have multiple TVs, receivers, and other devices accessing your MCE PC at the same time. If you don't intend to do too much of this multitasking in the beginning — or you simply don't have a lot of devices in your home — you can get by with a lower-speed processor, fewer interfaces, and less hard drive space. But if you can envision using MCE all over the house (we can), you'll want to get a powerful MCE PC to start.

Buyer's Guide Checklist

Certain characteristics differentiate Media Center PCs from different vendors. Some of these characteristics are the look of the machine, the processor, the size of the hard drive, the supplied interfaces, the bundled components, the price, the comprehensiveness of the warranty, and the on-site maintenance plan. In this section, we describe each of these items.

Most vendors enable you to customize your machine by adding hard drive space, upgrading the processor, and more. This type of customization is more common and flexible when you buy your MCE PC on the Web rather than in a brick-and-mortar store.

Appearance

We hate to start our discussion of buying criteria with something as superficial as appearance, but some people can be downright finicky about the way their entertainment area looks. Even with rounded edges and chrome molding, Media Center PCs look like, well . . . PCs.

Some manufacturers, however, are more creative in the design of their units. For example, you can use Viewsonic's M2000 vertically or horizontally. Alienware — a company that started manufacturing MCE PCs, stopped for a while, and has promised to return to the MCE PC marketplace — has modern, stylish PC cabinets. ZT Group's products are so small (a 12-by-8-by-6-inch cube) that they look more like a small photo file cabinet than a computer and can be easily placed on a shelf alongside your CD collection.

To top that, Toshiba's Satellite 5205-S705 MCE PC is a laptop (see Figure 3-2)! Its TV tuner fits in the device's media bay, and it has a built-in recordable DVD drive. You can record TV shows and save them to the 60GB hard drive or to DVD.

Figure 3-2:
Toshiba was
the first on
the market
with a
Windows
XP MCE
laptop.

PCs are becoming smaller, more attractive, and more flexible, and MCE PCs will ride the same development curve. Before long, we expect to see black-matte, stereo-like MCE PCs, to match your fancy home-theater system.

Processor

What can you say about processors? The faster the better. Period. When shopping for Windows XP MCE PCs, you'll likely run across the Intel Pentium 4 or the AMD Athlon XP processor (or their successors). Unlike in the past, the Pentium 4 is now similar in price to the Athlon XP, so we think you'll be happy with either one.

You're more likely to have to make a decision as to *clock rate,* and again, faster is better. Because you pay a high premium for the latest processors on the market, the best value is to buy a processor one or two steps below the fastest processor available. Unless you buy the lowest clock speed, you'll still have a fast machine for almost all your applications.

The price difference between the 2-GHz processor and the 3-GHz processor is about $250 street price. The *street price* is the price you encounter in a store or on the Web. The *list price,* which is almost always higher, is the price the manufacturer places on a product.

You're likely to run across the term *hyperthreading* when shopping for Media Center PCs. Hyperthreading is a new Intel technology that improves the performance of multithreaded software products (that is, software that does many things at once, in parallel). In the past, threading was enabled in the software by splitting instructions into multiple streams so that multiple processors could act upon them. Hyperthreading, however, uses processor-level threading, in which *one* processor efficiently does many things at once, such as recording a TV show while playing music. Because of the multitasking nature of Windows XP MCE, performance is clearly improved in a hyperthreading environment. Although XP is designed to take advantage of hyperthreading, MCE is not. Therefore, the XP portions of your MCE PC may perform better with Intel hyperthreading-enabled processors than with the Athlon.

If you want to know more about the nitty-gritty of processors, check out Tom's Hardware site (www.tomshardware.com), a great source for information on all sorts of computer topics.

Hard drive

How big a hard drive do you need? The easy answer is, "As big as possible!" However, the largest drives cost more per gigabyte than the smaller drives (about $1.50 to $2.00 per gigabyte), so you're paying more per gigabyte as you go up in size.

The correct answer for you depends on how you intend to use your MCE PC. Some customers prefer a large hard drive for storing full seasons of their favorite TV shows and only a recordable CD drive for making music CDs. Those with a set-top DVD player might not need as much internal storage if they choose a recordable DVD writer to make DVDs of recorded TV shows and home movies.

One complicating factor is that Windows XP MCE 2004 doesn't treat all storage space the same. Depending on your use of the software, you might need different levels of storage. Some MCE modules, such as My TV, make you set aside huge chunks of space on a particular drive (defined storage). Other modules let you put content wherever you want (dynamic storage). This makes for an uneven use of hard drive space. Some defined storage areas can be almost empty (if, for example, you don't record TV shows), while the rest of your hard drive is packed full of dynamically situated content.

How big is big enough? Let's answer that by looking at the ways that MCE deals with different types of content.

Storing audio

Windows XP MCE 2004 makes extensive use of Microsoft Media Player to find, catalog, and play audio and video content. Media Player 9 operates by searching your local and network hard drives and attached network devices for content. Media Player then either links to the content from your MCE PC, if you're on a home network, or copies the content to your designated directory on your local hard drive for playback. If it finds 1000 songs across your drives and home network, for example, you might transfer those 1000 songs to the designated drive on your Media Center PC. Therefore, if you have a lot of CDs and want them stored locally on your MCE PC, you'll need a lot of space on your MCE PC. What's more, if you want others to be able to play those songs, you have to put shortcuts in your Shared Music folder to avoid creating duplicates of the same songs on your hard drive.

Also, as with any media content on your MCE PC, file size depends on the quality of the recording. For CD-quality sound, expect to use 3MB to 4MB for each song. Perfectly acceptable but less pristine recording formats use about half the space. We talk more about recording, storing, and playing your audio files in Chapter 10.

Storing home videos

To view home movies on MCE PC, they must be on your MCE PC in the My Videos folder in My Documents. Home videos share the same issues as recorded TV — namely, the size of the file increases as the quality increases. In addition, home videos are often of poorer quality, so you might use higher-quality levels when converting them to a format readable by your computer. This will result in larger file sizes. The file sizes listed for recorded TV — a range from 1GB to 3GB per hour of video — are a good estimate for home video. For more on home-video recording, see Chapter 13.

Storing TV and radio content

Recorded TV and radio are nothing more than recorded video and audio. Following are the "costs" for different levels of recording quality:

- Best recording quality for TV shows uses about 3GB per hour.
- Better quality uses about 2.5GB per hour.
- Good quality is about 2GB per hour.
- Fair quality is about 1GB per hour.

In addition to setting the recording quality level, you set the amount of storage space (entered as a percentage of the total hard drive) that you want to allocate for recording TV shows. The more you allocate, the less that's available for use by other programs, whether you use the space or not. If you plan on recording many TV series, you'll need a lot of hard drive space.

Radio storage requirements are a lot less, roughly the same amount as lower-quality CD recording. Because the Radio module only temporarily records 30 minutes worth of audio (Radio doesn't keep this data recorded for you to access later), there's not a lot of concern for drive space for this module.

Recorded TV is stored on the main or C: drive of your MCE PC. However, you can change where these files are stored if you want to add supplemental storage in the future.

To add more storage capacity, you can add an new internal hard drive, if space permits, or connect an external one through your FireWire (IEEE 1394) or USB 2.0 connection. (When formatting the drive, choose the NTFS option.) You could have, for example, a 100GB external hard drive dedicated to recorded TV programs and your internal drive for all your other MCE storage needs. We discuss recording TV in more detail in Chapter 9.

Storing DVDs

Windows XP MCE assumes that you're going to only play DVDs, not record or copy them to your hard drive. This probably won't stop a lot of people from wanting to back up their DVDs to their hard drive so that they can access them easily from their newfound "video server."

If you regularly download movies and TV shows from the Internet, you're familiar with their file sizes. Your DVD video file sizes can range substantially depending on the recording quality and whether all the additional content from the DVDs is included with the download. A DVD disc can hold up to 17GB, and publishers cram as much as they can on the discs. The largest hard drives in the MCE PCs at the time of this writing are only 200GB, so you won't be able to fit too many movies on your hard drive at DVD-quality levels. We talk more about DVDs and backing them up to your hard drive in Chapter 12.

Storing photos

If you scan pictures into Windows MCE or save pictures from your digital camera, Windows XP stores them in the My Pictures folder in your My Documents folder, unless you tell it otherwise. Photos from other media, such as Compact Flash cards, can be viewed directly from those media, without having to copy them first to the My Pictures or Shared Pictures folder.

There is no standard for photo size, and the file size varies greatly depending on the format. The issue again is file size versus quality. A 35mm 24-exposure film at resolutions commonly provided by film processors (1200 dots per inch, or *dpi*) takes up about 100MB on your hard drive.

As we discuss in Chapter 11, if you scan your photographs, you're in control of the stored resolution and therefore the file size. We suspect that most of you are like us: If you're bothering to scan your pictures, you select as high a resolution as possible. A 35mm 24-exposure roll of film at 4000 dpi takes up more than 1GB on your hard drive. This is one part of your hard drive storage requirements that may grow quickly, especially with the fast pace of product development in digital cameras that has driven down camera prices and moved digital photography to other devices, such as your cell phone.

The bottom line

We expect future versions of MCE PC to be much more flexible in where you can store files and in how you manage available hard drive space, especially as the MCE PC expands to cover other types of devices around the house. Then, if you need additional space for any of your modules, you can just add some storage capacity through your FireWire or USB connection or use the storage capacity on other network-connected devices.

The price of hard drives is dropping so fast that it doesn't make sense to buy too much more capacity that you think you'll use in the near term. In general, to get a lot of flexibility, you want a minimum of 80GB to 100GB of hard drive space. If you need more capacity internally as well as externally after you've purchased your MCE PC, you can always swap out the hard drive in favor of a larger drive. Another option is to offload some content to recordable DVDs and CDs.

You'd be surprised how fast your hard drive will fill up. Video eats up storage space — especially if you're recording series of shows. After you start recording TV and audio, you might never stop! We've been storing digital content for years, and we've always filled up every hard drive we've owned.

A final note on hard drives. You'll see *rpm* (revolutions per minute) in reference to hard drives. The faster the rpm, the faster the drive read/write rate. You want as high an rpm rating as possible.

Interfaces

Microsoft defines a minimum level of audio and video connectivity for any MCE-outfitted machine. As a result, the minimum *interface* capabilities that allow you to connect your MCE PC to your TV or your set-top box, such as S-video or analog audio connections, are similar from machine to machine. However, fancier cards, such as those found in high-end MCE PC packages, add more processing capacity, extra interface *ports* (the jacks on the interface cards where you plug your cables in), and extra software features for your video-display and audio-rendering capabilities.

We talk about audio and video interface cards in Chapter 2. Here's what you should look for in video cards:

- ✔ **More memory:** The more memory on the video interface card, the faster your card can perform the processing required to translate video into something the computer understands.

- ✔ **Enough analog and digital connections:** Make sure that you have enough VGA, DVI, and S-video connections for your MCE PC. In Chapters 4 and 5, we describe how to set up your system. In addition, check out the diagrams in the appendix for information on setting up your particular system. That way, you can establish a set of minimum connection requirements for your MCE PC.

A note on terminology: Some PC makers refer to their video cards as *graphics cards*. However, your MCE PC has another video interface card called the TV tuner, or Video In, card that accepts inbound signals. We don't talk about the TV tuner card in this section because it usually can't be customized. However, you can customize the video card, which is the video interface/graphics card we've been talking about up to now.

Windows XP MCE 2004 has FM radio capability, but some PC vendors are shipping tuner cards without the extra coaxial interface for your FM antenna input. The ATI AIW 9000 card is an example. So if you plan on using the FM Radio capability, make sure your tuner card has both Video In and FM input connection ports.

The quality of your video interface card affects the quality of your MCE experience. The difference in price between the minimum Microsoft-specified video capability and a souped-up video capability can be as much as $200, buy we think it's worthwhile to get the best possible video interface card you can. The top of the line for us, as of this printing, is the 8X AGP NVIDIA GeForce FX 5900 Ultra 256MB with DVI and TV Out ports. Nice!

The biggest difference in audio boards is in how they support multichannel (or surround-sound) audio. Some MCE PCs come with integrated surround-sound systems with built-in connections for the six speakers (five main speakers and a subwoofer for that room-shaking bass). Many PC manufacturers bundle high-end, six-speaker surround-sound computer speaker systems with the MCE PCs (more on this in the next section). If you want to move beyond small computer speakers and hook up your MCE PC to your home-theater system, look for a system that has digital audio output on the back of the audio card. (These may be called Digital Audio Optical or Digital Audio Coaxial ports.) The digital audio connection lets you use an inexpensive optical or coaxial connector to hook your MCE PC's audio directly into the back of your fancy home-theater receiver.

You can hook up two basic types of speakers to your MCE PC:

✔ **Computer-oriented active speakers:** These tend to be smaller units with their own amplifier, so they can be plugged directly into the audio interface card port on your MCE PC. This is the type of speaker that's often bundled with your MCE PC.

✔ **Entertainment-center-oriented or traditional passive speakers:** These are the speakers you usually find in stereo and entertainment stores. A separate amplifier is required to power the sound to the speakers.

Many MCE PCs use a SoundBlaster Audigy audio card. We like the Audigy2 Platinum card, available as an upgrade on many built-to-order MCE PCs. This is top-of-the-line stuff, and sounds great in a fancy home theater. It should cost about $150 to upgrade to a top-of-the-line audio interface card.

In addition to differences in audio and video cards, MCE PCs differ also in the availability of other interfaces. To maximize your use of the MCE PC, look for the following:

✔ **Front-panel interfaces:** This interface consists of a bay of interface ports on the front (not back) of the MCE PC for plugging in your cables — are handy. A good front panel interface will provide a USB, RCA composite, and FireWire connection, which saves you from having to turn your MCE PC around just to plug in your camera or camcorder to download pictures.

✔ **Extra USB interface ports:** Because more and more devices are standardizing on USB as their interface to the PC, figure out how many USB ports you're going to need. These days, printers, Web cams, computer mice, keyboards, and more sport USB interface connectors instead of older, lower-speed and bulkier serial and parallel interfaces. You can find MCE PCs that ship with eight USB 2.0 ports as standard equipment, with some of these ports on the front of the unit! We explain USB and USB 2.0 in Chapter 2.

If you're short on USB ports, an *external USB hub* adds extra USB interface ports to your PC. A four-port hub can connect four devices to a single USB port on the PC. You can get a four-port USB hub from your local computer store for $20 to $30. You can stack (daisy-chain) these too, if you get a stackable hub.

Bundled components

Some manufacturers bundle certain components with their basic system; others sell these same components separately at an added cost. For instance, HP sells for $19.99 a Media Center PC Accessory Bundle that contains a 12-foot S-video cable, an RCA-stereo-miniplug-to-two-phono-RCA-plugs adapter cable, and a coaxial two-way splitter. Viewsonic gives you the S-video cable and RCA miniplug adapter with each Viewsonic MCE PC product. It pays to read the specifications so you'll know which cables and other paraphernalia are included with your purchase.

We suggest that you read the specs not so you can save money but because it's a hassle to unpack your new MCE PC, get excited about installing the system, and then find that you need to purchase a cable separately. We hate that!

Some manufacturers include a 6-in-1 media reader (see Figure 3-3), which allows you to read Compact Flash Type I and II, IBM Microdrive, SmartMedia, SD Card, MultiMediaCard and Sony Memory Stick media. Other manufacturers suggest that you buy a USB or internal add-on unit, which can add up to $70 to the price of your system.

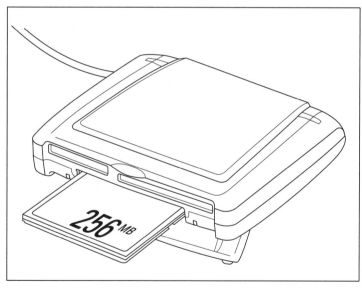

Figure 3-3:
A 6-in-1
USB-
connected
media
reader for
your cam-
corder and
camera
memory
cards.

Manufacturers differ also in the surround-sound packages they include with their system or their special-offer packages. You'll find packages with no speakers, just two little stereo speakers, or full-fledged surround-sound systems. Some offer all these options. HP, for instance, bundles a Klipsch ProMedia 5.1 THX-certified, 500-watt, 6-piece computer-speaker audio system, powered by a Creative Labs Sound Blaster Audigy 24-bit sound card with Dolby 5.1 and analog surround sound. Cool! But HP does so on only its highest-end MCE PCs (see Figure 3-4); lower-end MCE PCs don't have bundled speakers.

We don't have room here to go through the ins and outs of home-theater speakers (we wrote *Home Theater For Dummies* for that), but we can tell you that these Klipsch speakers are excellent add-ons. You might find (as Danny did) that you'll get rid of the old speakers in your home-entertainment system and use the Klipsch speakers exclusively. After all, with all the TV, radio, DVD, and other capabilities of your MCE PC, you might find that your existing entertainment system can't do the things that your MCE PC can do. Heck, Danny even uses these speakers for outdoor movies. They're that powerful!

Figure 3-4: The HP Media Center 884 PC ships with a complete home-theater sound system.

Some audio interface cards work only with specific types of audio entertainment gear. Therefore, if you already have a set of computer speakers or a receiver-based audio system that you intend to use with your MCE PC, make sure it's compatible with the audio interface card. For instance, the Klipsch speakers just mentioned require input from *three* 3.5mm-miniplug cables for its five channels, and some audio cards support only two channels through two 3.5mm cable ports. Ask the salesperson or check online to see whether you need to buy a different audio interface card.

Finally, remember that most MCE PC packages do not come with a display. The manufacturers assume that you already have a display, or are going to pick one up separately, or are planning to use a high-quality plasma or other display to serve as both the TV set and the computer monitor.

Support

We want to stress that you should not buy from anyone without 7x24 support. You're likely to need support at odd hours — when cuddling in bed, in a rush in the morning, or on a rainy weekend day. These times are hardly compatible with a 9-to-5 customer support line.

Check out who gives you unlimited telephone support and how long that support lasts. Gateway and Viewsonic served as our evaluation platforms for the beta trials of the new 2004 software, and we called their customer service lines at all hours of the day and night. They solved our problems quickly and directly each time. We hope you have similar experiences.

Warranty

Check out the warranty period because the various vendors have substantial differences in their limited warranties. Some vendors have only a 15-day money-back guarantee. iBUYPOWER, however, provides a full 30-day money-back guarantee (not including shipping, handling, and rush service fees). Note that shipping costs are often the customer's responsibility.

Make sure you keep all the original packing material for your MCE PC. If you ever have to ship it back to the vendor, many of the ground shipping companies won't insure the system unless it's in its original packaging.

You can buy extended warranty packages. Some vendors have additional forms of warranties you can buy too. For example, Gateway has an Accidental Damage Protection plan that covers you against damages when Little Susie knocks over the Media Center PC, which was delicately balanced on top of the TV set, or Jack Junior trips with his hockey stick, ramming it into the back of your MCE PC. Gateway covers the system for three years at a cost of $99. If your spouse is accident prone, consider this. Toshiba has the same plan, but calls it the SystemGuard plan. Check with your vendor to see what's available.

Some on-site repair plans have distance limitations. For instance, Toshiba's plans apply only if you're within 75 miles of one of their service center cities. Make sure you're eligible before you sign up for a plan.

On-site maintenance

Doctors may have given up making house calls, but PC technicians have not. Most vendors have an option for making house calls to fix your machine. When you consider the hassle and cost of shipping the unit and waiting for its return, these on-site maintenance plans start to look pretty good. They're not that expensive to add to your existing warranty (under $100 per year).

These support packages are location specific. Before you buy, make sure that you're within their service area; there are distance and special instance limitations where they won't come on-site. (For instance, they won't come to Danny's vacation house on an island two miles off the coast of Maine.)

Price

In general, you can expect to pay around $1000 for an entry-level Media Center PC. You can pay up to $4000, for the Gateway Media Center PC with a 42-inch plasma TV. The average price is about $1500, plus any extra costs for a monitor or a speaker system.

Prices change all the time, so we provide updates at our Windows XP Media Center Edition 2004 PC for Dummies Web site at www.smarthomesbook.com.

Want to know more about buying a MCE PC? It pays to surf around. CNET has a good site for generic advice on buying desktop computers. Go to

```
reviews.cnet.com/Desktops/4520-3118_7-5021315.html?tag=cnet.fd
```

Also, as we mention in Chapter 19, check out the Buyer's Guides at www.thegreeenbutton.com and www.xpmce.com.

Where to Shop for Your MCE PC

The correct answer to the question of where to shop for your MCE PC is "It depends." We suggest that first you visit the Web site of each computer you're interested in. Figure out the exact model and configuration you want. Some sites have online system configurators that help you craft the system you want.

Then, armed with that information, check out manufacturer's Partners pages to find their online distributors. Some manufacturers won't have any — instead, you buy directly from them online. Other manufacturers sell through many channels so check to see who has the best special for your selected package.

Part II
Integrating Your Media Center PC

The 5th Wave   By Rich Tennant

Don't get your hopes up, Ted. The other end may not be plugged in.

In this part . . .

The Media Center Edition PC is a cool gizmo. Take it out of the box, plug in all the pieces and parts, and you're ready to listen to music, watch videos, and more. But to get the most out of your MCE PC, you'll want to hook it up to various devices and gadgets in your home. After all, the MCE PC can be the centerpiece to your home-entertainment system, if you let it. (It's the little PC that *could* — you just need to give it a push.)

In this part of the book, we tell you how to connect your MCE PC to your home-theater or home-entertainment system. The MCE is a powerful machine, so why not enjoy it with your biggest and best screens and speakers?

We also talk about getting your MCE PC online, including a discussion on how to get online with a broadband connection (such as DSL or a cable modem). Pay attention here, because MCE has been optimized to work with a fast Internet connection.

Finally, we walk you through configuring the MCE PC to your liking. You set user preferences, tell your MCE PC where in the world you live (vital for TV viewing), and more. After you've finished this part, you'll be ready to get down to business and start using your MCE PC for fun!

Chapter 4

Cables, Connectors, and Components

. . . .

In This Chapter

▶ Confirming that you have what you need

▶ Wading through cable spaghetti

▶ Making the audio connection

▶ Connecting your TV and display

. . . .

*R*ipping open that Media Center PC box is like unwrapping the best present you ever got! We get goose bumps just thinking about it.

In this chapter, we tell you what you should expect to find in the box with your Media Center PC and what you might need to run down to the Radio Shack or local computer store to get. You find out what all those cables in the box do and why you need them. Finally, you get some instructions for connecting your Media Center PC to your audio and video equipment.

Inventory Time

Let's start with a checklist of lessons learned. When taking your Media Center PC out of the box

✔ Be careful if you're using a knife to open the box because many manufacturers slip last-minute documentation updates on top.

✔ Lay a white sheet on the ground under the box, and put things from the box onto the sheet. This way, nothing gets lost.

✔ Make sure you have everything. Somewhere in the box is an inventory checklist. Some MCE PC makers provide the inventory list on a poster-like installation and connection sheet.

✔ Keep all packaging materials. Most manufacturers won't accept (and shipping companies won't insure) returns unless you ship them in the original box and packaging.

Different vendors bundle different items with their MCE PCs. Regardless of what brand you buy, each MCE PC has extensive audio and video capabilities, including a TV tuner card for receiving video signals from your cable or satellite system, a video card to drive your computer and TV displays, and an audio card to drive your sound system. However, there's often more than one way to connect things. Different vendors provide different combinations of cables and connectors, which can make things a bit confusing. In this section, we talk about all the most common ways of connecting audio and video systems.

When you open the box of a typical Windows XP MCE PC, you should find most or all of the following items in addition to the PC itself. Look for these items (if you don't find them in the box, you may need to go out and buy a few of them to get things up and running):

✔ Remote control with batteries

✔ Power cord for the PC

✔ RJ-11 telephone cord if your MCE PC is configured for a modem connection

✔ CAT-5e RJ-45 network cable if your MCE PC is configured for a home-network or broadband connection

✔ Coaxial cable, one each to connect to the TV, cable or satellite service, and the VCR

✔ S-video-to-composite-adapter cable to connect your PC to your TV

✔ Composite-video cable to connect your PC to your TV

✔ DVI-VGA adapter to connect your PC display to your PC

✔ Digital audio coaxial cable to connect to your stereo system

✔ Digital audio optical cable to connect to your stereo system

✔ Analog audio cable to connect to your stereo system

✔ Stereo miniplug-to-RCA audio cable to connect to your stereo system

✔ IR remote emitter control cable to connect to your cable or satellite box to change channels

Even the biggest MCE PC box might not have all the little accessories and connectors required when you install your Media Center PC. You might also need the following:

✔ Remote sensor for picking up IR signals if you're not in line-of-sight with your PC IR pickup

✔ Speakers with speaker cables for a true surround-sound-5.1 experience

✔ USB-connected or internal 6-in-1 memory adapter for a digital camera and other digital storage cards

✔ Powered cable signal splitter; if you use a VCR, you need one or two of these

✔ Coaxial A/B switchbox, if you plan to hook up your VCR to your MCE PC

✔ RCA A/B/C/D switchbox if you plan to hook up a lot of devices that use RCA or composite-video connections, such as an Xbox or electronic toys that require video

Finally, we advise you to get the following connectors at Radio Shack or elsewhere:

✔ Three female-miniplug-to female-miniplug connectors (the miniplug also called a ⅛-inch or 3.5mm plug)

✔ Three female-miniplug-to-male-RCA-plug connectors

✔ Three male-miniplug-to-female-RCA-plug connectors

We recommend that you buy high-quality surge-protector power strips, such as Monster Cable's Powerbar (www.monstercable.com). When you plug in an AC adapter on that expensive power strip, however, it ends up covering one or two slots. We've found a solution to this problem: the Power Strip Liberator and Y-Splitter Liberator adapter cables from ZIO Tek (www.ziotek.com) as shown in Figure 4-1. They're like a handy 1-foot extension cord from your surge protector to your AC adapter.

Where should you put your Media Center PC?

The current version of Media Center is designed to be used in one area of your house. In Part 4, we help you connect your MCE PC to a home network and access the media on your MCE PC from anywhere in the house. In future versions of the software, we expect Microsoft to add wireless distribution capability. But even though you can connect a Media Center PC to a network to access files stored on its hard drive, you can't access the Media Center interface itself from remote locations.

So, where do you put your Media Center PC? If you plan on using it not only for entertainment but also for traditional PC stuff such as crunching numbers in spreadsheets, put it where you'll feel comfortable working. It's nice to be able to use the remote from the bed, but we wouldn't want to type a long report from there.

Our advice is to set up your MCE PC next to your TV first. After you get everything working, you can add wireless or long-range connections to equipment located across the room or even in other rooms.

Figure 4-1:
ZIO Tek's
Liberators
take the
hassle out
of power
adapters.

At a bare minimum, you need surge protection in your setup. But surge protection doesn't protect you from other issues. For example, voltage drops can lower the output of the amplifier powering your speakers. Improperly grounded electrical systems can cause a hum in your audio and lines on your video display. Consider investing in a *power conditioner,* which improves and stabilizes your AC power. For example, Monster Cable's Home Theater Power Centers provide surge protection, voltage stabilization, and noise filtering. Check them out at `www.monstercable.com/power`.

Cables and Connectors 101

We're as impatient as anyone. We like to rip open a box and just plug everything together, with the full expectation that it will work. If it doesn't, we turn to the documentation.

However, the recent proliferation of new cable types and the related increase in the complexity of the configuration have made us take a more thoughtful approach. Many cables look the same but are used for different purposes. Other times, you can plug the right cable into the right interface, but it won't work because that interface isn't *enabled* (or turned on) for the purpose you are using it for (connections that aren't enabled sometimes pop up when you are making video connections). And in other cases, you can use the wrong cable, have it look like it works, but with poor results. You might encounter any of these problems when working with your MCE PC, so we're including an introduction to audio and video cables.

In the rest of this chapter, we talk in detail about the different kinds of audio and video connections you might have available to you on your MCE PC. Table 4-1 is a brief rundown of these cable types and connectors. We describe these in more detail next.

Table 4-1	Cable and Connection Types	
Category	*Type*	*Connector*
Audio interconnects	Analog audio interconnects	RCA connector
	Digital audio interconnects	
	Toslink optical	Toslink cable connector
	Coaxial	RCA connector
Speaker cable	12-, 14-, and 16-gauge cable	Pin connectors, spade lugs, or banana plugs (or bare wire, which is not recommended)
Video interconnects	Analog video interconnects	
	Composite video	RCA connector
	S-video	S-video connector
	Component video	RCA connector
	VGA	VGA connector
	Digital video interconnects	
	FireWire	
	DVI	

If after reading this chapter you want to know more about audio and video cables, check out our *Home Theater For Dummies* (published by Wiley Publishing, Inc.).

Audio Interconnects and Connectors

Most of the connections you'll make to your MCE PC are *short runs* — that is, connections between devices and components sitting just a few feet from each other (or at least in the same room). The cables you use for these connections are called *interconnects*.

An *interconnect* cable is simply a short run cable (used for making audio or video connections). With all the *connects* we're throwing around, it's not hard to get an *interconnect* confused with a *connection* or a *connector*.

Analog audio interconnects

The most common type of cable in any home-entertainment application is the standard *analog audio interconnect*. You've probably used these to connect a VCR to your TV set, for instance. Traditionally, audio interconnects came in pairs, for two-channel (stereo) audio connections, but in the realm of the home theater — with its multiple surround-sound channels — you might use an individual cable (such as the cable that connects a subwoofer to the receiver or the controller) or a big bunch of cables (such as the six cables that connect an advanced digital DVD player to the receiver).

Audio interconnects use a standardized jack known as an *RCA jack,* so any audio interconnect will plug into a corresponding RCA plug on a piece of A/V equipment. Figure 4-2 shows the RCA plugs and jacks on a stereo (dual) pair of audio interconnects.

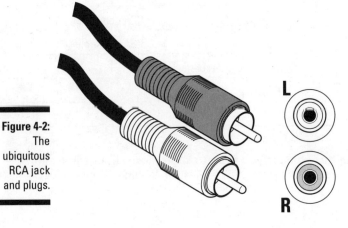

Figure 4-2:
The ubiquitous RCA jack and plugs.

Miniplug connectors

Standard audio interconnect cables are not the only analog audio cables used by computers. You'll often also find mini-RCA-like interconnect cables with 3.5mm (⅛-inch) connectors called *miniplug* connectors (see the figure).

As you might guess, these miniplugs are smaller than RCA plugs. They're often found in portable audio gear (for connecting headphones to iPods and similar devices).

A typical sound card for surround sound 5.1 might have three 3.5mm connections — one for the center speaker, one for the front left and right speakers, and one for the rear left and right speakers. These cables connect to the powered subwoofer, which then connects through 3.5mm (or other format) speaker cables to the speakers themselves.

If you go shopping for audio interconnects, you'll find a huge array of cable constructions. The typical audio interconnect is a *coaxial cable* (a cable containing two electrical conductors) with a shielded jacket. The shielded jacket keeps stray electromagnetic energy from getting into the conductors and causing interference with the audio signal. Other audio interconnects are made of unshielded, twisted cable.

 Although you can use the audio cables included with your MCE PC, we think you might eventually want to upgrade them if you want to refine your picture quality. However, we don't think you need to pay $1000 a foot for double-secret-mojo cold-fusion reactor-type cables. There's a happy medium. Look for cables that have oxygen-free copper (OFC) conductors and jacks with gold-plated surfaces, which resists corrosion. Use the shortest run of cable possible; the longer the run, the greater the chance that the audio signal will be degraded by interference or *attenuation* (the weakening of the signal as it travels over any cable).

 You can buy high-quality cables from dozens of companies, including Monster Cable (www.monstercable.com), Kimber (kimber.com), and Audioquest (www.audioquest.com).

Digital audio interconnects

Digital surround-sound systems (such as Dolby Digital and DTS) have made the digital audio interconnect commonplace. Microsoft doesn't require that MCE PCs have a digital connection, but the company *strongly recommends* that they do. All MCE PCs that we've seen have one.

If you want to use your MCE PC with a surround-sound home-theater receiver and you want to watch DVDs using Dolby Digital or DTS surround sound, you must use a digital audio interconnect.

Digital audio interconnects are used to connect DVD players, HDTV tuners, video game consoles, and more to the A/V receiver or controller. The two main types of digital audio interconnects are Toslink optical and coaxial. Your MCE PC card will probably have one or both of these interconnection options.

A *coaxial cable* looks like a single (mono) audio interconnect, with RCA jacks on either end and a coaxial cable in-between. Put a coaxial cable and a mono audio cable side-by-side on a table, and you wouldn't be able to tell them apart. But the conductors inside coaxial digital audio interconnect cables are different than those in analog audio interconnects to handle the higher frequencies of digital signals. You shouldn't use a standard audio interconnect instead of a coaxial digital cable.

Composite video and component video cables, which we discuss shortly, also look the same as audio interconnects, but each type uses different internal conductors and designs.

A *Toslink optical interconnect* uses fiber optics instead of copper cabling, and carries the digital signal as pulses of light instead of as an electrical signal. Viewed head-on, the connector on a Toslink cable looks like a house, but with a flashing laser. Figure 4-3 shows the Toslink interconnect.

Figure 4-3:
Fiber optics in your house! The Toslink inter-connect.

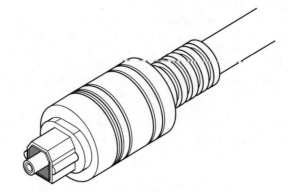

The female Toslink connector (on your receiver or DVD player or wherever you're plugging in a Toslink) is usually covered by a removable dust cap. If you don't take this cap off, you're going to curse like a sailor trying to get that cable plugged in.

Speaker Cables and Connectors

Another cable that you'll find in just about every surround-sound setup is speaker cable. *Speaker cables* connect the outputs of the power amplifier or the amplifier section of the receiver or PC audio card to the speaker, and carry the higher-powered electrical currents required to move the internal components of the speaker. You need one pair of speaker cables for each speaker in your system, except the subwoofer. (The vast majority of subwoofers have their own amplifier and need only a single audio interconnect cable, not a pair of speaker cables.)

Speaker cables (the conductors within, to be precise) are thicker than interconnects because they have to carry signals over longer distances and also carry more electrical current. Thicker conductors have less electrical resistance to the current flowing through them. That's a good thing, because too much resistance can alter the audio signal. The longer the cable, the greater the resistance to the signal traveling over the cable.

The thickness of a speaker cable is referred to as its *gauge* (using a standard system called AWG, or American Wire Gauge). The lower the gauge, the thicker the conductor. We recommend cables no more than 16 gauge; our preference is 14 gauge. For longer runs of 40 to 50 feet or more — for example, to surround-sound speakers in a large room — we recommend 12-gauge cables if they fit your budget.

Unlike the different types of audio interconnects, which share the common RCA connector, many connector choices are available for speaker cables. (These connectors are sometimes called *terminations*.) The simplest approach is to use the bare wire itself (stripped of any insulation), but we recommend that you don't do this — the connection isn't as good and the bare wire ends can corrode over time, making the connection even worse.

Following are the three main types of connectors for speaker cables:

- ✓ **Pin connectors:** These look like their name — a straight or angled pin at the end of the wire. Pin connectors work best with the spring-loaded clip type of speaker connectors on less expensive receivers and speakers, but they work also with the five-way binding posts found on better models.

✔ **Spade lugs:** These U-shaped connectors fit behind the screws on a five-way binding post. You slide the open part of the U over the post and then screw down the plastic nut. Spade lugs provide the tightest, most reliable connection because they're screwed down.

✔ **Banana plugs:** If you squint really hard, you might think that banana plugs look like bananas. To us, they look like pin connectors that are fat in the middle. Banana plugs come in single and dual configurations. The dual configuration is simply two banana plugs (one for each wire in the speaker-wire pair) stuck in the same housing.

Figure 4-4 shows the pin, spade lug, and banana plug. Figure 4-5 shows a five-way binding post.

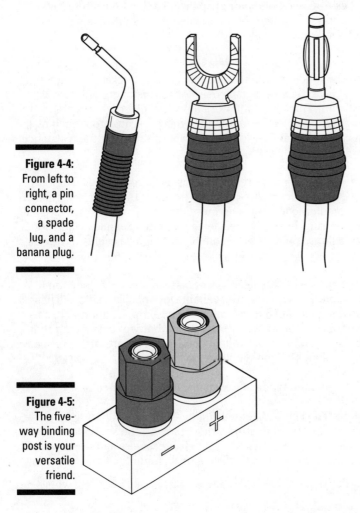

Figure 4-4:
From left to right, a pin connector, a spade lug, and a banana plug.

Figure 4-5:
The five-way binding post is your versatile friend.

Which type of speaker wire termination you use depends on which kind of termination your speakers will accept. Unlike fancier home-theater speakers, some speakers for computers don't have five-way binding posts. In this case, you might not be able to use your own speaker cables, and instead have to use the speaker cables that came in the box with your MCE PC or speaker system.

Video Interconnects and Connectors

The two components of a video signal are the luminance and the chrominance. The *luminance* provides the video display with the brightness information that determines which parts of the screen are darker or lighter. The *chrominance* adds information about what color each segment of the screen should be.

Analog video interconnects

You'll find three types of short-run analog video connections in a home theater. There is a definite hierarchy among these connections — one is visibly worse (in terms of picture quality) than the other two, and between the two superior methods, one is better (though not as significantly) than the other. In order from worst to best, these connection types are as follows:

- ✔ **Composite video:** Both luminance and chrominance are combined in a single signal. A comb filter inside the display separates these two components and sends them to the appropriate internal circuitry.

- ✔ **S-video:** Luminance and chrominance are separated onto two separate signal paths, so the signal can bypass the comb filter in the TV. This usually results in a much clearer picture, with more defined colors and images.

- ✔ **Component video:** The signal is separated even further, providing one path for luminance information and two separate paths for chrominance information. Component video connections can be further enhanced in a *wideband* component video connection, which allows the higher frequencies needed for HDTV to travel from the source (such as an HDTV tuner) to the HDTV monitor.

We haven't seen an MCE PC with component video connectors yet. But that's not surprising because component is most useful for HDTV, which MCE PCs do not yet support.

The big difference between composite video (the lower-quality video signal) and S-video and component video is that the better connections carry luminance and chrominance information separately. Why is this a big deal when the comb filter in the display separates the signal? Well, comb filters do an imperfect job and can leave visible *artifacts* in your picture (objects have fuzzy edges). You want the sharpest, most colorful picture you can get, don't you?

Composite-video cables and component-video cables use standard RCA connectors and look similar to audio cables (and the digital coaxial cable, for that matter). Composite-video cables are loners (you need just one); component-video cables travel in small packs of three (often labeled Y, Pr, and Pb).

Composite-video cables are usually color-coded yellow (that is to say, the connector has a yellow ring around it, or the rubber boot around the connector is yellow).

S-video is an unmistakable cable with its own S-video connector, which has four pins that correspond to four holes on the S-video plug on your gear. Figure 4-6 shows an S-video connector and plug.

S-video connectors can be difficult to line up and connect. The bottom set of pins is spaced slightly wider than the top set. If you're having trouble with the connector, check to see that you aren't trying to push the connector in upside down. A little plastic doohickey keeps you from destroying the connector, but bent pins are far from unknown to first-time S-video users.

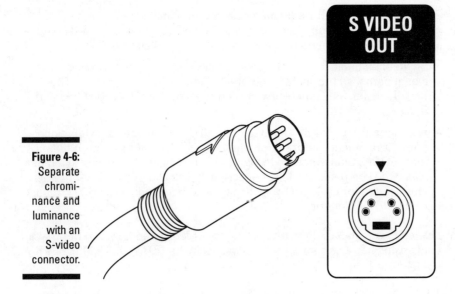

Figure 4-6:
Separate
chromi-
nance and
luminance
with an
S-video
connector.

VGA all the way

If you've ever owned a computer that *didn't* have an integrated monitor (like a laptop does), chances are pretty good you've dealt with VGA video connections. VGA (Video Graphics Array) was developed by IBM a long time ago (in the '80s!) as a standardized system for connecting PCs and monitors.

VGA is actually a specific display mode (640 x 480 pixels), but the term has become more generic and is used to describe any analog computer monitor cable that uses a standardized connector (called a *DB-15 connector*).

The vast majority of MCE PCs use a VGA cable to connect the MCE PC to a standard computer monitor (an exception is described in the upcoming "DVI" section).

For the most part, you won't use VGA to connect your MCE PC to a TV — most TVs don't have a VGA port. However, you might be able to use a VGA connection to connect to a projection TV system. If you have this option, we recommend that you use it, unless you also have one of the digital video connections we list in the next section. (If you have digital, use it instead.)

Digital video interconnects

The video-connection systems we've discussed are all analog systems — they carry analog video signals, not digital ones. Analog connections are more susceptible to interferences and other losses of signal quality when compared to digital connections. And in the case of digital signals (such as HDTV and other ATSC digital television broadcasts), there's no reason to convert to analog until the very last minute (inside the display itself). As Dick Vitale would say, "Keep it digital, baby!"

Some analog connections (particularly component video) require multiple cables per connection. If you want to connect the component video output of an HDTV tuner card to your receiver and then on to your display, for example, you'll need six cables (three for each link). Add a DVD player using component video into the mix, and you have six more cables. Pretty soon you have spaghetti.

In addition, analog connections don't have an inherent copy-protection system. If there's one thing that content providers (movie and television studios) want to prevent, it's people copying their content.

To satisfy all these requirements, the consumer electronics industry (in association with the content providers) has been working overtime to develop digital-video interconnection systems. We discuss these next.

FireWire

One of the first systems for digital video crossed over from the computer industry: FireWire (also called IEEE 1394, or i.LINK). FireWire was developed by Apple Computer for connecting peripheral devices to Macintosh computers. Companies such as Sony picked up on the technology and began incorporating it in their camcorders and PCs, and it grew from there. (The FireWire in camcorders is often called *DV.*)

Some HDTV tuners and HDTV-ready displays (as well as a few other devices such as JVC's D-VHS) include FireWire connections. However, it appears that FireWire will become less common as a means of connecting HDTV devices together.

The only place that FireWire is being used on MCE PCs today is *not* for connecting to the television. Instead, many MCE PCs have a FireWire connection that lets you hook your digital camcorder to the MCE PC. (See Chapter 13 for more on camcorders.) We mention FireWire here mainly because it's a common system for connecting HDTVs to external HDTV tuners, and you might have a FireWire connection on your own high-definition TV. With today's MCE PCs, you can't use that connection for the PC-to-TV hookup.

Next up is FireWire's biggest competitor in the digital video connection world: DVI. It looks like DVI is winning the war and will become the most common digital video interconnect. Battles are still being fought, however, so don't count FireWire out yet.

DVI

One reason that FireWire is becoming less common in the digital video world is the success of its competitor, *DVI* (Digital Visual Interface). DVI is another technology adopted from the computer world, where it was developed as a means of connecting computers to digital LCD screens. Figure 4-7 shows a DVI connector.

The main reason DVI is becoming more popular than FireWire has nothing to do with performance or technology. Instead, it's because DVI systems used for HDTV allow much stronger *copy protection* (meaning the TV provider can keep you from recording shows). So the TV and movie studios are pushing the copy-protected version of DVI onto the industry.

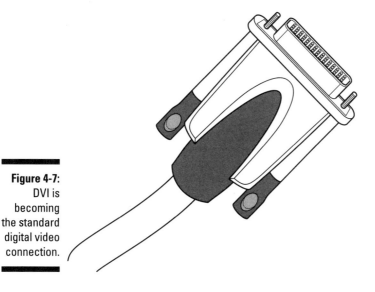

Figure 4-7:
DVI is
becoming
the standard
digital video
connection.

Along the way, DVI picked up a strong copy-protection system called *HDCP* (High Definition Copy Protection), and became a favorite of the HDTV industry. The HDCP system makes DVI a relatively *dumb* connection — all it does is send video in one direction (for example, from the tuner to the display), and it won't let you make a digital copy of what you're watching (so forget taping that *CSI* episode on your digital VHS tape deck).

Not all devices with a DVI connector incorporate HDCP. (For example, you connect an LCD computer monitor to MCE PC using DVI without HDCP.) If you use a DVI cable to connect an HDCP-enabled HDTV tuner to a non-HDCP display, you will not get a full HDTV signal. Instead, the signal is converted to a lower resolution.

DVI connections are becoming standard on digital high-definition televisions and are popular for computer monitors as well. That's probably not too surprising, because many large flat-panel computer monitors (such as LCD displays) operate in a similar way as flat-panel TVs. Many new MCE PCs use DVI instead of the older, traditional VGA analog connectors to connect to flat-panel digital computer monitors.

In Chapter 5, you take some of this cable knowledge and put it to work by doing the plugging and connecting needed to get your MCE PC ready to go.

Chapter 5

Hooking Up Your Media Center PC

● ●

In This Chapter

▶ Planning your connections the right way, the first time

▶ Plugging in a display (or two)

▶ Ensuring all video sources link to your MCE PC

▶ Extracting 5.1 surround sound from your system

▶ Connecting peripherals, IR devices, and more

● ●

*I*n this chapter, we describe the process of hooking up your Media Center PC. Each manufacturer approaches the process in a slightly different order, but the result is the same. Linking all the different elements of your MCE PC package together and then hooking your MCE PC to your entertainment system aren't difficult tasks, but you need to look out for some serious gotchas. We help you with those in this chapter.

Planning Your Connections

Most PC manufacturers provide you with diagrams showing the different ways you can configure your system. If you've put together any sort of entertainment system, such as an Xbox or a DVD player, you're probably familiar with these types of diagrams.

When figuring out the connection scheme for the MCE PC and your entertainment devices, you might run into trouble in two areas: connecting a VCR and connecting speakers.

Microsoft decided not to support a VCR connection to the MCE. If you have a VCR, chances are you would think it appropriate to connect the signal cable to your set-top box (if you have one), then to your VCR, and then to your MCE PC. That way, any signals coming from the VCR are treated as inbound signals to the MCE. This would allow you to record onto the PC any home movies stored on VCR tapes. For more information on editing, viewing, and storing video tapes on your MCE PC, read the "MY VCR" sidebar in this chapter.

My VCR

Microsoft left out the VCR in its architecture because of the fast move to digital and the complexity of supporting the many brands of VCRs on the market. Still, with all the video tapes out there, we think Microsoft should have included the VCR in some fashion.

But Windows XP MCE doesn't have a My VCR feature, so you have to kludge your cabling plan and recording habits to view and capture VCR-resident content through your MCE PC. In Chapter 9, we talk about how to tape from the VCR to your MCE PC. Here, we tell you how to cable your VCR and MCE PC together so that you have a smoother interface between them.

You need to split the signal back to the PC by inserting another powered splitter (such as a Radio Shack model 15-1196 bidirectional CATV amplifier, $39.99) in-line between the VCR and the TV set, and then running a patch cable to a coaxial switchbox (such as a Radio Shack model 15-1968 remote control A-B switch, $29.99) that sits in front of the PC. (A switchbox allows you to switch between signal A and signal B.)

Only one signal should go into the PC at any time, and this setup gives your PC access to the VCR signals. Now, you might ask, "Then why split the signal at the cable box to the VCR and the PC to begin with?" With this setup, you can both watch your VCR and tape a show with your PC — if the VCR and MCE PC were in-line, you'd be limited to one or the other function at a time.

Another challenging area is in connecting your speakers to your PC. You have a choice that you've never had before: You can run your speakers directly from your MCE PC or from an intermediate receiver that's part of an entertainment system.

Only in the past few years have audio systems for your PC become so sophisticated and on par with speakers for entertainment systems that you would consider using them instead of a separate audio system. The Klipsch speakers mentioned in Chapter 3, for instance, rival similarly priced and sized speakers that you could connect through your receiver. Your MCE PC, with its CD/DVD drives, links to video and radio signals, and picture slide shows, gives you an alternate entertainment center — you don't need a lot of other expensive audio gear.

If you've already invested a lot of money in your entertainment system, there's no question about what to do: Route the audio through that system. If you have an old or low-end receiver and speakers, however, you might think about driving the sound from the MCE PC instead of your present receiver. After all, the FM tuner on board MCE 2004 provides almost as much capability as your stereo receiver — everything but AM radio.

If you go this latter route, all sorts of speakers and speaker connections are available. We get into more detail about speakers later in the chapter, but in general, if you purchased an MCE PC with a speaker package, your cables and card interfaces should match. If you didn't buy them together, you could be in for some trips to Radio Shack for connectors.

Connecting to the Monitor

Perhaps the first things you connect to your PC are your local PC cables for your keyboard, mouse, and monitor. These connections are basic — most new PCs even have color-coded ports and cables to make it as easy as possible to connect the right cable connectors to the right cable ports.

If you have a wireless mouse and keyboard, you might need to attach a transmitter to the back of the machine. If you do have a transmitter and you notice that your mouse doesn't move fast enough or skips around when you move the cursor, make sure that nothing is blocking the transmitter. (You might have inadvertently stacked stuff behind the PC.) Check that your wireless transmitter cables aren't intertwined with a power cable — this can cause interference and make your mouse not work properly. Also check the batteries — sporadic movement of the cursor or missed keystrokes could mean that the batteries are low in power and should be replaced.

You're probably going to want to connect both a computer monitor and your TV set to your MCE PC. We recommend this highly, especially if you don't have a new, large LCD or plasma screen — small computer type is hard to read on regular TV sets. Setting up both a PC monitor and TV display, however, can get a little tricky depending on your video interface card and the cables supplied by your PC manufacturer. In some instances, where it might appear that you should plug one cable connector into a certain port, you actually shouldn't because of other system issues. So please read this section closely if you're using both a TV and a PC monitor.

Your MCE PC has one video card, which handles outbound video signals from the PC. The video card handles one signal (your MCE PC's desktop, in other words) distributed across its two active ports, so you can attach two displays and see the same thing. (This capability is a base requirement of Microsoft's MCE PC license.)

A graphics card is just another name for a video card.

For example, Danny's Viewsonic MCE PC and Pat's Gateway both have an NVIDIA graphics card that supports three video output signal formats (S-video, VGA — the standard analog computer monitor video connection — and digital video using the DVI connection system). At any particular time, two of the three Out ports on the video card can be in use, one for a TV and one for a PC monitor.

Because card manufacturers have to match two outbound signals with three ports, two of the ports must share a signal. This means your video card can support only certain combinations of simultaneous output port connections. Here are the options for Danny's NVIDIA card:

	Display 1	Display 2
Option 1	DVI	S-video
Option 2	DVI	VGA
Option 3	DVI-to-VGA adapter	S-video

In this example, DVI (digital visual interface) is the primary output source signal and VGA and S-video share the secondary output source signal. Now suppose that Danny's TV doesn't have a DVI connection, and his computer monitor doesn't have an S-video connection — it has only VGA. That means his only option is to hook up the PC monitor to the DVI port using a DVI-to-VGA adapter, and use S-video for the TV.

This example is important because it's non-intuitive to most of us. If you were just plugging in cables without reading the fine print in the manuals, you would probably plug the VGA cable from your PC monitor into your video card's VGA port, and plug your S-video connector into the S-video port. But as you can tell from the preceding table, that won't work.

Note that in Chapter 3 we mention an S-video-to-composite adapter. Does your TV have only has the three colored RCA-composite jacks (white and red for audio and yellow for video)? If so, you'd have to use the S-video-to-composite adapter (in the preceding example) to send video to your yellow video port on your TV.

You may find more about your specific video card's capabilities buried in troubleshooting areas or in FAQs on the vendor's Web site. This information was not in the main body of any of the PC manufacturers' user manuals that we reviewed for publication.

Connecting to the TV

In one sense, connecting your TV to your PC is simple. You run a cable or cables from point A to point B. Keep in mind our advice from earlier in the chapter about the relative hierarchy of video connection cables: component video is best, then S-video, then composite video.

One of the most frequent complaints that we hear from people about hooking up their TV set to their PC is a statement of dismay that they don't have the same resolution on the TV as on the computer display. That's because many

TV sets struggle to give you 480 x 440, but many computer displays have a 1024 x 768 resolution, if not 1260 x 1024!

As a result, you can't read small print well on a traditional TV, so Web surfing can be tough. There's not much you can do about this limitation, except buy one of the new TV sets with high-resolution-display technologies. The good news is that LCD and plasma TV displays — the type required to act as large computer monitors — are available for lower prices each month. For example, you can now get a 20-inch LCD TV for around $1100, and a full 42-inch plasma-screen TV from Gateway for less than $3000.

When connecting your MCE PC to both a monitor and a TV, attaching the cables is only one step. The other step is telling the computer that you have two displays — and making sure it "sees" both of them.

In this section, we walk through an example of what you need to do, using the HP Media Center computer with Microsoft Windows XP Media Center Edition and the NVIDIA GeForce4 video card, which is a common video card. The procedure for your setup should be similar. Check the manual that comes with your MCE PC to see whether the exact steps you should follow.

The following steps are *not* performed inside the full-screen, remote-controllable Media Center interface. Instead, you do the following in the regular keyboard-and-mouse Windows XP interface:

1. **Turn on the computer and the television.**

2. **Make sure your TV is set to the right input source.**

   Your source is the MCE PC. Your TV settings should be the same as with your present video signal. Most TV sets have a Video/TV toggle button on the remote control or the front of the TV. If you have problems seeing an image during this process, try switching the input source setting (usually line 1, video 1 or S-video on your TV screen).

3. **Right-click anywhere on an open area of the Windows XP desktop and choose Properties.**

4. **Click the Settings tab, and then click the Advanced button.**

5. **Click the tab whose title matches the name of your video card, as shown in Figure 5-1.**

6. **Choose Clone, click Apply, and then click OK.**

7. **If a Monitor Settings dialog box appears after the screen properties change, click Yes.**

8. **In the Display Properties dialog box, click OK.**

9. **If a Monitor Settings dialog box appears after the screen properties change, click Yes.**

This will *clone,* or recreate exactly, the image on your desktop to the TV.

These steps will be different on your MCE PC if you have a different video card. We *very strongly* recommend that you check your PC and video card manufacturer's Web sites for assistance if you have a different card than the one we describe here.

If you follow these steps and don't see the signal on both screens, check that the Video Out cables are connected to the correct jacks on the back of your MCE PC.

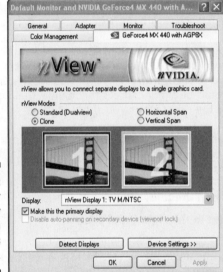

Figure 5-1:
Cloning your display signal in Windows XP MCE.

Connecting to Your TV Signal Source

Now it's time to connect your content signals to your MCE PC. After all, connecting your PC to your TV helps when you want to play home videos and DVDs, but it won't do much for recording TV shows.

If you have a set-top box, antenna, or other source for your TV signal, connect that source to your PC using the TV or Video In port on your PC. If you have a coaxial connection from, say, a cable set-top box, you'll find a complementary coaxial interface on a card in the back of the PC. If your source is outputting an S-video or composite-video connection, use the S-Video port (using an S-video-to-composite-video adapter cable).

If you use an S-video or composite-video cable to connect to your TV source — instead of using the coaxial cable connection — you also need some separate cables to carry the audio signals that correspond with your TV video (in other words, the dialogue and soundtrack). In this case, you plug your audio cables into the PC using red (right) and white (left) audio interconnect cables.

Be sure to read the "My VCR" sidebar earlier in this chapter for more information about including a VCR as a signal source in your setup.

Tying in Your Speakers

Different audio interface cards have different ports. Most MCE PCs are designed for folks with an existing stereo system or a set of PC computer speakers — and either two-channel stereo or 5.1 surround sound.

Your audio card in your Media Center computer outputs a high-quality but nonamplified signal. If you're using conventional speakers — the type that you'd connect to your stereo system — make sure they're self-amplified or that you have an amplifier somewhere in your system. (This amplifier can be a stand-alone audio amplifier, or in a home-theater receiver, or in a regular stereo receiver.) Computer speakers that come with MCE PCs have their own built-in amplifiers, so you don't need an external amplifier like the one in a receiver in a home-entertainment system.

Speakers with built-in amplifiers are often referred to as *active loudspeakers*. Conventional stereo-connected speakers without built-in amplifiers are called *passive loudspeakers*.

Audio cards vary in terms of their capability to output different types of signals. You get three major forms of sound from these cards:

- ✔ 2 channel (stereo)
- ✔ 4 channel (quad stereo)
- ✔ 6 channel (5.1 surround sound)

You also may see some vendors pitching a *2.1 system,* which is a left and right channel with a derived bass signal to a subwoofer. A *derived* signal means that the processor is filtering out only specific frequencies from the other signals to create a signal for the subwoofer. Contrast this approach to a true *5.1 system,* in which an encoded special-effects channel in the audio signal goes to the subwoofer.

These three forms of sound are output on one of four connectors:

- ✔ Analog RCA connector
- ✔ Analog miniplug (3.5mm) connector
- ✔ Digital optical connector
- ✔ Digital coaxial connector

Connecting your computer speakers to your MCE PC is a matter of connecting the speaker cable connectors to the appropriate ports on the audio out cards.

Hooking up your MCE PC to your stereo system

If you have a newer or high-end stereo system, you'll probably want to tie your MCE PC to your receiver or preamplifier using the digital optical or coaxial interfaces. If your receiver has only RCA Audio In jacks, you'll use either the analog RCA or miniplug connector (with a miniplug-to-RCA adapter — we told you that you'd need those adapters).

Integrating speakers into your MCE PC can become complex because some audio interface cards were designed to work with computer-oriented amplified speaker systems, such as the Klipsch ProMedia 5.1 (www.klipsch.com/, $499) or the Logitech Z-680 (www.logitech.com, $399) — two of the most commonly bundled speaker sets for MCE PC computers. From the cabling used to the color coding on the ports, these cards are often matched to computer speaker sets.

Take a look at the Sound Blaster Audigy card, one of the most popular cards for MCE PCs. This card has the following audio connectors:

- ✔ **Mic (Pink):** Connects your microphone
- ✔ **Line In (Blue):** Connects to an analog audio source
- ✔ **Line Out-1 (Lime Green):** Connects to an active stereo or multichannel speaker system, either as the single link to a 2.1 speaker system or as the first (front speakers) of three links to a 5.1 speaker system
- ✔ **Line Out-2 (Black):** Connects to an active stereo or multichannel speaker system, for the rear speakers of a 4 or 5.1 speaker system
- ✔ **Line Out-3 (Orange):** Connects to an active stereo or multichannel speaker system, for the center speakers and subwoofer of a 5.1 speaker system
- ✔ **Digital Out (same connector as Line Out-3):** Connects to a digital device such as a preamp or a stereo receiver that has a digital input port

So depending on what speakers you have, you might be using one, two, or three cables, and either analog or digital ports. Whew.

Another example of an MCE PC's audio connections is the Viewsonic M2000, which offers two analog RCA ports (for a 2.1 speaker system), as well as optical and coaxial digital outputs (for 5.1 signals). But if you have an amplified 5.1 computer-speaker system that doesn't take anything but a miniplug interface, there's no way to connect the two without going through some sort of interface device, such as a preamp. You'd need to have speakers like the Logitech Z-680, which can accept the S/PDIF optical or coaxial digital output from your MCE PC.

After you connect your speakers physically, your next step is to configure your MCE PC to support the type of audio setup you have. It would be a shame to have a 5.1 surround-sound system installed but be outputting a simple, stereo two-channel signal. Your audio should be set correctly for your speaker system by default from the factory, but it's a good idea to check it to be sure.

After you boot your system (see Chapter 7), you should check the following configurations on your MCE PC:

1. **Open the audio card utility program that comes with your PC and set the speakers to the appropriate setting, such as 2 Speaker or 5.1 Surround Sound.**

   If you have an Audigy card, choose Start➪All Programs➪Creative➪Sound Blaster Audigy, and then click AudioHQ to access the audio card settings.

2. **Launch the Media Center interface (press the big green button on the remote) and set the speaker preferences in the system Settings folder.**

   a. **From the main Media Center screen, choose Settings➪TV/DVD➪ DVD➪Audio.**

   b. **On the Audio tab, make sure that the correct speaker/channel option is selected.**

   c. **Click Apply and then click OK.**

3. **Open the Windows Control Panel and select right speaker/channel mode.**

   To do this:

   a. **Choose Start➪Control Panel➪Sounds➪Speech and Audio Devices, and then choose Sounds and Audio Devices.**

   The Properties window appears.

   b. **Click the Volume tab. In the Speaker settings, click the Advanced button.**

   c. **Click the Speakers tab. In the Speaker Setup area, choose the correct channel combo from the pull-down menu.**

   d. **Click Apply, and then click OK.**

Now your PC should be configured not only for Media Center usage but also for any other audio or video application on your PC.

Connecting headphones and mics

You can connect headphones to your PC. Generally, most headphones have a ⅛-inch (3.5mm) male miniplug connector that you plug into your equipment. So you would plug this connector into a headset 3.5mm port, a Line Out port, or the speaker system itself. (Look for the port with the little headphone icon next to it.) Not much to it really — just plug the headphones in and that's it.

Because you'll probably be sitting back a few feet from the MCE PC when you're using the headphones, you might consider buying a set of wireless headphones. Freedom of motion (and freedom from tripping over that darned wire) is a beautiful thing.

You can hook up a microphone to your system as well. Most PCs have a small 3.5mm port for a microphone jack. Some manufacturers color code the jack (HP's is pink). You don't need the microphone for any MCE functions we discuss here, but it can be handy if you want to use your MCE PC and Internet connection for voice chat or Internet telephony.

Connecting Peripherals

Your remaining peripherals — printer, USB devices, cell-phone data cord, and so on — plug into the MCE PC according to the installation process laid out by the manufacturer. Your MCE PC is just another Windows XP machine, so if a peripheral works on a normal XP PC, it will work on your XP MCE PC.

So many types of peripherals and vendors are available that we can't give you explicit instructions here on how to connect them, other than to note that peripheral devices generally connect to the PC through its USB, parallel, or serial ports. For more on USB (and the two variants of this technology — USB 1.1 and USB 2.0), see Chapter 1.

We recommend that you wait until you fully set up the software component of Windows XP Media Center Edition before attaching any peripherals unless they're needed to turn on the machine for the first time. Otherwise, Windows will detect and start to install these devices when it sees them, possibly interrupting the MCE installation process.

Recent advances in plug-and-play should make it even easier for you to connect new devices, so we don't have a lot to write about in this section. Microsoft has had great success in expanding the number of peripheral devices that truly are plug-and-play. And because Media Center is based on Windows XP

Professional, Plug-and-Play works just as well with an MCE PC as it does with any XP computer.

You might have problems plugging older gear into MCE PC. If your hardware is not on the Windows Hardware Compatibility List (HCL), search the vendor's site for updated XP drivers. The drivers should be easy to find because most hardware vendors have developed compatible drivers for their older equipment — look at the support pages of the vendor's Web site.

You can check the compatibility of your hardware (and software for that matter) at the Microsoft Compatibility Web site at

```
www.microsoft.com/windowsxp/upgrade/compatible/
```

or by choosing Start➪Help and Support. When the Help and Support Center window appears (it's also called HelpSpot), click the Find compatible hardware and software for Windows XP link.

You might have difficulty also if you're plugging into a USB 2.0 slot older gear that uses a USB 1.1 interface in. The combination of older and new equipment on the USB 2.0 connection might cause some attached USB devices to not work, particularly if you're using an external USB 2.0 hub, a device that adds interface ports to your MCE PC.

USB 1.1 runs a slower speed than the newer 2.0 specification. Because USB is a serial communications channel, everything connecting to that channel has to use the same protocol and work at the same speed. The computer doesn't have a problem with this requirement, but the devices might. Many devices (cameras, scanners, mice) can "speak" only one language (USB 1.1 or 2.0). If you combine a USB 1.1 device and a USB 2.0 device on the same channel, one takes precedence (by being the first to communicate with the computer) and sets the language that will be used. In almost every case, the newer device wins out because the faster 2.0 protocol is always the first to communicate with the computer. The older device will not work, even though it's plugged in correctly (and even if its indicator lights indicate a valid connection).

You do have a way around this problem: The XP MCE PC has two USB slots on the back. Each has a unique channel, so one could "speak" USB 1.1 and the other could "speak" USB 2.0. Just make sure that all your older devices go on one channel and all your newer devices go on the other. To do this, use two dual-mode USB hubs. Connect all USB 1.1 devices to one hub, and connect that hub to one of the USB ports on the PC. Connect all USB 2.0 devices to the other hub, and connect that hub to the other USB port on the PC. Now every device should be happy.

All those cables ... and the cat!

Do you have pets and are worried that they might go after your cables? You can try a few things:

✔ **Organize your cables:** Viewsonic has a wonderful, built-in hood, or cover, for its MCE PCs that protects your cable connections (by keeping the cat away from them, for example) and ensures that all the cables exit in a common area, making it easier to bundle them. For cables going to the same place, such as to your entertainment center or across to a network connection jack, think about binding them with plastic tubing or Velcro straps. Check out the great list of cable and wire organizers at www.online organizing.com.

✔ **Make your cables taste bad:** We use Grannick's Bitter Apple spray to keep pets away. We've heard that it tastes so horrible that even pets won't try it (and we've seen our dogs taste a lot of questionable stuff). It's available in your nearby pet store.

In the next few years, you should see wireless cables — little wireless adapters that create a high-speed, wireless link between connected devices. (For more in this topic, see Chapter 19.) We simply can't wait for that!

Connecting to the Telephone Line or Network

After you've made all the local connections, it's time to connect your MCE PC to the outside world. In Chapter 6, we go into detail about connecting to the Internet. In this section, we focus on the physical aspect of plugging in your connections so that you can do all the configurations we talk about in Chapter 6.

Included with your MCE PC is a telephone line cord, with RJ-11 connections (the little plastic jobbers) on each end. Connect one end of the telephone line cord into the modem port on your PC and the other into a nearby phone jack. There, that was easy.

Some MCE PCs come with modem cards that have both a Line In and a Line Out RJ-11 jack, so you can share your wall jack with a phone. You run a phone cable (with two RJ-11 jacks) from the wall jack to your PC Line Out jack, then you run another phone cable from the PC to the wall. Now, both your PC and your phone can work at the same time.

If your PC doesn't have a Line Out jack and you're using the wall jack next to your MCE PC for your phone, buy a 2-to-1 splitter adapter from Radio Shack. The splitter allows you to connect both the MCE PC and a phone to a single wall outlet.

You connect to a cable modem, DSL line, or satellite modem using either the USB connection or the Ethernet connection on your MCE PC. Most PC Ethernet cards have a little green LED that will light up if you have a valid connection.

We continue the discussion of the configuration of your Internet connection in Chapter 6. For now, it's sufficient that all your cables are connected.

Connecting Your IR Devices

Your MCE PC is outfitted with IR-sensing capability for taking input commands from the remote control. This sensor is part of the computer, part of the monitor, or an attachable remote sensor connected to your computer with a cable.

An attachable remote sensor allows you to extend your IR-signal-receiving capability, so you can tuck the PC away in a corner and not worry about having to point your remote control at the front of the PC or the monitor.

The remote sensor is smaller than a deck of cards and connects to your PC using (in almost all cases) a USB cable. Locate the remote sensor in a position that's visible from all areas of the room.

If you have a cable TV, satellite, or other set-top box that controls your TV signal, you need to use an IR-sensor control cable that will allow your MCE PC to control that set-top (so that the MCE PC can change channels to record a program for you). If you have a remote-sensor box, this control cable will connect to the back of that box. Otherwise, the cable connects to the back of your MCE PC.

Remote-sensor control cables have a little, clear IR-emitting head that you should position over the IR-sensor eye on your set-top box. You have to remove the tape backing on the IR head of the remote-sensor control cable and then stick it to the IR sensor eye of the set-top box. Hold it there for a little while to make sure it sticks.

In addition to taping the IR head to the sensor eye on the set-top box, tape the sensor cable itself to the set-top box so that the cable doesn't get yanked loose. (The sticky side of the IR-emitter head on the cable can degrade over time.) It's common for the small IR-emitter head of a sensor cable to fall off, and you'll be mad if this happens at just the wrong time — say, when you're running into your room at 8:59 on a Sunday night because you forget to tell your MCE PC to tape *Sex and the City.*

If you have a set-top box whose IR sensor is hidden behind a large panel of smoked or red plastic, use a flashlight to see through the plastic panel and find the IR sensor. The sensor is typically shaped like a small circle, about ⅛-inch round, within a squarish frame.

Connecting Your FM Antenna

For your FM tuner in your new Media Center PC to work, it's going to need . . . ta-da . . . an FM antenna. All sorts of FM antennas are on the market, from the cheap, string-like, dipole antenna you can get from Radio Shack to expensive, roof-mounted FM directional antennas. One nifty unit from Radio Shack is its VHF/UHF/FM Antenna with IR Learning Technology (model 15-1870, $39). The antenna "learns" and remembers the preprogrammed position for the best reception for each FM station. Then, every time you select a station, the antenna automatically adjusts to the same position!

Connecting an FM antenna to your MCE PC is easy. Connect the antenna's leads to the FM jack on your PC's radio tuner card. The PC card typically requires a 75-ohm connection from the antenna, so make sure the antenna you choose has one of these connections (it looks like a cable TV connector).

You'll need to fiddle with the position of the antenna to find the spot with the maximum signal strength.

"Houston, We Are Go for Liftoff!"

You've assembled and connected your Media Center PC, but you need to do a few more things before everything is completely up and running. First, you need to get your Internet connection online. In the next chapter you find out about the different types of Internet connections you can use with your MCE PC (we recommend broadband), obtaining service, and getting online.

Then you need to boot 'er up and go through the setup programs, which we talk about in Chapter 7. We love configuring software so much that sometimes we reset everything and do it all over again, just for fun! We walk you through the things you see the first time you fire up your MCE PC (in Chapter 7) and then give you advice on how to configure and customize Media Center (in Chapter 8).

Chapter 6

Connecting to the Internet

*G*etting online. Connecting to the Internet. It's vital for any PC, including a Media Center Edition PC. Getting your MCE PC online gives you a window to the world of online music, pictures, and videos. And with new services such as the new, legal version of Napster, Listen.com's Rhapsody, and Movielink, you can get songs and movies online legally and inexpensively. In addition, accessing the on-screen program guide to see what's on TV and to program your My TV module so that you can record TV shows *requires* an Internet connection.

In this chapter, we talk about the two ways to connect to the Internet: slow dial-up and the much faster broadband. You find out how to get Internet service and how to connect your MCE PC.

Internet Connection Basics

At the most basic level, you can connect your MCE PC (or any PC) to the Internet in two ways:

✓ **Dial-up:** Using the analog modem built into every MCE PC, you can create a dial-up connection to an ISP (Internet Service Provider) such as AOL or Earthlink. This dial-up connection uses your existing phone line and connects you with your ISP at a speed of up to 56 kilobits per second (Kbps). Hardly anyone gets a true 56 Kbps out of his or her dial-up connection, however. For technical reasons we won't bore you with, most connections are 44 Kbps or less. And your dial-up connection is slower in the *upstream* direction (that is, from your computer to the Internet) than in the *downstream* direction.

✔ **Broadband:** Using the Ethernet port on the back of your MCE PC, you can connect to a broadband ISP at speeds that can be 20 or more times faster than dial-up connections With a broadband connection, you don't have to sit around and wait for hours (or even days) to download music and movies from the Internet.

We *strongly recommend* that you get a broadband connection for your MCE PC, if you can. The amount of entertainment content (songs, movies, videos, and pictures) that you can access online will only increase, and a dial-up connection simply can't handle many types of media because the files that you need to download are too big.

Did you know that some services won't even let you on their site if you don't have the right bandwidth? It's true. If you have a dial-up connection, try to log on to Movielink's site (`www.movielink.com`). It checks your connection as you log on and shunts dial-up users to a message saying that the connection is not fast enough for its service. That's harsh!

As you begin to connect your MCE PC to the Internet, you might come across a few unfamiliar terms. To demystify them, we provide the following list of definitions:

✔ **IP address:** Every computer (actually, every device) on the Internet has an IP address. (IP stands for Internet Protocol — it's the common language used by everything on the Internet.) Your *IP address* is sort of like your telephone number for the Internet.

When you surf the Web, your computer and Web browser program send out small requests for data (Web pages) to the IP address of the computer (or server) hosting the Web page you want to look at. These requests include *your* IP address, so that the Web server can send the Web page data back to your computer and your Web browser. Everything you do on the Internet is based on the concept of computers communicating with other computers, using their respective IP addresses.

✔ **DNS:** An IP address consists of four sets of numbers separated by periods (for example, 64.236.16.116). When you want to read a Web page, you type something like `www.cnn.com` instead of 64.236.16.116. Because it's easy to remember `www.cnn.com`, but not many of us can remember `64.236.16.116`, the Internet powers-that-be were smart enough to set up something called DNS (Domain Name System). With *DNS,* you enter a regular text name (also called a *host name*) such as `www.cnn.com`. The DNS server at your ISP converts that name to the IP address so your Web browser or other Internet program can find what you're looking for online.

✔ **DHCP:** With the majority of ISPs, your MCE PC (or any PC) is assigned a new IP address every time you connect to the Internet using a system called DHCP (Dynamic Host Configuration Protocol). Because the IP address changes every time you go online, it's a *dynamic IP address.*

This is an automated and behind-the-scenes process, but we want to tell you about it because in certain cases (for example, if you want to host your own Web site on your MCE PC), you may want to pay a few bucks more a month to your ISP and get a static IP address instead of dynamic one. A *static IP address* never changes, which makes it much easier for other people to find online services you're hosting on your MCE PC.

DHCP is an important concept for people who are logging on to your home network as guests. DHCP allows your brother-in-law's kids to come over with their sleek wireless-enabled laptops and log on to your home network with relative ease. The laptops are considered another computer on your network requesting a temporary IP address to access the Internet. For more on home networking, see Chapters 15 and 16.

Dial-up Modem Connections

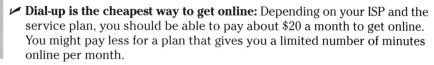

The easiest and quickest way to get online is to use a dial-up connection to your ISP, using the internal modem built into your MCE PC. The advantages of using a dial-up connection follow:

✔ **Dial-up is easy to do:** The modem is already installed in your MCE PC. You don't have to do anything special to your phone line (that is, neither you nor the phone company has to make any special preparations). Using dial-up is just plug and play.

✔ **Dial-up is available anywhere:** Just about every phone jack in the United States can support a dial-up connection. Even in the most rural areas with rotary phone dialing, you should be able to dial up your ISP, although it might be a long-distance call.

If you're new to the Internet and are using a dial-up connection to your ISP, be sure to check whether it's a toll call.

✔ **Dial-up is the cheapest way to get online:** Depending on your ISP and the service plan, you should be able to pay about $20 a month to get online. You might pay less for a plan that gives you a limited number of minutes online per month.

As we've already mentioned, dial-up is not ideal. Here are some limitations to dial-up compared to broadband ISP connections:

✔ **Dial-up is slow:** 56 Kbps is the maximum speed of a dial-up connection. As mentioned, usually the connection speed is lower, probably in the 40 to 45 Kbps range. To put this in perspective, an average quality MP3 music file is about 2MB. So downloading a single song using a modem can take 7 to 8 minutes. If you have a ten-song CD that you want to download, plan on spending an hour to an hour and a half. That's a long time! This slow downloading gets even worse when you start talking about video files and movies (where the files are exponentially larger).

✓ **Dial-up can be a pain:** Dialing into an ISP can sometimes be a quick and painless procedure, but often it's time consuming and slow. Busy signals are not unheard of with some ISPs; just when you need to dial in to send a quick e-mail or to check a sports score, you find that you can't get online. Even if there's no busy signal, you may end up taking more time dialing in than you will doing what you need to do online.

✓ **Dial-up connections block your phone calls:** Probably the biggest inconvenience you might experience with dial-up connections is that it ties up your phone line. For that reason, many people have second phone lines at home, dedicated solely to dial-up connections. That adds about $15 to $25 to your monthly bill (exactly the difference in price between dial-up and broadband, you'll notice).

Today, some ISPs offer an *Internet Call Waiting* service that displays a message when someone calls while you're online and offers you the option to suspend your online activities so you can answer the phone.

✓ **Dial-up connections don't play well with home networks:** If you have more than one computer (a work laptop maybe or a spouse's computer), dial-up can be inconvenient. It's difficult to share a dial-up connection among multiple computers, and even if you can get it to work, you'll find that the limited speed (bandwidth) is stretched even more thinly when two or three people are accessing the Internet simultaneously.

Well, now that we've said a few good things and a few bad things about dial-up Internet connections, let's say this: Not everyone can get a broadband ISP connection where they live, and not everyone who can get broadband can afford it. (Broadband connections cost $15 to $20 a month more than dial-up connections.)

Satellite Internet service reaches most of the United States and serves as a reasonable link to the broadband world. More than 90 percent of Americans have access to some sort of broadband connection (at least that's what the FCC tells us). We talk more about this in the "Other Ways to Get Online" section, later in this chapter.

If you're going to use a dial-up Internet connection, the first step is to choose your ISP. A few years ago, ISPs were set up in just about every corner of the globe, with small Mom-and-Pop ISPs serving a large percentage of Internet users. In the intervening years, the ISP market has undergone a lot of consolidation, meaning that a few big players have bought up the smaller ISPs or driven them out of business.

There are still some local dial-up ISPs around, and they can offer good service. If you have some geeky friends, ask them whether they know of any local ISPs in your area and get their recommendations. You can also look at your local computer paper (you know the one — it's stacked by the door at your local coffee shop or computer parts store) to see what's available.

Your other choice is a national ISP that provides — you guessed it — service nationally. You might get less personal service with a national ISP, but it does have some advantages. First, it's more likely to have an access number (the phone number you dial into to connect to the Net) wherever you go. So if you move or travel with your MCE PC (remember, some MCE PCs are laptops), you'll be able to get online. Second, many also provide broadband ISP services. So if you decide to upgrade to broadband later, you may be able to do so without changing your e-mail address or going through the process of signing up with a new provider.

Some of the national ISPs that you might consider include the following:

✔ AOL: www.aol.com

✔ Earthlink: www.earthlink.net

✔ MSN: www.msn.com

✔ NetZero: www.netzero.com

You can also get dial-up service from your local phone company (such as SBC, BellSouth, Verizon, or Qwest). In many cases, the local phone company works with another company — for example, SBC offers a dial-up service with Yahoo!, and Qwest works with MSN. If you get your Internet access from your local phone company, you may find that you can get a discounted price if you buy a bundle of services from the company.

Our favorite online source for information about dial-up and broadband ISPs is CNET. Check out its ISP information page at www.cnet.com/internet.

DSL Connections

The local phone company offers you an even better way to get online using your phone lines: DSL (Digital Subscriber Line) service. *DSL* is a digital modem technology that takes advantage of the unused frequencies on your phone line (specifically, the frequencies above those used to carry your voice over the phone line) to give you extra bandwidth, or speed, on your Internet connection.

Many variants of DSL technology are available, such as ADSL, SDSL, and IDSL. The most common by far is ADSL (Asymmetric DSL). If you go to your local phone company or your favorite ISP to buy DSL, 99 percent of the time you'll get ADSL.

Filtering out noise

We mentioned that DSL — particularly the ADSL technology used in residential DSL — uses different frequencies on the phone lines than your voice telephone service. Unfortunately, things aren't always that tidy in the real world — systems that operate at different frequencies may still send out stray frequencies that interfere with each other. So even though your phone (on the lower frequencies) and your ADSL modem (on the higher frequencies) are not supposed to interfere, overlap occurs.

Early DSL modem installations used a device called a POTS splitter to keep your voice and the DSL modem on different segments of the phone wiring in your house. This brute-force approach of keeping things separate solved the interference problem but came with a price. A phone technician had to come to your house to install this splitter, and you ended up with only one phone outlet in the house that could accept your DSL modem.

The current solution is more elegant. When a DSL modem is installed, you simply plug a small filter into your wall outlet between the phone and the outlet. This filter is called a *low-pass filter* because it lets only lower frequencies through. The low-pass filter corrects any interference problems and lets you plug the DSL modem into any phone outlet in the house. You can also do the installation yourself, which saves you time and money.

ADSL is called asymmetric because the *downstream* speed (from the Internet to your MCE PC) is typically much faster than the *upstream* speed (from your MCE PC to the Internet). Although some computer-savvy folks find that they need a lot of upstream bandwidth (to host their own Web servers and the like), the asymmetric bandwidth of ADSL is not a problem for most users. That's because most of the large files you want to access (such as movies and music) are coming in the downstream direction. All that's headed upstream are relatively small bits of data requesting those files.

So, how fast is ADSL? It depends on the provider and what service you choose, but most ADSL services offer downstream speeds of 500 Kbps or faster — on up to multiple megabits (thousands of kilobits) per second. In other words, DSL ranges from a *lot* faster than dial-up to a *whole helluva lot* faster than dial-up.

DSL pieces and parts

Unlike dial-up ISP connections, which use an analog modem built into your MCE PC, DSL ISP connections use a separate external DSL modem. This modem connects to your MCE PC using an Ethernet port (the most common connection) or USB (Universal Serial Bus — a common computer connector also used for things such as printers, mice, and digital cameras).

If you have a choice (and you usually will), go for the DSL modem that includes an Ethernet port. A USB-only DSL modem isn't useful if you want to start creating a home network for more than one computer. Many DSL modems include both a USB connection and an Ethernet connection, so there's no choice to be made. Easy as can be!

For the most part, DSL modems are not available off the shelf like other computer accessories. Instead, you obtain a DSL modem that's set up to work with your DSL provider. Typically, when you order your DSL service, the provider ships the modem to you. You either buy the modem from the DSL provider (for about $100), or they lease it to you as part of the service and you have to give it back if you cancel the service. In a few parts of the country, you can buy a DSL modem at stores such as Circuit City or Fry's — the DSL modem is offered in conjunction with the DSL providers, so you buy the modem and sign up for a specific service at the same time.

Choosing a DSL provider

Two general types of DSL providers are available:

- ✔ Your local phone company
- ✔ A group of competitive phone companies called *CLECs*

If you haven't been paying attention to the news in the Internet business lately, you might not have heard that CLECs have had a tough run the past few years. Most have gone out of business or focused solely on the business (not consumer) marketplace. The one remaining large CLEC is Covad Communications. That means you usually have a choice between your local phone company and Covad for getting DSL.

Your options depend on where you live, but generally you can choose between Covad (www.covad.com) and one of the following companies:

- ✔ **Verizon:** www.verizon.com (serves the Northeastern U.S. and a few markets elsewhere in the U.S.)
- ✔ **BellSouth:** www.bellsouth.com (serves the Southeastern U.S.)
- ✔ **SBC:** www.sbc.com (serves much of the Central and Southwestern U.S.)
- ✔ **Qwest:** www.qwest.com (serves the Rocky Mountains area and Northwestern U.S.)

If you live outside the service areas of the "big four" local telephone companies listed here, your phone company is probably a smaller local one (often called an *independent*, because it was never part of the Bell system). If so, you're lucky — many independents are excellent providers of DSL services and have wider availability and better services than the big guys.

When you choose a DSL provider — such as Covad or your local telephone company — you usually have a choice of ISP. The DSL provider gives you the connection, and the ISP provides Internet services such as e-mail, Web site hosting, and music services.

Most DSL providers offer their own ISP service, but you can also choose from both local ISPs (in most cases) and big national ISPs. Some of the bigger ISPs who focus on DSL services are

- **Earthlink:** www.earthlink.net
- **Speakeasy:** www.speakeasy.net
- **AOL:** www.aol.com
- **MSN:** www.msn.com (available through Verizon and Qwest)
- **Yahoo! Broadband:** sbc.yahoo.com (available through SBC)

Which to choose? We recommend that you look at the options and prices and try to find the ISP that offers the services that best fit your needs. This is not exactly earth-shattering advice, but each of these ISPs has their own specialties and services.

We like to choose ISPs that explicitly support home networks. Many will often provide you with networking hardware, extra e-mail boxes (one for each person in the house), and other neat Internet features such as fixed IP addresses (helpful if you want to use applications such as videoconferencing) and firewall services (to keep the bad guys out of your computer). ISPs offer their own packages of music and video services that help you get entertainment content for your MCE PC. Check them out and see which one has the services you want and the price you can afford.

Expect to pay between $30 and $50 a month for DSL service, depending on the provider and the connection speed.

Many DSL ISP connections are *always-on* connections, meaning that the DSL modem makes an initial connection to the Internet and stays connected at all times. You don't need to log on or enter a user name and password when you want to access the Internet on your MCE PC. Some DSL providers, however, use a system called *PPPoE* (or Point to Point Protocol over Ethernet) that forces you to enter that user name and password every time you restart your computer or want to get online. If you have a choice, we highly recommend that you avoid PPPoE and find a DSL ISP that offers a true always-on service.

Many people who use AOL don't want to upgrade to DSL or a cable modem because they want to keep their AOL e-mail address and interface. No problem. AOL sells high-speed Internet access in select areas, so you might be able to buy it from them. AOL also offers a subscription package that allows you to add AOL on top of any broadband connection for $9.95 per month. That means you keep your AOL e-mail address and AOL service, but you access AOL over a broadband connection instead of dial-up.

Cable Modem Connections

The other common way to make a broadband Internet connection is to use a cable modem. The *cable modem* connects to the Internet over your home's cable TV wires, not the phone lines used by DSL or dial-up connections, and offers the same always-on, high-speed connection offered by most DSL providers. Like DSL, cable modems offer downstream speeds measured in megabits per second, not the kilobits per second that dial-up connections offer. So, like DSL, cable modems are a fast broadband alternative to dial-up connections.

 We've seen many arguments (in advertising, in online forums, and the like) about DSL versus cable modem — which is faster, which is better, and so on. We've used both systems in our homes and offices over the years, and think they're roughly equivalent. What's important is the service offered by your local providers — check out the speeds and prices and see what suits your needs best. We highly recommend www.broadbandreports.com as a source of consumer reports and recommendations for broadband services.

Cable modem services, such as DSL services, typically range from $35 to $50 per month, depending on your cable company and what speed you choose (some providers offer higher speed services for more money). And like phone companies, cable companies tend to offer discounts if you buy that bundle of services (in this case, high-speed Internet plus cable TV, digital cable, or even cable telephone service). It's most likely that your best economic solution will come from your existing provider of telephone or entertainment (cable or satellite) services. The incremental cost of adding broadband to your phone service or your cable TV service is a lot less than buying it separately.

Cable modems for everyone

Cable modems, like DSL modems, are external (they sit on the shelf near your MCE PC). Because the cable modem industry has done a better job than DSL providers of standardizing their systems nationwide, you're more likely to be able to just go to the local electronics superstore and buy your own cable modem off the shelf (but check with your cable company first). Most cable companies will also sell or lease you a modem, just as the DSL providers do.

The majority of cable modems have either USB or Ethernet connectors — a few have both types of connectors. Again, we prefer the Ethernet modem or Ethernet and USB combination modem because they're more flexible if you decide to start a home network or already have one. The USB-only modems are simple to set up but too limited in their capabilities.

When you're buying an external broadband modem, you'll find some that include other functionality such as a router or a wireless access point. These can be no-brainer add-ons depending on what you plan to do with your home networking strategy. We urge you to read Chapters 15 and 16 on wired and wireless home networking options before you buy or lease a particular model.

Getting your hands on cable modem service

Getting cable modem service is a simple task. Unlike the telephone company world, the cable world doesn't have competition; only one cable provider is in any given location. Most of the United States is served by a local cable company that is affiliated with or is a subsidiary of a national cable company (or MSO, multisystem operator). Some smaller towns and more rural parts of the country have smaller, local cable companies, but increasingly, the cable business is run by a few large, nationwide MSOs.

The most common cable (and cable modem) service operators follow:

- ✔ **Comcast:** www.comcast.com (the largest MSO in the United States; acquired AT&T's cable business as well)

- ✔ **Time Warner Cable:** www.timewarnercable.com (the cable modem service is called Road Runner, at www.rr.com)

- ✔ **Cox Communications:** www.cox.com

- ✔ **Charter Communications:** www.charter.com

- ✔ **Cablevision:** www.cablevision.com

- ✔ **Shaw Cable:** www.shaw.ca (Canada's biggest cable operator)

- ✔ **Rogers:** www.rogers.com (the other large MSO in Canada)

For the most part, when you order cable modem service from your local cable company, it also acts as your ISP (providing your e-mail mailboxes and other ISP services such as a personal Web page). In some areas, particularly those controlled by Time Warner, you may have a choice of ISPs.

For example, Pat is a Road Runner customer, but he can also use AOL or Earthlink as his cable modem ISP. If you want to use a different ISP for your cable modem service, we suggest that you check the Broadband Reports Web site (www.broadbandreports.com) or check the Web pages of individual ISPs (such as www.Earthlink.net) to see whether they offer cable modem service.

Other Ways to Get Online

Dial-up, DSL, and cable modems are the way the vast majority of us get online, but they're not the only ways. Alternative broadband technologies such as wireless ISPs are beginning to pop up in a few locations. Chances are, you won't be able to get online with these technologies today, but here's a quick overview for future reference:

- **Wireless ISPs:** Some ISPs have grown sick and tired of dealing with phone companies or cable companies and want to provide their own connection to customers' homes, without relying on someone else's wires and cables. Dozens of new companies are offering wireless Internet access systems to these wireless ISPs (WISPs) or to traditional ISPs who are considering becoming WISPs. Different technologies are being offered but all involve a small antenna and receiver that you can place in your window (or on your roof) to pick up a wireless signal from the WISP's own antennas. These systems then connect to your MCE PC or home network using an Ethernet connection.

- **Satellite Internet:** If you live out in the boonies (or anywhere where DSL and cable are not available), you might consider using a satellite connection to get online fast. The most common satellite Internet service is offered by DIRECWAY (www.direcway.com), the ISP arm of DirecTV. DIRECWAY uses a special two-way capable satellite dish (which is slightly larger than the DirecTV dish used for TV only) and a special DIRECWAY receiver (which connects your MCE PC to the Internet through this dish). DIRECWAY service (which can be purchased directly through DIRECWAY or through Earthlink) offers relatively fast download speeds (up to 400 Kbps) and slower upstream speeds (60 Kbps), which doesn't quite match up to faster DSL or cable connections. The service is available just about everywhere in the U.S. for about $70 a month. DIRECWAY has a few disadvantages:

  - Satellite connections have a lot of latency: *Latency,* or delay in the connection, is inherent in satellite connections because of the long distance that the signals must travel. So certain applications, such as audio and videoconferencing and online gaming, don't work well on a satellite Internet connection.

  - You can't use DIRECWAY with a home network. DIRECWAY can be connected only to a single PC. If your MCE PC is the only computer in your house, you'll be okay, but if you want to set up a home network, you're out of luck.

✔ **Electrical utility (powerline) services:** Not very common in the United States or Canada today but becoming popular overseas (particularly in Europe), powerline services use the electrical wires coming into your house to carry high-speed, broadband Internet services. A powerline modem is connected to your electrical panel, and then uses Ethernet to connect to your MCE PC or home network. This new technology is not widely available, but some electrical utility companies are beginning to look seriously at offering such a service.

✔ **Fiber to the home:** The backbone of the Internet itself runs primarily on super-high-speed, fiber-optic connections, which use beams of light from lasers, instead of electrical signals, to communicate. Phone companies and cable companies also use fiber in almost all their networks as well — except for the copper-wire piece of the network that connects to your house. FTTH (fiber to the home) providers extend this fiber right to the side of your house, offering Internet access at speeds in excess of 10 Mbps (and potentially much faster). FTTH deployments are extremely limited (because it costs a lot of money to dig trenches and run fiber) but are beginning to appear in new developments. All the major phone companies have decided that their long-term future revolves around this FTTH network, so they've begun planning how they will deploy such a network to their customers.

Making the Online Connection

One of the great things about Windows XP Media Center Edition 2004 — or any version of Windows XP, for that matter — is how easy Microsoft has made the process of setting up an Internet connection. Windows XP was designed as an Internet-friendly operating system, and Media Center Edition is no exception. The most important tool included with MCE is Microsoft's New Connection Wizard — an easy-to-follow, step-by-step system for getting your MCE PC online.

If you're installing your MCE PC as part of a home network rather than connecting it individually to an ISP, you can skip this section and go to Chapter 15. That chapter discusses the ins and outs of home networking, including how to use a home-networking router to connect multiple PCs to the Internet — which is what you'll need to do to get online with your networked MCE PC. If you're using your MCE PC in a dorm room or another location that has an Ethernet connection for getting online, skip to the same chapter.

The first step to getting your MCE PC on the Internet is to choose an ISP. If you skipped right to this part of the chapter and don't have an ISP already, skip right back and read through the sections on dial-up, DSL, and cable modem connections. Go find an ISP that you like, and *then* come back here.

If you've chosen a broadband connection (DSL or cable modem), you need to start with the DSL or cable modem installation. We can't tell you exactly what this will entail because every provider's installation is a bit different, but in most cases you can do the installation yourself. (The DSL or cable modem ISP will send you a self-install kit with the modem as well as all the accessories you need.) Generally you need to connect your broadband modem to the wall (your cable TV or phone line), to an electrical outlet (use a surge protector strip!), and finally to your MCE PC using an Ethernet cable (which should be included in the self-install kit).

If you're unsure of how to do all this plugging in and setting up, you can pay your cable or DSL provider to come to your house and set up your broadband service. They'll install all the hardware and then configure your computer to get online. Installations are usually $100 or more; self-installs are typically free or inexpensive (about $25 for the kit).

If you're going the dial-up route, you don't have to do any special wiring or modem installation. Instead just connect a standard phone cord to the modem port on the back of your MCE PC and to an empty phone jack in your wall. If your MCE PC has two jacks on the back, use the one labeled Line, not the one labeled Phone. See, we told you that dial-up connections were a bit easier!

If your ISP requires that you have a user name and password, and you already know these items, make sure you have them handy because you need them in the following set of steps. If you don't have the user name and password from your ISP yet (perhaps because you're connecting to the ISP for the first time), the New Connection Wizard will give them to you. Dial-up connections also require a local *access number,* or phone number for your modem to dial into.

After everything's plugged in and turned on, use the following steps:

1. **Open the New Connection Wizard by choosing Start⇨All Programs⇨ Accessories⇨Communications⇨New Connection Wizard.**

   The wizard appears and says "howdy." Actually, it doesn't say howdy, but it does tell you what's coming next, as shown in Figure 6-1.

2. **Click Next.**

3. **Choose the Connect to the Internet option and then click Next.**

   Remember, if you're connecting through a home network (or other Ethernet network like the one in a dorm), you don't want to choose Connect to the Internet here. Instead you want to choose "Connect to the network at my workplace (for the dorm)" or "Set up a home or small office network (for your home network)." We give some tips on running the Microsoft Home Networking Wizard in Chapter 15.

Figure 6-1:
Starting
the New
Connection
Wizard.

4. **Choose one of the three options shown in Figure 6-2 (based on the advice we give next) and then click Next.**

   a. **If you don't already have an ISP account** (from another computer, for example), you'll probably select the "Choose from a list of Internet service providers (ISPs)" option. The wizard then dials up a toll-free number using your modem, displays a list of locally-available ISPs (at least a list of locally-available ISPs who have cut deals with Microsoft to be included in this list), and asks you to choose one. When you do, the wizard automagically finishes your ISP setup by itself and gets you online.

   b. **If you already have an ISP account,** choose the "Set up my connection manually" option. Continue with Step 5.

   c. **If you have a CD from your ISP,** choose the "Use the CD I got from an ISP" option. This ends the wizard installation and launches your CD's installation program. Follow the on-screen instructions. Many larger national ISPs (such as AOL) use these CDs, and most broadband ISPs include a similar CD in their self-install kits.

5. **If you chose the Set up my connection manually option, select the option that describes how you're connecting to the Internet. Then click Next.**

   a. **If you're using a dial-up connection,** choose the "Connect using a dial-up modem" option.

   b. **If you're using broadband and your broadband ISP (requires you to use a user name and password to get online** (it'll tell you when you sign up), click the "Connect using a broadband connection that requires a user name and password" option.

Figure 6-2:
Choices
galore in
the New
Connection
Wizard.

c. **If your broadband provider doesn't require a user name and password to get online** (our favorite kind), click the "Connect using a broadband connection that is always on" option. Click Next, and you're finished!

6. **In the text box, type a name for your ISP. Then click Next.**

The name can be just a name you'll remember rather than the actual name of your ISP. If you end up with multiple ISP connections on your MCE PC (for example, if you have a laptop computer MCE PC and take it to different locations), you'll be able to choose the appropriate ISP connection by selecting this name.

7. **Type the phone number for your ISP and then click Next.**

This is the local access number for your dial-up connection. If you're using broadband, you skip this step.

8. **Type your user name, and type your password twice (see Figure 6-3).**

If you're using a broadband connection that requires a user name and password or if you're using a dial-up connection, this is where you type the user name and password you've been saving all this time.

9. **Leave all three check boxes at the bottom of the screen checked, and then click Next.**

The "Use this account name and password when anyone connects to the Internet from this computer" option means that even if you set up multiple *users* on your computer, they'll be able to get on the Internet without having to go through all these steps and recreating this connection. (User accounts allow everybody who uses the MCE PC to have their own customized settings.)

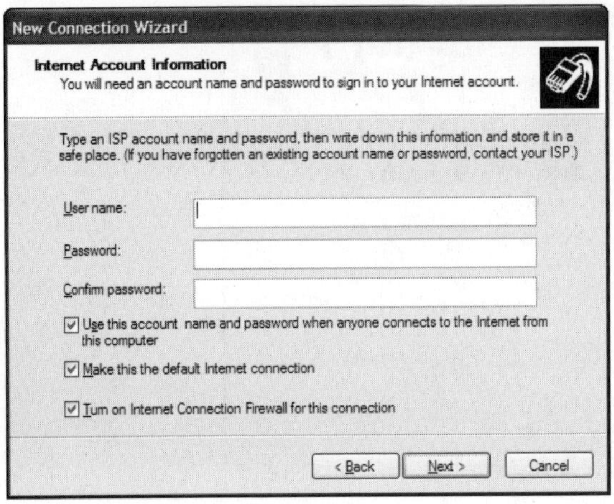

New Connection Wizard

Internet Account Information
You will need an account name and password to sign in to your Internet account.

Type an ISP account name and password, then write down this information and store it in a safe place. (If you have forgotten an existing account name or password, contact your ISP.)

User name:

Password:

Confirm password:

☑ Use this account name and password when anyone connects to the Internet from this computer

☑ Make this the default Internet connection

☑ Turn on Internet Connection Firewall for this connection

[< Back] [Next >] [Cancel]

Figure 6-3:
Complete your Internet connection by entering your user name, password, and preferences.

The "Make this the default Internet connection" option simply means that the computer automatically uses this connection when you try to go online. In the future, if you add additional connections, you may not want them to be the default connection. For example, if you take your MCE PC to your in-laws' house for the holidays, you'd want to set up a connection from there that's *not* the default — unless you like your in-laws a lot!

The "Turn on Internet Connection Firewall" option enables XP's internal *firewall* system, which helps keep out the bad guys who want to sneak into your MCE PC.

10. Click the Finish button.

You're finished. Windows XP MCE connects you to the Internet, and you're online.

If you want to make sure that you're connected, just open Internet Explorer by choosing Start➪Internet Explorer — it's right there on top. By default, Internet Explorer should display the MSN home page; if MSN loads, you're online and all set.

If you decide to move to a different ISP or add additional connections, just fire up the New Connection Wizard again and run through these same steps.

If getting online is a complicated procedure for you (perhaps you have a special setup in mind), check out *The Internet For Dummies* by John Levine et al. (published by Wiley Publishing). It will turn you into an Internet pro.

Chapter 7

Starting MCE for the First Time

*Y*ou're sitting on the floor, staring at your fully-configured MCE PC, and it's just ready to be powered up. The anticipation is enough to make you want to just fire it up and start playing — but we recommend that you take a more measured approach.

In this chapter, we guide you through the process of starting your MCE PC for the first time. You are also introduced to the Media Center environment. We walk you through the first screens that appear when you launch Media Center and go through the MCE startup wizard. We end with a discussion of how to turn your PC off — a topic that might seem unnecessary but is a point of confusion among new users.

Powering Up Your MCE PC

When you turn on any PC for the first time, you're in the realm of the PC vendor. That vendor decides what you see, when you see it, and where you see it. When you turn on your Windows XP MCE system, you may have to go through a Windows XP setup process. You may be presented with the Welcome to the Windows XP Setup Wizard. You may have to fill out a registration screen. You may be prompted to sign up for an Internet service, in the hopes that you don't have an ISP yet. The vendors spent a lot of time refining their startup process to minimize the calls to customer support, so it's best to just let their screens guide you through the setup process.

During setup, you'll probably be prompted to activate your Windows XP MCE software. This is part of Microsoft's efforts to cut back on software piracy. (If you want to activate the software at another time, do so by choosing Start⇨All Programs⇨Activate Windows.) Note that *activation* is not the same as *registration*. You have to activate XP within 30 days to use your system. Registration with Microsoft is optional.

We don't want to dwell on the XP side of things, except as it affects Media Center and its operation. We're biased. We think the *real* configuration starts when you start the Media Center interface for the first time.

Starting your PC is not the same as starting the Media Center interface. When you've completely started your system, you'll see a normal Windows XP desktop, with shortcut icons, a Start button, and a taskbar. This is the normal Windows XP Professional OS — just like you'd find on any of the millions of new PCs sold every year. What *is* different is that this version of Windows has a green Media Center shortcut button that activates your Media Center interface.

The Media Center Edition Interface

Before we get into the details of the MCE startup process, we want to take a quick detour to the "Tell me about the Media Center user interface" rest stop. We highlight the main features of the user interface so that you'll know where to find what you need as you go through the startup process.

We tell you about the main elements of MCE's *look and feel* — that is, the navigational and graphical elements that help you get around the program. We also introduce you to your MCE remote control, which is the main device you use to control MCE.

But first, you need to open Media Center itself. You can do this in one of three ways: by double-clicking a shortcut on the desktop, by clicking the Start button on the taskbar of your desktop and choosing Media Center, or by pressing the green button on your MCE remote control.

MCE Start menu

When you enter Media Center for the very first time, Windows XP MCE sends you into a setup wizard, which we talk about in the following section. However, before we do that, we wanted to introduce you to some of MCE's navigation and usage standards, so you know what to expect when you see the MCE interface — wizard or not — for the first time. So in this section, we talk about the overall look and feel of XP MCE, even though we're not launching MCE just yet. Be patient and read this section — you launch the application in the next section.

When you enter Media Center, you see the main Media Center Start menu (see Figure 7-1). This screen presents you with a single, unified, full-screen portal for all your entertainment needs. Everyone should have one, don't you think?

The date and time are prominently displayed in the center of the screen, with the Media Center modules listed alongside. The modules are in a loop, so you can cycle through them.

At the bottom left of the screen is an *inset window* that shows the media currently playing. This window is called, not surprisingly, the Now Playing window. The *media playback toolbar* is below the inset window. (Microsoft refers to this toolbar as the *desktop controls toolbar,* but we — and everyone else, it seems — prefer the name media playback toolbar.) The media playback toolbar gives you direct access to the entertainment in the forefront of your screen. Here you can change channels (- and +), pause, play, stop, rewind, fast forward, mute, and change volume (- and +). This playback toolbar appears whenever you move your mouse

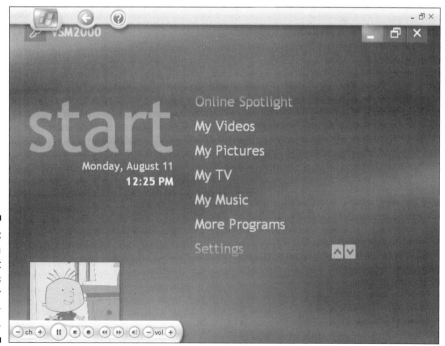

Figure 7-1: The Media Center Start menu is your jumping-off point.

At the top left of the screen are three buttons. From left to right, they

🖈 Let you quickly log off to end your Media Center session or to switch users

🖈 Return you to the main Media Center Start menu, like the Go Back button on your remote

🖈 Access Media Center Help

An on-screen volume control gives you a visual view of the volume level and indicates when the audio is muted. This volume control shows up when you adjust the volume using the remote control and disappears after a few seconds. In addition, a phone call notification (using Caller ID) shows you who is calling and the phone number — you need to have a phone line plugged into your MCE PC for this to work, of course.

For the Caller ID feature to work, you also need Caller ID service from your phone company (you probably guessed that) and *TAPI*-compliant modem in your MCE PC. TAPI (Telephone Application Program Interface) is a Microsoft standard for modems that lets them do regular phone stuff, including Caller ID. Check with your MCE PC vendor if you don't know whether the modem you have is TAPI compliant.

The upper right of the screen has the standard Windows tools for minimizing, resizing, and closing the window. You can use the minimize capability to keep Media Center running while you work in another program elsewhere on the screen.

Navigating in Media Center

At the beginning of any software project, programming firms create a document that defines the *usage conventions* for the software. As programmers develop the code, they reference these conventions so that the process of moving, scrolling, selecting, adding, deleting, and so on is similar throughout the program. Here are the key usage conventions used in MCE:

🖈 **Navigating:** To move around and select menu items, you use the arrow buttons on the remote control, the arrow keys on your keyboard, or the mouse. You can get everywhere in MCE using only the arrow buttons on the remote. To see everything in long Media Center menus or option listings, you use the arrow buttons (or arrow keys or mouse) to select the scroll buttons at the bottom-right side of the screen, as shown in Figure 7-2.

🖈 **Highlighting:** MCE indicates that you have successfully navigated to an item by highlighting it in green. The highlight is different depending on the item. An item represented by a thumbnail or an icon — a picture, movie, folder, file, and so on — becomes outlined with a bright green border. A button or a check box turns green.

✔ **Selecting:** To choose an item or an option, navigate to it (the item or option becomes highlighted), and press the OK button on the remote control, press the Enter key on the keyboard, or click the mouse button.

If a media selection is playing in the Now Playing inset window, you can switch to full-screen mode by navigating to the inset window (the frame turns green), and then clicking the OK button on the remote.

When you're navigating in the MCE interface, just remember three things: arrow buttons, green highlight, OK button. Selecting is that simple.

MCE remote control

The core component around which the entire Media Center concept revolves is the remote control, shown in Figure 7-3. Microsoft is perfecting the 10-foot experience for users — the ability to access content from 10 feet away. To that end, Microsoft has minimized the number of buttons on the remote to keep your interface with the program as simple as possible.

Central to this remote control, as you've undoubtedly noticed, is the big green button. It's so prominent that there's even a Windows MCE Web site named after it (www.thegreenbutton.com). This button always brings you to the main Start menu for Media Center.

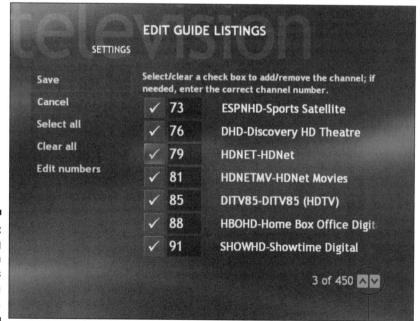

Figure 7-2:
Scrolling through long menus in Media Center.

Scroll up or down

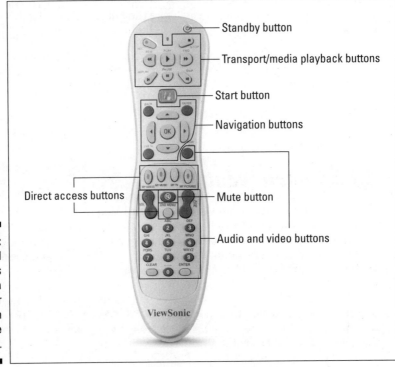

Standby button

Transport/media playback buttons

Start button

Navigation buttons

Direct access buttons

Mute button

Audio and video buttons

Figure 7-3:
A typical
Windows
XP Media
Center
Edition
remote
control.

The MCE remote control has the following four groups of buttons:

- **Direct access buttons:** My Videos, My Music, My TV, My Pictures, and DVD Menu provide direct access into these particular functions. One tap and you're there — no need to navigate. The *standby button* — the power button denoted by a circle with the vertical slash through it — puts your PC and monitor into a power-reduced state.

- **Navigation buttons:** These buttons move the cursor around and do specific actions in Media Center. The arrow buttons move the cursor up, down, left, and right. The OK button selects the task highlighted on the screen (just like an Enter button). The Back button (we use this one a lot) returns you to a previous window — keep clicking it to go back several steps. The Guide button displays your television program guide. Live TV is a shortcut button that launches full-screen live TV.

- **Audio and video buttons:** You use the CH/PG button to change channels, the VOL button to increase or decrease the volume, the mute button to mute the audio, and the More Info (or Details) button to access data on what you're watching, such as the title, the artist, or a TV show summary.

The Clear button clears any numbers or letters you've entered on the screen. The Enter button works like the Enter key on a keyboard. Finally, the numeric keypad works like a cell phone keypad when tapping in text (press the 2 button once for A, twice for B, and so on).

✔ **Transport/media playback buttons:** These buttons control the recording and playback of CD, DVD, and TV content. You use these to play, rewind, fast forward, skip, replay, stop, pause, and record, as follows:

- **Record:** The REC button is the neat one here because you can just tap the button, and the TV show you're watching is recorded from that point on.

- **Fast forward and fast rewind:** Press the FWD or REW button once after your CD, DVD, or video content has started, and the fast forward or rewind process, respectively, moves at double the normal speed. With video content (DVD, recorded TV, or video) press the button a second time or a third time, and you increase the speed by 40 times and 250 times, respectively — that's fast. Press the FWD or REW button a fourth time to return to double normal speed. Pressing PLAY resumes the selection's normal playing speed. Pressing PAUSE freezes the video image on the screen.

  With audio content, pressing FWD moves the pace forward at 1.4 times the normal speed. Pressing FWD again moves the pace to 5 times the normal speed, and pressing FWD a third time resumes the playing at normal speed.

  The REW button doesn't do anything in audio programs (such as CDs or music files you have in My Music). Only FWD works with music files.

- **Skip ahead or backward:** Press the Skip button to move to the next audio or video track or to skip ahead 29 seconds when watching recorded TV. (Hmmm, how long are those commercials?) Press the Replay button to go back 7 seconds. Hold down the Skip or Replay button for 2 seconds and the media moves ahead or backward, respectively, by several minutes. Hold either button down longer and the media moves to the end or the beginning, respectively.

Not all MCE PC remote controls follow these same groupings, but almost all have the same general functionality. You might find the DVD Menu button located by the navigation buttons on an HP remote control, for instance, but sandwiched between the VOL and CH/PG buttons on the Windows-standard MCE remote. The DVD Menu button works the same in both instances, however, taking you straight to the main menu of the DVD movie.

Fighting over who turns off the PC? You need his-and-her remote controls! Order extra Philips remotes from your manufacturer or from www.newegg.com, which sells them for $32.

Other MCE interfaces

The remote control is not the only way you can control your Media Center. Here are some other possibilities:

- **Shortcut buttons on the front of the PC:** Across the front of some PCs, such as the HP, are shortcut buttons that you can press to go to live TV, the program guide, your music collection, your pictures, or your videos. These are handy when you're working at the front of the PC downloading files or videos from your camcorder or other device and want to quickly check that the files were downloaded successfully into the system.

- **Keyboard shortcut buttons:** Across the top of your keyboard, you might have a similar lineup of shortcut buttons that will take you quickly into select functions of Media Center. Some of these are programmable, so you can customize your shortcut experience.

The Media Center Edition Start-Up Process

Now we're getting to the good part. When you start Media Center Edition for the first time, you're entering a whole new world.

The first time you press the green start button on your remote control, the Media Center Setup Wizard process begins. You're asked a series of questions that customize and optimize the MCE interface.

You need to know the following information to get through the Media Center Setup Wizard:

- Your zip or postal code.
- Your TV signal provider and, if you have a cable or satellite provider, the package you subscribe to. (You might need to grab your monthly bill.) A sample package might be the Platinum package from DirecTV or the Basic Cable Service package from Charter Communications.
- The manufacturer and model number of your set-top box, if you have one.

To download the TV programming guide data, you'll also need an active Internet connection. If you don't have your Internet connection hooked up yet, that's okay. Just come back to this step later by going to the MCE Start menu and selecting Settings⇨TV.

During the initial Windows setup process (not the Media Center setup), you'll be asked to specify the country or region in which the PC resides. This information is required in combination with your zip code information to download the television guide. If the country setting and the zip or postal code you entered don't yield a valid combination in the MCE database, you might see an error message on your screen. If this happens to you, do the following:

1. **Leave the Media Center interface and go back to the regular XP interface.**

   To leave MCE quickly, navigate to the top-right corner of the screen and click the minimize button. (It's the one on the far left.) Don't worry, your MCE session will be right where you left it when you return — you've just reduced the window to a button on the taskbar along the bottom of your XP desktop.

2. **Now that you're back in XP, choose Start⇨Control Panel⇨Date/Time/Language/Regional Options.**

3. **Click the Regional and Language Options tab.**

   Towards the bottom of the tab, the country appears in the drop-down list. If you're in the United States and speak English as your preferred language, this should be 'English (United States).'

4. **If the country is wrong, select the correct one, click Apply, and then click OK. If the country is correct, simply click Cancel.**

5. **Return to the Media Center interface.**

   To do so, simply click the minimized Media Center button on the XP Windows taskbar at the bottom of your screen.

6. **Check your zip code.**

   Navigate to Settings and choose Zip/Postal Code. Type your zip code again. If you changed the country in Step 4, you should see that new choice now. (If you don't, call your MCE PC's vendor's technical support line.)

7. **Click Next.**

   You're prompted for your TV signal provider.

8. **Select the provider, and then click Next.**

   You can now download your TV program schedule. MCE seeks out the appropriate databases from the master MCE databases at Microsoft. You can always update your TV guide manually by going to the MCE Start menu and choosing Settings⇨TV⇨Guide⇨Get Guide Data.

That's it . . . it's not a complex installation or startup process. So what's the first thing to do after installation? Read on and find out!

Time for Your Calibrations!

If you're connecting a TV to your MCE PC, you need to make sure that the display is calibrated correctly. Most TV displays come from the factory improperly calibrated. The brightness and color are set at unnatural levels to make the displays stand out on the showroom floor in a brightly lit store. Put one of those displays in a darkened home theater, and the picture looks awful. You'll be asking yourself why you spent so much money. Even if your display is not brand new or all that fancy, calibration can breathe new life into your picture quality.

The factory-set, overly bright settings can reduce the lifespan of a CRT (direct-view or projection) or plasma display.

Windows MCE comes with its own calibration program to guide you through the process of changing the various settings on your TV. Before we walk you through the calibration process, however, we define some terms you'll encounter.

The ABCs of calibrating your TV display

You, as a non-technician, can make five adjustments on the average display. A few displays let you adjust more, and service techs with the proper manuals and codes to get into the service menus of the display can adjust almost anything. We average folks can adjust the following:

- **Contrast (white level):** *Contrast ratio* is the ratio between the brightest and darkest images a display can create. In terms of display adjustments, your contrast control adjusts the *white level,* or degree of whiteness your screen is displaying.

  In video displays, whites and blacks are measured on a scale called the IRE (Institute of Radio Engineers — they must have named this a loooong time ago!) units. Black is 0%, and white is 100%. You can actually drive your TV beyond 100% if your contrast is improperly set. If you do this, white portions of your picture tend to bleed over into the darker portions surrounding them, reducing the quality of your picture.

- **Brightness (black level):** Now to throw in a counterintuitive statement, the brightness control on your display adjusts the *black level* that you see on the screen. Weird, huh? If the black level is set incorrectly, you won't be able to discern the difference between darker images on the screen.

- **Sharpness:** The sharpness control adjusts the *fine detail* of the picture — it's the TV's capability to display small details. If the sharpness is set too low, you have a fuzzy picture. If it's set too high, your picture appears *edgy,* often with blobs instead of clearly defined lines around the edges of objects.

- **Color:** Along with tint (which we discuss next), color is one of the two controls that you use to set the balance of colors on your display If your color setting is too low, images begin to appear as black and white. If the color setting is too high, images take on a reddish tinge. (For example, Nicole Kidman's face will turn as red as her hair.)

✔ **Tint (hue):** On most TVs, this control is labeled tint, but a few TVs use hue, which is the more technically correct label. The tint control adjusts your display's color in a range between red and green — your job is to find the perfect balance between them.

Almost every display has an on-screen indicator that shows the status of these settings. Typically, you see a horizontal bar with a vertical hash mark that moves as you change the settings, or the entire bar moves left or right as you increase or decrease the settings. Some displays also have a numeric display that shows the current settings.

These settings are performed using the controls directly on your monitor or TV. (You can often use your TV's remote control instead of buttons on the TV itself.) Media Center provides the pictures and instructions on the screen to tell you what kind of adjustments you need to make, but you have to do the adjustments yourself using the controls specific to your TV or monitor.

The Display Calibration Wizard

When Microsoft created MCE, it wanted users to think that this was the best way to watch video, no questions asked. But to do that, it had to rely on users to have their TVs set up correctly. Many don't.

So Microsoft included a Display Calibration Wizard in the MCE interface. To use it, follow these steps:

1. **From the MCE Start menu, choose Settings⇨General.**

2. **Select the Appearance button.**

   To do so, navigate to the button (it becomes highlighted in green), and then press OK on your remote.

3. **At the bottom of the Appearance page, select the Adjust display settings option, and then press OK on the remote.**

   This option is your doorway to the wizard.

We like the little movies that Microsoft has added here and there to provide information. In the Adjust Display system, Microsoft has a helpful video that explains what happens as you adjust your settings. To watch the video, just select Watch video and click OK on your remote. When the video ends, you're taken back to the same screen you were viewing before you watched the video.

4. **Select Next and click OK on your remote.**

   The wizard starts.

5. **Answer the wizard's questions, selecting Next and clicking the OK button on your remote after each step.**

The wizard asks you questions to extract the best viewing experience on your TV. It will ask about the type of display you have (such as CRT, flat panel, or plasma) and whether your TV has a wide-screen display. XP MCE adjusts the content it displays if it knows there is more space, which is the case with a wide-screen display. For instance, instead of showing 9 images of pictures in the My Pictures area, MCE shows 12 picture images because it has the room. Also, in the Programming Guide, MCE can now show an additional 30 minutes of Guide content.

Then calibration mode starts. You see a series of videos that help you adjust the tint, brightness, contrast, color, and sharpness. The program makes use of inset pictures that you compare with your generated picture in the larger portion of the screen, and uses tools such as on-screen images that disappear when the settings are correct.

You need to use the controls on your display itself (either on the front of the display or on the remote that came with it) to make adjustments to the display. You can't fine-tune the display with your MCE remote.

6. **When you've run through all the Display calibration settings, select Done and click the OK button on your remote.**

You've successfully calibrated your monitor!

Third-party programs

You can also adjust your video with a DVD home-theater calibration disc from a third party. Why do both? You can use the disc with all the TVs in the house, not just the MCE TV. Also, we've found that third-party programs add a little more accuracy to the settings.

We think that these discs (which cost about $50) are an essential part of the investment in your home-theater and home-computing environment, unless you've had a professional calibrate your system. Following are the most common home-theater calibration discs:

✔ **AVIA, Guide to Home Theater:** Available from Ovation Software (www. ovationsw.com) this disc contains a ton of great background material about home theaters. It also provides a series of easy-to-follow on-screen test patterns and signals that let you correctly adjust all the settings we discussed previously, as well as test tones for your surround-sound audio system.

✔ **Video Essentials:** Found online at www.videoessentials.com, this is the definitive calibration disc. Two versions are available — one standard disc and one for digital TVs.

✔ **Sound and Vision's Home Theater Tune-up:** This disc is produced by Ovation Software, this time with *Sound and Vision* magazine (one of our favorites, www.soundandvisionmag.com). This disc includes videos and tutorials that demonstrate aspect ratios and let you test the S-video and component-video outputs on your DVD player (to see which works better in your system).

We like all three discs and would be hard pressed to recommend just one. The AVIA disc and Sound and Vision disc are probably the best bet for people who aren't trained video calibrators. Video Essentials is geared more to the professional. AVIA is a bit more detailed and comprehensive, and the Sound and Vision disc is a bit easier for first-time users. All will give you a better picture.

Unlike Microsoft's package, these three include a blue filter. You use this filter to block out certain light frequencies when adjusting some of the color and tint settings on your display.

Using one of these discs is a simple process. We're not going to recreate it here step by step, because the on-screen instructions do a better job than we can in a book. However, before you adjust any settings, set up the room with the same lighting conditions you'll have when you sit down to play movies or watch TV. Ambient lighting has an immense effect on what you see on your screen (regardless of what type of display you have in your home). So lower the blinds, close the door, and dim the lights. Then just follow the instructions, step-by-step.

When you're finished, you'll notice that your picture looks different. (We sure hope it does!) It's going to look darker. If you're not accustomed to a calibrated video picture, this might be a bit disconcerting. Give yourself some time to get used to it. You'll notice a more detailed picture, one that looks more like the movies. And isn't that what you're after?

Windows Transfer Wizard

Suppose you want to keep all the files and settings from your old computer. How do you go about doing that? Windows XP MCE has a tool called the Files and Settings Transfer Wizard that walks you through the process of transferring the settings and files from your old machine to your new machine. Note that the wizard transfers only settings and files, not programs.

If your old machine has a lot of files — CD songs, videos, or pictures — you'd save yourself a ton of time if you transfer just the settings now, and make sure your machine is configured correctly. Then transfer the files using a home network or direct cable connection between the two — this is preferable to using floppy discs. (Danny's machine prompted him for 4177 floppy disks to do the transfer of his files and settings.)

Before you can transfer your settings and files, you need to have the same programs installed on the new machine as you have on the old machine. The wizard checks to see which programs must be installed on the new computer before you can proceed with the transfer, so you can double-check that they're all there.

You launch the wizard in the regular XP interface, not the Media Center interface, as follows:

1. **Choose Start➪All Programs➪Accessories➪System Tools➪Files and Settings Transfer Wizard.**

2. **When asked, Which computer is this?, choose the Old Computer option.**

   This is the computer from which you'll get the files and settings.

3. **Select a transfer method, and then click Next.**

   If you have a direct cable connection linking the two computers or a home network in place, the program senses this and provides those options. Otherwise, it prompts you for a removable media drive (such as an E: writable CD drive). Select the means by which you intend to move the files and settings from the old PC to the new one.

4. **Select the files and settings to transfer.**

   The default setting is to transfer global Windows settings for things such as taskbar options as well as specific folders such as Desktop, Fonts, My Documents, My Videos, My Pictures; files and settings for specific applications such as Outlook Express and Internet Explorer; and file type associations for your PC.

   We suggest that you accept the defaults. If want to customize what is transferred, choose the "Let me select a custom of files and settings when I click Next (for advanced users)" check box and follow the on-screen instructions that appear after you click Next.

5. **Click Next.**

   The wizard checks to see which programs must be installed on the new computer before you can proceed with the transfer. Some files and settings, called *program dependencies,* work only if a certain program is installed.

   If the wizard finds files that require programs to be preinstalled on the new machine, a Depended programs screen appears. If any of these programs are not on the new machine, dig out those programs' CDs and install them now.

   Otherwise, the wizard begins the process of collecting the files and settings from the old computer. This can take a while, so stand up and stretch but don't leave the computer, because it's not necessarily a one-step process. The collection process occasionally turns up a file that can't be transferred, such as a .dat file, and asks you what to do.

6. **If the computer asks you what to do with a file that can't be transferred, just click Ignore.**

   After the collection process is finished, you'll get a list of those files and settings.

   If a lot of files are listed, consider highlighting them, copying the list into Notepad (choose Start⇨All Programs⇨Accessories⇨Notepad), and saving the list for future use.

7. **Start the Files and Settings Transfer Wizard on the new target computer.**

   Choose Start⇨All Programs⇨Accessories⇨System Tools⇨Files and Settings Transfer Wizard.

8. **Indicate that this is the new computer by choosing the last option.**

   That option is titled: I don't need the Wizard Disk. I have already collected my files and settings from my old computer.

9. **Tell the wizard where to look for the collected items.**

   When your transfer is finished, you're finished! Your new computer is ready to go.

Turning Off Your XP MCE PC

It might seem silly to have a section about turning off your MCE PC, but we want to say a few things about this JSYK (just so you know).

When using MCE, figuring out when to use one of the "suspended" modes and when to turn off the machine can be challenging. The power management features in Windows XP are hibernate, standby, and the turned off state:

- ✔ **Turn off:** Shuts things down entirely. Anything saved in RAM (your computer's memory) is lost (of course, your hard drive retains its memory), and all loaded programs and states are *not* retained. Therefore, make sure you save any open files before you turn off the computer. To use the programs again, you need to *reboot* the MCE PC and start the programs. If you turn your computer off, it will *not* start itself back up to perform scheduled TV recordings. So if you have a TV recording scheduled during a time you're away from your MCE PC, use the Standby option described below instead.

- ✔ **Hibernate:** Saves an image of your desktop with all open files and documents, and then powers down your computer. When you turn power on, your files and documents are open on your desktop exactly as you left them. We don't recommend that you use the Hibernate option unless you have the 2004 version of Media Center — Media Center won't wake up to begin recording shows unless the PC is in standby mode (or actively running).

✔ **Standby:** Reduces power consumption by cutting power to hardware components you're not using. Standby can cut power to peripheral devices, your monitor, and even your hard drive, but it maintains power to your computer's memory so that you don't lose your work.

You can turn off your XP MCE PC at any time by going to the XP Start menu (if you're in Media Center, minimize or close it) and choosing Turn Off Computer➪Turn Off. This completely shuts down your PC. When you want to turn on your MCE PC again, press the On (power) button on your computer, and wait for the PC to reboot.

You can also put the computer in standby mode. This eliminates the rebooting process by keeping memory alive, but saves power by turning off your display and hard drive. To put your computer in standby mode, simply choose Start➪Standby. Or if you don't want to get out of the Media Center interface, simply push the remote's standby (or power) button.

To wake up the computer from standby mode, do one of the following:

✔ Briefly press the On button on the MCE PC

✔ Press the Esc key on your keyboard (or the Standby key, if your MCE PC keyboard has one)

✔ Press and hold the Standby button on the remote control for a few seconds

When you see the Windows XP startup menu, press the green button on your remote to launch MCE or click any MCE window running in the Windows taskbar along the bottom of the screen.

If you plan on using the PC to record TV shows while you're *not* using the computer, be sure to put the PC in standby mode so that the computer can wake up at the right time, change the channel as needed, and start recording.

To check your power management settings, choose Start➪Control Panel➪ Performance and Maintenance➪Power Options. Work your way through the various tabs there to make sure the settings are correct. You might want to set the Auto-Standby option to 30 Minutes of inactivity. Set Hibernate to Never unless you're using the 2004 version of Media Center — and even then we recommend that you use Hibernate only if you have a laptop MCE PC).

When powering down your system, check the drives for CDs, DVDs, and anything that might be in your 6-in-1 card reader. It's not a good idea to leave anything in a PC — you never know what might get overwritten or corrupted. Also, having disks in the reader might cause an error on reboot, because the system tries to interpret the disk or content as it boots up.

Chapter 8

Customizing Your MCE Experience

· ·

In This Chapter

▶ Setting up XP your way

▶ Personalizing Media Center

▶ Tweaking your audio system

▶ Adding third-party programs

· ·

Computers have come a long way from the old days of command-line prompts and DOS, when that flashing C:\> prompt was as sophisticated as the user-computer interface got.

We know that some computer users *enjoy* memorizing arcane text commands and using just the keyboard to control and manipulate data, but most of us were glad when Windows (and the Mac) came along and gave us a mouse and a nice graphical user interface (GUI) to control the PC. Windows XP Media Center Edition is a further refinement of this GUI, designed for use with a remote control (but also fully supporting the mouse and keyboard, if you want to use them).

The coolest thing about MCE is that it's not "one size fits all." You can customize your interface and a lot of the behind-the-scenes settings to make MCE work the way you want it to.

In this chapter, we discuss how to handle some basic settings in Windows XP, such as setting up your mouse the way you like it. Then you find out about the many ways you can customize settings in the MCE interface. Finally, we talk about some third-party software you can add to your MCE PC to further customize your Media Center environment.

When we say you should *select* something, it's shorthand for this: Use the arrow buttons on the remote to move the cursor to that item and then press the OK button on the remote.

Setting General XP Preferences

Before we get into customizing the Media Center interface, let's run through some of the basic customizations you can make in the regular XP interface — such as setting up your mouse, keyboard, and monitor. These settings influence how your MCE PC reacts when you're using it in regular computer mode and also carry over to the MCE interface (when you use the mouse and keyboard instead of the remote).

You change these settings in the XP interface (the one you see when you start your MCE PC) — so don't press that famous green button on the remote yet.

Mouse customization

In Windows XP, you can customize how your mouse behaves so that it works at the same speed that your eyes, brain, and fingers do. You can make the cursor move more quickly or slowly on the screen, adjust how fast you need to push the button for a double-click, and even adjust your mouse for left-handed use.

If you change the mouse for left-handed use by swapping the functions of the left and right mouse buttons, remember that whenever we use *right-click* you should use your left mouse button, and vice versa.

Customizing the mouse is easy:

1. **In Windows XP, choose Start⇨Control Panel.**

2. **Click the Printers and Other Hardware icon.**

3. **Click the Mouse icon.**

   The Mouse Properties dialog box appears, as shown in Figure 8-1.

4. **Click each of the five tabs in turn to access and change the different settings.**

   For more information on the various options, read ahead a few paragraphs.

5. **When you're finished, click the OK button at the bottom of the screen to save your settings.**

In most dialog boxes, including the Mouse Properties dialog box, you can see the results of your modified settings without saving them. Just click the Apply button to use your mouse with the new settings. If you like the settings, click OK to save them; if you don't like them, click Cancel.

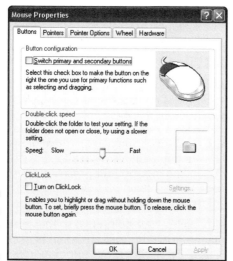

We won't walk you through each of the settings step-by-step — mainly because you'll probably want to leave many of these settings alone. Instead, we describe each one briefly. Remember that when you finish making your changes, click the OK button to save your new settings.

Following are the mouse properties that you can adjust to your own personal likes and dislikes:

- **Buttons:** This tab helps you adjust the buttons on your mouse. You can switch from left- to right-handed operation. The specific areas in this tab follow:

  - **Button configuration:** Click the Switch primary and secondary buttons option to swap the left and right button functions.

  - **Double-click speed:** Click the slider bar with your mouse and drag it left to slow down your double-click speed or to the right to increase the speed. You can practice on the little folder icon to the right — when you've successfully double-clicked at the speed you've set, the folder pops open.

  - **ClickLock:** The Turn on ClickLock option lets you click your mouse once (and let go) when you're dragging items around the desktop or selecting text (or other data) in a file. We never use this, but you might want to try it out.

- **Pointers:** This tab lets you customize your mouse's *pointer,* which is the cursor or arrow on the screen that your mouse manipulates and moves around. Some people like to turn the pointer into a Mickey Mouse icon or a rocket ship. You can select from a long list of *schemes* (options) by clicking the pull-down list. Or if these choices aren't enough, you can make up your own pointer scheme.

✓ **Pointer Options:** This tab lets you further customize your pointers. You have the following choices:

- **Motion:** You can adjust how quickly the pointer moves across the screen relative to your hand moving the mouse. Click the slider and move it to the right to increase the speed and to the left to decrease the speed. We like to set this option for really fast speeds — if your eyeballs can't keep up or you need to do a lot of precise mouse movements, you may want a slower speed. We think you should always click the Enhance pointer precision check box below this slider because this function helps the mouse handle small movements more accurately.

- **Snap To:** This option makes your pointer go to the default button in a dialog box (usually the OK button). This can be handy, but it takes some getting used to. We like move our cursor manually, so we leave this option unchecked.

- **Visibility:** Sometimes, when you're using your mouse (or haven't used it for a few minutes), you lose track of the pointer on the screen. The Visibility area provides three options. The Pointer trails option means that ghost images of the pointer remain on the screen for a few seconds, following the trail of the pointer. The Show location of pointer when I press the CTRL key option displays a bull's-eye when you press the Ctrl key. And the Hide pointer while typing option doesn't help you find the pointer but does keep it out of the way when you're using the keyboard.

✓ **Wheel:** Most mice that come with MCE PCs have a *scroll wheel* that lets you move up and down a Web page, a Word document, or almost any document without using the scroll bars on the right side of the document window. This tab lets you adjust that behavior and customize how many lines of text you want the wheel to move. You can also click the One screen at a time option, if you want the wheel to page down or page up when you use it.

✓ **Hardware:** You probably won't need to do anything in this tab, unless you've installed a different mouse and are having trouble. This tab lets you select the mouse you've installed. You can also configure *drivers* (the software that lets the mouse and computer work together) and troubleshoot mouse problems here.

If you've installed a special mouse on your MCE PC (or the manufacturer has provided a special mouse), your Mouse Properties dialog box might be different. In some cases, the dialog box stays the same, but you'll have an additional program with controls for the extra buttons and features of your mouse. To see that extra program, choose Start➪All Programs, and look around — typically you'll see a folder that contains the manufacturer's name (such as Logitech).

Keyboard customization

In addition to customizing your mouse in Windows XP Media Center Edition, you can customize your keyboard. Just follow these steps:

1. **Choose Start⇨Control Panel.**

2. **Click the Printers and Other Hardware icon.**

3. **Click the Keyboard icon.**

   The dialog box shown in Figure 8-2 appears.

Figure 8-2:
Customizing
keyboard
behavior.

4. **Click the two tabs to access and change the different settings.**

   For more information on the various options, read the description after this set of steps.

5. **Click the OK button at the bottom of the screen to save your settings, or click Cancel to revert to the original settings.**

You can change only a few keyboard options:

✔ **Speed:** Like some electric typewriters (remember them?), the keyboard on your MCE PC repeatedly types a key if you hold it down. Use the Speed tab to customize the response speed of your keyboard:

   • **Repeat delay:** This determines how long you have to hold a key down before XP starts repeating that key's character. Move the slider to the right for shorter delays or to the left for longer.

- **Repeat rate:** This determines how fast the character is repeated as you hold down the key. Move the slider right for a faster repeat or left for a slower one. There's even a text box below the slider where you can practice. If you are a mystery novel writer and need to type Aaaaaaaaaaaaaaaaaaaah a lot, cranking this speed up can increase your productivity.

- **Cursor blink rate:** The only reason why your cursor blinks is to help your eye find it amongst all the text on the screen. Use the slider in the Cursor blink rate area of the Speed tab to set the blink from no blink to the fastest blink.

✔ **Hardware:** Like the Hardware tab on the Mouse dialog box described earlier, this tab lets you select and troubleshoot your keyboard hardware. If you start having problems with the keyboard, go here and click the Troubleshoot button.

If your MCE PC came with a keyboard that has special function keys and buttons (such as volume controls and keys that provide one-touch access to programs or modules in MCE PC), you'll probably have additional software on your PC to tweak these extra settings. Sorry, but you probably have to read the manual to find out what kind of extra keyboard software you have, where it's located on your hard drive (try Start⇨All Programs), and how to use it.

Desktop and monitor customization

Now that your input devices are customized, it's time to customize your output devices — the monitor and the desktop that appears on it. To do so, follow these steps:

1. **Choose Start⇨Control Panel.**

2. **Click the Appearance and Themes icon.**

3. **Click the Display icon.**

   The screen shown in Figure 8-3 appears.

   You can open this dialog box also moving your cursor to an open spot on your desktop, right-clicking, and choosing Properties.

4. **Click each of the tabs along the top of this dialog box and make changes.**

   We describe each tab in detail shortly.

5. **When you're finished, click the OK button at the bottom of the dialog box.**

   Your changes are saved and applied.

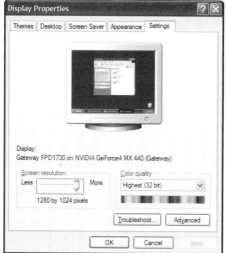

Figure 8-3:
The Display
control
panel.

The Display Properties dialog box has five tabs:

✔ **Themes:** Microsoft makes it easy to overhaul the appearance of your MCE XP desktop by providing several themes. These *themes* define the colors of windows (the foreground, the background, the borders, and so on.) and the system sounds. We leave ours in the Windows XP theme (who has time to mess around with this stuff?). If you'd like to try other themes, simply click the arrow to the right of the pull-down menu and make your selection.

✔ **Desktop:** This tab lets you customize the picture on your desktop — that is, the image you see in the background behind all the icons and other elements. Just click the picture you want to use and you're all set. You can also use any picture from your digital camera, any JPEG or GIF image someone sends you, and more. Just copy the image to your My Photos folder.

If the picture isn't exactly the right size to fill your desktop, you see a small pull-down menu on the right. You can center the picture, tile it (the picture is repeated to fill the screen), or stretch it. If you center your picture or select the None option, use the other small pull-down menu to select a color to fill in the uncovered space.

If you have a picture somewhere on your hard drive that you want to use, just click the Browse button. A Find File dialog box appears. Use this dialog box to navigate your hard drive, find the picture, and select it.

✔ **Screen Saver:** In the old days, when all monitors were CRTs (cathode ray tubes, like traditional televisions), you could burn-in (leave permanent images on) the screen if you left the same image on it. To prevent damage to the screen, many people put *screen savers* on their computers — if your PC is idle for a while, it times out to a screen-saver program, which displays moving images on your display to avoid having any particular image burn into your screen.

This problem isn't much of an issue any more because many MCE PCs use an LCD screen, which is not susceptible to burn-in problems. However, it can be an issue for your TV set if the TV display is connected to the PC. We recommend that you use XP's screen-saving capabilities to avoid any burn-in problems.

If you run a screen saver, just select it from the pull-down menu. There are also buttons to adjust the settings of the screen saver (Settings) and to preview the screen saver you've selected (Preview). You can use the input box below the screen saver menu to set how long your MCE PC must be idle before the screen saver starts up, and you can create a password that must be entered before the screen saver is turned off. (If you have a snooping roommate, this is for you.)

✔ **Appearance:** This tab lets you get to the nth degree of customize by changing the appearance of various Windows elements (such as the size and shape of borders and arrows). We don't get much out of this setting, but you might.

We want to point out one setting, however, for those with an LCD computer monitor (not an LCD TV). Click the Effects button. When the Effects dialog box opens, go to the area of the screen labeled Use the following method to smooth edge of screen fonts. Make sure that check box is checked (click it if it's not), and then click the pull-down menu and choose ClearType. Click OK. ClearType is a special system in XP that makes fonts (text characters) appear smoother and less blocky with LCD monitors. It's worth using.

✔ **Settings:** This tab lets you select the display size in pixels, which are individual points of light in your display. The more pixels you choose, the more stuff you can see on your screen at once. Here are the options:

- **Screen resolution:** This slider lets you select the number of pixels displayed on your monitor. Check your documentation before you mess with this too much. Some monitors have specific screen resolutions that work best and other resolutions that don't work at all. Slide the slider to the right to increase the number of pixels and to the left to decrease the number.

It may seem like a good idea to show as many pixels as possible, but this isn't always the case. If you cram too many pixels onto the display, the picture isn't sharp. And if you're eyes aren't what they used to be (perhaps too many late nights in front of the screen writing books?), you might want to use a lower resolution because this makes everything on the screen appear bigger.

- **Color quality:** This menu lets you select the color quality (or color depth) displayed on your monitor. The color quality is measured in bits (the same kind of bits that you think of when we talk about bits and bytes of data). The higher the number of bits, the greater the number of color gradations shown. It's always best to select the highest number of bits. You usually have a choice of Medium (16 bit) and Highest (32 bit). With some computers, you need to select a lower color quality so that performance doesn't suffer, but MCE PCs have such butt-kicking video cards that you can happily select Highest and go on your way.

You should always use the Highest (32 bit) setting for the best possible picture and user experience with MCE.

At the bottom of the Settings tab, note the Advanced button. We mention this button in Chapter 5 when we discuss supporting two displays. You click the Advanced button to begin the process of setting up your video card to support a television as your second monitor.

If you change anything in the Settings tab (which controls things such as the resolution and color depth of your monitor), the changes are temporarily applied, and you see a dialog box asking the following: "Your desktop has been reconfigured. Do you want to keep these changes?" If the new desktop looks okay to you, click Yes. If it looks funky, click No or just wait (it reverts to your previous settings after 15 seconds).

Setting General Media Center Preferences

All the stuff we've discussed so far in this chapter provides you with a means of customizing the traditional Windows XP interface in your Media Center PC (though some of these settings also affect the Media Center interface as well).

Now we dig into the different settings and customizations that you can do *within* the Media Center interface. To access these settings, follow these steps:

1. **Start Media Center.**

   Click the green button on your remote, or choose Start➪Media Center.

2. **In the Media Center Start Menu, select Settings.**

   Navigate to the Settings option and press the OK button on the remote. The Settings window appears, as shown in Figure 8-4. You see six options: General, TV, Music, Radio, DVD, and Pictures.

Adding users to your XP MCE PC

Adding users to your system isn't difficult. In XP, choose Start⇨Control Panel⇨User Accounts, and then click the Create a new account option. A wizard appears for adding a new user account. Simply follow the on-screen instructions.

Your big decision as you add users is whether to make them computer administrators or give them limited accounts. An administrator can do more stuff, such as add programs, install hardware, and change system-wide settings, but they can also do more damage to the system when making these changes. You need at least one administrator (the first person to use the computer is usually set up as the administrator). We recommend that you use limited accounts for the kids and guest users of your Media Center PC. That way, they can still set their own preferences and create their own user environment, without affecting your favorite settings or adding and removing programs without your permission.

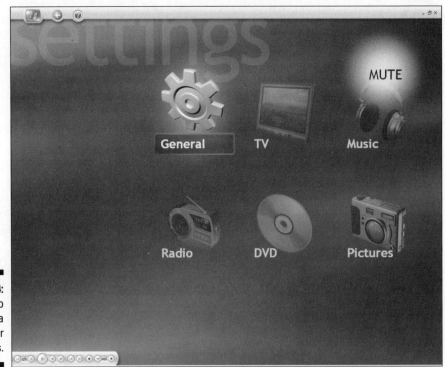

Figure 8-4:
Getting into
your Media
Center
Settings.

Not all of these settings can be manipulated by all users. Windows XP can be used with multiple users, with different levels of assigned privileges. Users who have administrator privileges can adjust all the settings we describe in this section. Other users can't adjust items such as parental controls and privacy settings. If you have several people who will be using your PC, we strongly advise that you set up your system to support multiple users. To find out more about adding and changing user settings in XP, see the "Adding users to your XP MCE PC" sidebar in this chapter.

Each user of the Media Center system can have his or own settings in the Media Center interface. One user can turn on animations and turn off phone call notifications, for example, and those settings will not affect the settings of the other users.

The General MCE settings are just what they say. They're general settings that apply throughout the Media Center interface. Figure 8-5 shows the General Settings window.

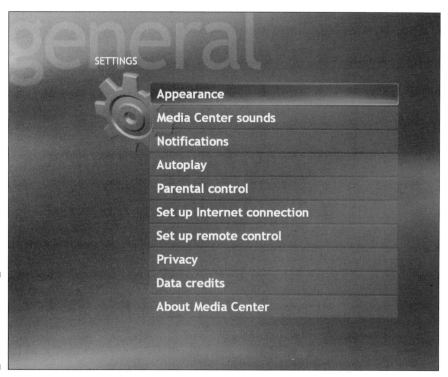

Figure 8-5:
Tweaking the General settings in MCE.

To select a setting in the General Settings window (or any of these windows, for that matter), simply navigate to the setting you want and press OK on the remote control.

Keeping up appearances

First up in the General Settings window are the Appearance settings, which are shown in Figure 8-6. These settings let you adjust some effects and the color of Media Center on your screen.

Figure 8-6 contains the three types of controls in MCE:

- ✔ Check boxes
- ✔ Radio buttons
- ✔ Plus and minus controls

Check boxes work much like they do in the traditional XP interface — click them with the mouse, or select them with the remote (by using the arrow buttons and pressing OK). You can select multiple check boxes in a window.

Radio buttons, on the other hand, are either-or settings. When you select one (with the mouse or the remote), you automatically deselect the other (or others) in that section of the screen.

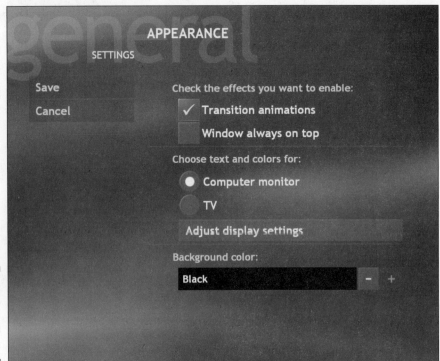

Figure 8-6:
You can
determine
how objects
appear.

The plus and minus buttons let you select from a list of options (similar to a pull-down menu in the traditional Windows interface). The plus sign moves in one direction in the list, and the minus sign moves in the other direction. With the remote, just select either plus or minus, and press OK repeatedly until you get to the setting you want. (When you get to the end of the list in the plus or minus direction, the opposite button is selected so that you can start moving your way back through the list.)

The options in the Appearance window follow:

- ✔ **Check the effects you want to enable:** This option has two choices, and because they're check boxes, you can select one or both. They are

  - **Transition animations:** Select this check box to enable transition animations, which basically just give a fancy appearance to your MCE by animating the screen when you switch between functions and screens — this isn't necessary, but it sure looks smooth and cool when you're navigating through menus.

  - **Window always on top:** Select this check box if you want your reduced size MCE window to always be on top of whatever you're looking at in Windows XP. We like to keep this one turned off, but some people can't miss a minute of *Oprah,* so they keep this window on top even when they're working.

- ✔ **Choose text and colors for:** This option is a pair of radio buttons labeled Computer monitor and TV. Select the one that you'll use most in the Media Center interface, and MCE adjusts the picture so that it looks best on your selected monitor type.

- ✔ **Background color:** This option (which uses the plus/minus controls) lets you select the background color that surrounds your video picture when you're watching TV and movies. Some programs may appear with bars on the screen (letterboxing) because they're designed for screens with a wider or narrower format than the one you're using. You can select the color for those bars using the Background color option. We like black, but choose your own favorite.

To save your changes in the Appearance settings screen (and all the others we're about to discuss), select the Save button and then press OK on the remote (or click Save with your mouse). The General Settings window reappears.

If you don't want to save your changes, select Cancel and press OK on the remote.

Setting sounds

The next item in the General Settings window is Media Center sounds. This is an easy one — in fact, it's so easy we're not going to waste valuable trees by including a picture of the window.

Media Center sounds are the little bings, bongs, and boings you hear through the speakers when you select items in Media Center. It's just aural feedback to supplement the visual feedback on your screen. The window for Media Center sounds contains a single pair of radio buttons for choosing to keep sounds on or off.

As usual, select Save and then press OK to save your changes, or select Cancel and press OK to not save them.

1 want to notify

The next item in the General Settings window is Notifications. This item allows you to customize when Media Center notifies you of issues, events, and the like. Figure 8-7 shows the Notifications Settings window.

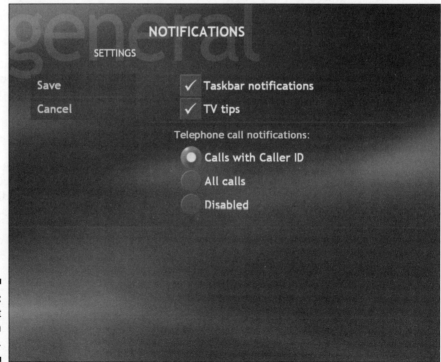

Figure 8-7:
You can set your own notifications.

The Notifications window contains the following options:

- ✔ **Taskbar notifications:** This check box lets you turn taskbar notifications on and off. Basically, MCE can keep you appraised of certain activities (such as downloading the TV Guide) or situations (such as running out of hard drive space to record TV programs) in the Windows taskbar.

- ✔ **TV tips:** The TV Guide includes little pop-up tips that help you learn how to use it. After you've used the Guide for a few hours, you'll grow weary of these tips and want to shoot the people who put them there. Don't bother. They were smart enough to include this check box to disable the tips, preserving your sanity and their safety.

- ✔ **Telephone call notification:** Media Center can tell you who is calling by displaying a notification (if your telephone line is plugged into your computer's modem line). Three radio buttons let you turn this function on only when a Caller ID signal is received, turn it on all the time, or turn it off. We use the first setting — if there's no Caller ID, it's probably one of those pesky telemarketers. (On an unrelated note, make `www.donotcall.gov` your first Internet destination on your new MCE PC, and get yourself on the national Do Not Call list.)

Caller ID requires a special kind of modem (a TAPI modem) that not every MCE PC has installed. If your MCE PC doesn't have this special modem installed, you won't see this Telephone call notification

Play Misty for me, automatically

When you launch a file or insert a disc of a certain type, Media Center can automatically start and play that content for you. You don't even have to lift a finger. The Autoplay settings window contains two check boxes that enable (or disable) autoplay for two specific types of content:

- ✔ **Enhanced Media Center content:** Check this box if you want Media Center to automatically open and play any enhanced Media Center content. This will typically be content that you received on a CD or (more likely) downloaded from Online Spotlight.

- ✔ **HighMAT player (if installed):** HighMAT (High-performance Media Access Technology) is a new system developed jointly by Microsoft and Matsushita (the humungous Japanese consumer electronics company that makes Panasonic, among other brands). HighMAT makes it simple to share content between computers such as MCE PCs and consumer electronics (such as CD players, DVD players, and video camcorders). Windows Media Player 9 — which is the underlying program for a lot of what Media Center does — can play these specially-coded HighMAT discs. By checking this box, you can set up Media Center to automatically open and play any HighMAT disc you put in your system.

Putting the kids in their place

We don't know what you watch with your MCE PC. We don't even care. But you may — just may — have content on your MCE PC that you don't want the kids to watch. Maybe you just bought the entire season of *Sex and the City* on DVD. Well, with the Parental control option, you can set up your MCE PC to keep the kids from watching that DVD as well as other TV shows and movies based on their ratings in the Guide.

There are just a few steps here:

1. **In the General Settings window, select the Parental control option and press OK on the remote.**

   A window appears with a single request, to enter your four-digit code.

2. **Using the number buttons on the remote, type a four-digit code.**

   Use a number that you'll remember, but don't use 1-2-3-4 or the month and date of your birthday — your kids are smarter than that. The first time you do this, another text box appears asking you to confirm that number.

3. **Retype the four-digit code.**

   A new window appears with the parental control settings.

You can choose one of three options in the Parental Control window:

- ✔ **DVD Ratings:** Adjusts your DVD blocking function

- ✔ **TV Ratings:** Adjusts the TV program blocking function

- ✔ **Change four-digit code:** Lets you select a new code (for when the kids figured out that you *did* use 1-2-3-4 after all)

- ✔ **Reset parental controls:** Lets you start over from scratch

If you choose the DVD Ratings option, the window shown in Figure 8-8 appears.

In this window, you can select the following options:

- ✔ **Turn on movie blocking:** This check box lets you enable or disable the movie blocking function of MCE for your DVDs.

- ✔ **Block unrated movies:** Not all movies are rated, and in some cases, even if the movie itself has received a rating, the DVD may not carry that information. This check box lets you block access to any movie on a DVD that doesn't include rating information.

- ✔ **Maximum allowed movie rating:** Use the plus and minus controls to set the particular MPAA (Motion Picture Association of America) rating that you're comfortable with. Any rating above the one you've selected is blocked.

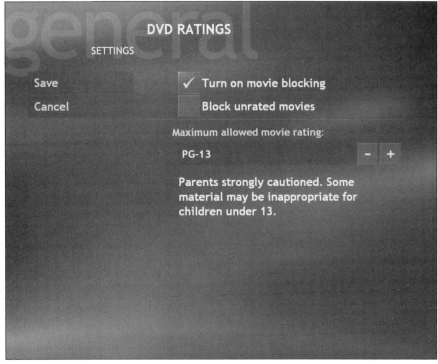

DVD RATINGS

SETTINGS

Save

Cancel

✓ Turn on movie blocking

Block unrated movies

Maximum allowed movie rating:

PG-13   − +

Parents strongly cautioned. Some
material may be inappropriate for
children under 13.

Figure 8-8:
Keep the
kids away
from inap-
propriate
movies.

Setting the TV ratings option is almost identical. Select TV Ratings and you'll
see a screen that mimics the one in Figure 8-8. The only real difference is that
TV uses a different ratings system than movies and DVDs — we discuss this TV
ratings system in more detail in Chapter 9, in the "Parental controls" sidebar.

Keep in mind that these settings do not keep *you* from watching this material.
When you try to tune in a movie with a rating above the maximum rating you
set, a window appears so that you can enter that double-secret, triple-dog-dare
code and watch away!

Getting MCE online

The next item in the General Settings window, Set up Internet connection,
helps you get MCE online — primarily for the purposes of downloading program Guide information. Whether you're downloading the Guide for the first
time or updating it, follow these steps:

1. **In the General Settings window, select the Set up Internet connection
   option and press OK on the remote.**

   The Set up your Internet connection window appears.

2. **Select the Next button and press OK.**

   Media Center spends a minute looking at your MCE PC's Internet connection (we discussed how to set that up in Chapter 5), and then displays the window shown in Figure 8-9.

   If you're using a dialup connection or some kind of connection that requires a password (in other words, you're not using a broadband, always-on connection), an intermediate window might appear, asking you to enter your password or username or both).

3. **Choose to download when you connect to the Internet or manually:**

   • **Download when connected:** Media Center automatically downloads the Guide whenever your PC is connected to the Internet — maintaining the next 14 days' worth of data in the Guide. This is the way to go, unless you have a pay-as-you-go connection.

   • **Manual download:** This option forces you to go into the My TV module and manually download the program Guide. (We tell you how in Chapter 9.)

4. **Select the Next button and press OK.**

Figure 8-9:
Choosing how you download your TV Guide.

A window appears to confirm your setting. If you want to change it, press the Back button and make your correction.

5. **If you want to check that your Internet connection is working, select the Test button and press OK.**

   Media Center checks out your Internet connection and confirms that it's working.

6. **Select Next and press OK.**

   Media Center tells you that you're all set.

7. **Select Finish and press OK.**

   You're returned to the General Settings window.

Readjusting your remote control

The next item in the General Setting list is Set up remote control. You already set up your remote control when you ran through the Media Center Setup Wizard (in Chapter 5). If you buy a new or second remote control, however, select this item and follow the steps to get the remote set up and working with MCE PC. We won't repeat the steps here because they're simple. Just follow the on-screen instructions.

It ain't nobody's business

Now for the final General Settings item, Privacy. Well there are two more, but they're just credits and an About screen, for those who want to read about all the people and companies behind Media Center.

If you have problems with Media Center and are on the phone with tech support, you might need to know which version of Media Center you're using. For that answer, select About Media Center to displays the version and build of your Media Center.

To configure your privacy settings, perform the following steps:

1. **In the General Settings window, select Privacy and press OK on the remote.**

   A window appears with three options. We encourage you to read the privacy statements for MCE and the Guide, but the action is behind the third option, Settings.

2. **Select Settings and press OK on the remote.**

   The window shown in Figure 8-10 appears.

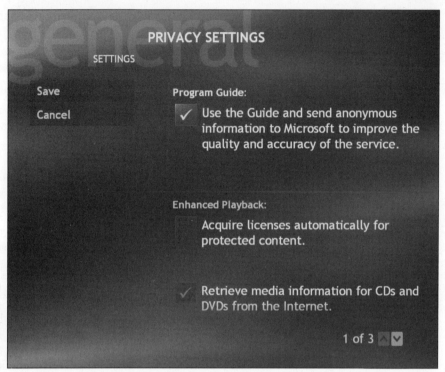

Figure 8-10:
Go public or
keep it
private.

3. **Make your selections on this page. Then select Save and press OK.**

   Read the following paragraphs for more information on these options.

You can turn three privacy-related functions on or off:

- **Use the Guide and send anonymous information to Microsoft to improve the quality and accuracy of the service:** This one is a mouthful, but it's also a no-brainer. We think you should check this box, even though we're both uptight about privacy.

- **Acquire licenses automatically for protected content:** This falls into the confusing world of *DRM* (or Digital Rights Management). Media Center uses the DRM functionality of Windows Media 9 to allow online content providers to sell you content (music, movies, and so on) with a license describing how you can use that content. For example, a provider might allow you to burn a CD with songs you paid to download.

   If you check this box, Media Center automatically acquires licenses to this protected content, and you'll be able to use it. If you don't check this box, you might have to stop and answer screens asking whether you accept the licenses for content you're downloading or playing — screens that might be hidden behind Media Center. This setting does *not* affect your own content (such as audio CDs that you own and copy to your MCE PC). We recommend that you check the Acquire licenses automatically box.

✔ **Retrieve media information for CDs and DVD from the Internet:** If you select this check box (we did), Media Center automatically goes out to the Internet to gather information about the CDs and DVDs you insert in your MCE PC. This feature makes it easy to get the cover art and song names of each CD when you copy it to the MCE PC. We describe this process in detail in Chapter 10.

Other Media Center Settings

When you've finished configuring the General Settings, press the Back button on the remote control and you'll find yourself in the Settings window (refer back to Figure 8-4). Here you'll see the TV, Music, Radio, DVD, and Pictures settings.

You can get to these settings also from each module. When you're in a particular module, just navigate to the menu on the left side of the window, select Settings, and press OK on the remote.

We describe each of these settings in their respective chapter in Part III. For example, we talk about the Music setting in Chapter 10.

Some adjustments to Media Center are made not in Media Center but in XP. The setting you're most likely to adjust is the autoplay setting for CDs and DVDs. (In the Autoplay settings in the MCE interface, you set up autoplay only for special file types.)

To make Media Center your default program for playing audio CDs and DVDs, do the following:

1. **Close or minimize Media Center.**

   Use the close or minimize button in the top-right corner of the Media Center window.

2. **With your mouse, choose Start⇨My Computer.**

   Figure 8-11 shows the My Computer window.

3. **In the Devices with Removable Storage area of the window, right-click your optical drive and choose Properties.**

   In the example, the optical drive is DVD-RAM Drive (D:), but yours may differ.

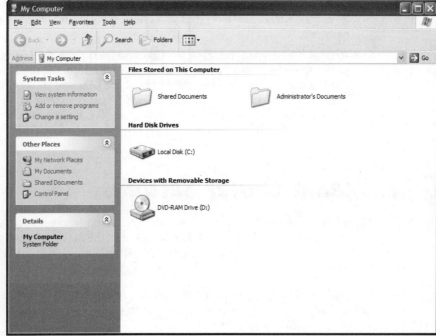

Figure 8-11:
My
Computer —
yours
should look
similar.

4. **Click the Autoplay tab.**

5. **In the drop-down menu at the top of the tab, choose Music CD.**

6. **Click the Select an action to perform radio button, and then click Play Audio CD using Media Center.**

7. **Click Apply.**

8. **Still in the Autoplay tab, select DVD in the drop-down menu.**

9. **Click the Select an action to perform radio button, and then click Play DVD Video using Media Center.**

10. **Click OK.**

Now every time you put a music CD or DVD movie into your MCE PC, Media Center will launch it and start playing it. Cool, huh?

Part III
Using XP Media Center Edition

The 5th Wave   By Rich Tennant

TROUBLE ON THE SET

©RICHTENNANT

All the software in the world won't make this a great film. Only you can, Rusty. Only you and the guts and determination to be the finest Frisbee catching dog in this dirty little town. Now come on Rusty—it's magic time.

We're losing the light, Dad.

In this part . . .

*I*f you're going to read only one part of the book (and we hope you'll read it all), this is the one. We get down to the nitty-gritty details about how you can use and enjoy a Windows XP Media Center Edition PC. Microsoft made the MCE PC easy to use, but we think you might still appreciate advice from someone who's been there (we have) and done that (we did).

We start with a discussion of how to get from point A to point B in plain old Windows XP, because every MCE PC is built upon the XP foundation. So if you're moving up from Windows 98 or ME (or something older), you'll be able to get a feel for how Windows XP reacts to your mouse and keyboard.

Then we discuss the fun stuff: using the MCE interface. You find out how to use your MCE PC to watch TV, record TV, pause live TV, and more. It's the ultimate in TV watching! Then you discover how your MCE PC handles audio and how you can get your favorite tunes into your MCE PC.

Following that, we talk about using your MCE PC to take your photography into the digital age. We also tell you how to watch DVDs using an MCE PC (it's easy!) and how to play around with digital home movies (and other digital video on your MCE PC).

Chapter 9

Watching TV

··

··

*W*atching TV is, in our minds, what the MCE PC is all about. We're not giving short shrift to the audio, DVD, digital photography, and video functionality built into Media Center — we love that stuff too! But we think that for most owners, the TV functionality that Media Center provides is its most compelling feature. That's why we recommend (in Chapter 3 and again here) that you use the MCE PC with your TV.

In this chapter, you set up My TV, the Media Center module for watching and recording TV. Then you find out how to use the on-screen program guide — once you use it, you won't want to live without it. We give you the information you need to know to watch live TV and tell you how to record TV shows on your MCE PC. The chapter ends with a section on archiving recorded TV shows onto blank DVDs, so you don't run out of hard drive space when you become addicted to My TV.

As mentioned in other chapters, when we say that you should *select* something, it's shorthand for this: Use the arrow buttons on the remote to move the cursor to that item and then press the OK button on the remote.

Setting Up My TV

Before you start playing around with My TV too much (the fun part!), we recommend that you take a few minutes to configure it. A properly set up and customized My TV environment will make it easier to use the Guide, find programs, and watch and record TV shows.

We cover how to get your MCE PC configured for your particular TV service provider (setting up the channels and Guide) in Chapter 7, where you start your MCE PC for the first time and use the Media Center Setup Wizard. If you ran that wizard, you already have a working TV connection and a Guide that shows your specific regional TV listings. If you haven't run the wizard yet, do the following:

1. **Press the My TV button on the remote.**

2. **Select Settings.**

3. **To configure your TV connection, select the Set up TV signal option and follow the on-screen instructions.**

4. **To configure the Guide, select the Reset Guide lineup option (in the Settings menu), and follow the on-screen instructions.**

We discuss the actual steps in these two wizards in Chapter 7, in the section "The Media Center Edition Start-Up Process."

The first step to setting up My TV is launching it. You can do this in one of two ways:

✔ Press the My TV button on the remote control.

✔ Open Media Center, navigate to My TV on the Media Center Start menu, and press OK on the remote.

Parental controls

In Chapter 8 we discuss setting up parental controls for your Media Center PC. These controls let you keep the kids (or anyone) from watching movies that are above a certain rating. This function is mainly for DVD movies (that's what we talk about in Chapter 8), but you can set rating limits also for My TV.

Setting rating limits for My TV is identical to setting them for DVD movies, with one exception: TV uses a different rating system than movies. Instead of G, PG, PG-13, and so on, you have both show ratings (TV-G, TV-13, and so on) and specific *content* warnings. So you might find a show that is rated TV-13 and also includes a *V* in the rating, for violence. You can set up your parental controls for both overall ratings and these content warnings. Check out www.tvguidelines.org for more information on the ratings.

You can set your rating limit as follows:

1. **In the Media Center Start menu, select Settings.**

2. **Select General.**

3. **Select Parental Control.**

4. **Type your secret code.**

5. **Select TV ratings.**

6. **Select the maximum rating you want your kids to see.**

When My TV is launched, you see a window similar to the one shown in Figure 9-1. From here, you'll configure your My TV settings, starting with the Recorder settings. These settings tell Media Center how you want it to handle the recording of individual TV shows and series.

These are global, or universal, settings for all My TV recordings. In other words, anytime you record something in My TV, these settings will apply. However, you can override these settings on a case-by-case basis using the Advanced record option, which we discuss in the "Doing the time shift" section later in this chapter.

Controlling your recordings

To configure your My TV recording options, just follow these steps:

1. **From the main My TV screen, select Settings.**

   The Settings screen appears, as shown in Figure 9-2.

2. **Select Recorder.**

   The Recorder Settings screen appears.

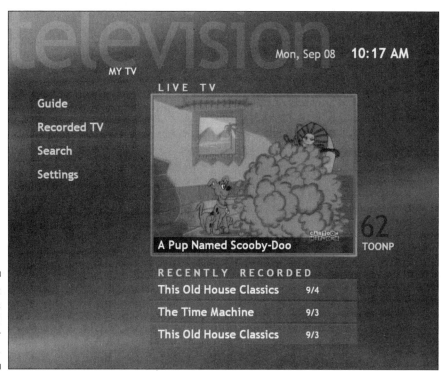

Figure 9-1: This is where it all starts for My TV.

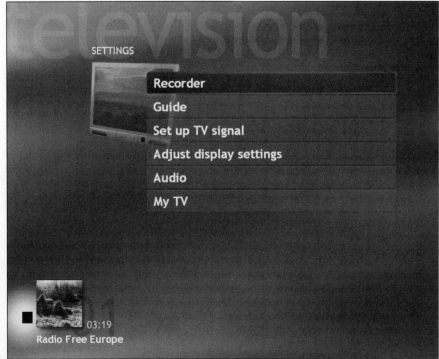

SETTINGS

Recorder

Guide

Set up TV signal

Adjust display settings

Audio

My TV

03:19
Radio Free Europe

Figure 9-2:
All the
settings you
need are
accessible
from this
screen.

3. **Select Recorder storage.**

The Storage Settings screen appears, as shown in Figure 9-3.

4. **If you have more than one hard drive in your MCE PC, navigate to the Record on drive setting's plus or minus button. Press OK repeatedly to scroll through the available drives until you find the one you want to use.**

Typically, you'll have extra drives only if you installed one (or ordered your MCE PC from the factory with an extra hard drive). See Chapter 3 for details. If you don't have an extra drive, skip this step.

5. **Navigate to the Disk allocation setting's plus or minus button. Press OK repeatedly to change this percentage if you want.**

By default, the disk allocation is set to 75%. If you want to allocate less of your hard drive space for video (perhaps you have a lot of audio files that you want to put on your MCE PC), set this option lower. If you just want to fill your hard drive up with TV, make it higher. As you change the percentage of the disk that's available for video, the numbers in the Maximum recording time and Unused recording time change accordingly.

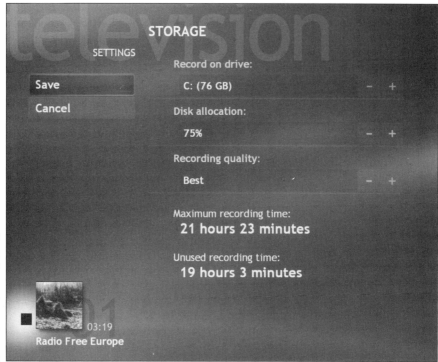

STORAGE

SETTINGS

Save

Cancel

Record on drive:

C: (76 GB) — +

Disk allocation:

75% — +

Recording quality:

Best — +

Maximum recording time:
21 hours 23 minutes

Unused recording time:
19 hours 3 minutes

03:19
Radio Free Europe

Figure 9-3:
Set up your recorded video storage preferences here.

6. **Navigate to the Recording quality setting's plus or minus button. Press OK repeatedly to change this setting.**

   The higher the quality setting, the better the picture you'll see, but the more space it takes up on your drive because the files are larger. We keep ours at the highest setting (Best), but we don't keep a lot of old recordings on our MCE PC. (We move them to DVD.) Again, the Maximum recording time and Unused recording time change as you alter this setting.

7. **Select Save.**

   If a dialog box appears asking whether you want to save these settings, select Yes. This dialog box may appear after each group of settings you make — just select Yes each time.

8. **Select Recording Defaults.**

   The Recording Defaults screen appears, as shown in Figure 9-4.

9. **Navigate to the plus or minus button next to each of the following settings and press the OK button as many times as needed to select the setting you want:**

- **Keep:** This setting determines how long recorded programs remain on your hard drive. If you want Media Center to keep recorded shows until you run out of space for new recordings, select Until space needed. Or you can tell Media Center to keep the show for a week, until you watch it, or until you manually delete it. We keep our recordings until we manually delete them — we like to store (or archive) our shows to DVD and then delete them from the hard drive.

- **Quality:** This is the same as the Quality setting you selected in Step 6. You can set the recording quality in either place. (We don't know why it appears twice, but it works fine in both places.)

- **Start when possible:** This setting lets you tweak the time when a scheduled recording will begin — you can start it On time (in other words, when the show begins in the Guide), or you can tell Media Center to start recording earlier (if you're paranoid about missing a minute or two of the show). As long as your MCE PC's clock is correct (see the "Going atomic" sidebar later in this chapter), we think you can stick with the On time setting.

- **Stop when possible:** This setting does the same thing as the Start when possible setting, except it does it on the other end of the recording time frame — at the end of the show. We also keep this one set to On time.

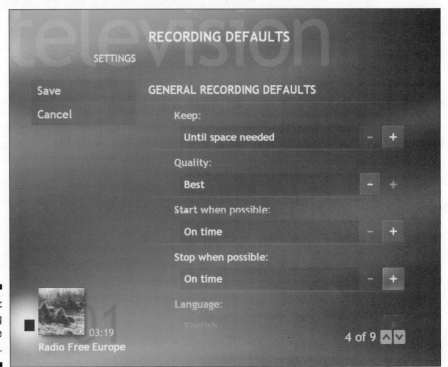

Figure 9-4:
Recording defaults are set here.

- **Language:** Sometimes, a program may be aired in one or more languages, at different times. In the Language option, you can specify if you want to record only English programs or other languages as well (for example, on HBO's Spanish Channel).

10. **If you told your MCE PC to record an entire series as opposed to a single show, navigate to the plus or minus button next to each of the following settings and press the OK button as many times as needed:**

   - **Show type:** This setting tells Media Center whether you want to record only the first run (in other words, new episodes) of a series, or both first runs and reruns. Media Center pulls this data from the Guide database.

   - **Record on:** This setting tells Media Center from where you want to record a show. (You might want to record only from a movie channel that doesn't have commercials, for instance.) This feature also helps when you run into scheduling conflicts with other show recordings. If you've selected other times or channels, the program can schedule around the conflict.

     If you select the first option, One channel only, the show is recorded from only the one channel you selected in the Guide and only within four hours of the scheduled time you've selected.

     The One channel, anytime option means the show is recorded on the channel you selected anytime it is on.

     The final option, Any channel, anytime, means all available showings of the program are recorded by Media Center.

     Customizing the Record on setting is handy also if you record a show that appears on multiple channels, such as a show in syndication or a show on a movie network that's played on all eight of that movie network's channels (such as *The Wire* on HBO). This setting stops you from getting eight recordings of the same episode as it's aired on each of the channels during the week.

   - **Daily recording limit:** You can tell Media Center how many times in a single day you want it to record a particular show. Select No limit if you want each showing of the series recorded in a single day. Select Once per day if you want only a single showing recorded.

   - **Keep up to:** Use this setting to tell Media Center how many recordings of a particular series you want it to keep. You can select 1, 2, 3, 4, 5, 6, 7, or 10 recordings, or you can select No limit to keep as many as you can record.

     The more recordings you keep for any particular series, the more hard drive space you'll use and the less you'll have left for other purposes.

11. **When you've adjusted all the Recording Defaults settings to your liking, select Save.**

Customizing your Guide

Next, you configure your Guide settings. The on-screen Program Guide is Media Center's primary interface for finding TV programming to watch or record. In Chapter 7, you set up the main functions of the Guide while running the Media Center Setup Wizard. Follow these steps to set up a few additional items:

1. **From the main My TV Settings screen, select Guide.**

   To get to the My TV Settings screen, select My TV and then select Settings.

2. **Select Edit Guide listings.**

   The Edit Guide Listings screen appears, as shown in Figure 9-5. You can remove channels so that they don't appear in the Guide. The channels are still available to view, but you won't see them when you're scrolling through the Guide.

3. **Uncheck the channels that you want to remove from the Guide.**

   Use the arrow buttons on the remote to scroll through the listings of the channels. Press OK to uncheck any channels that you don't want to appear on the guide.

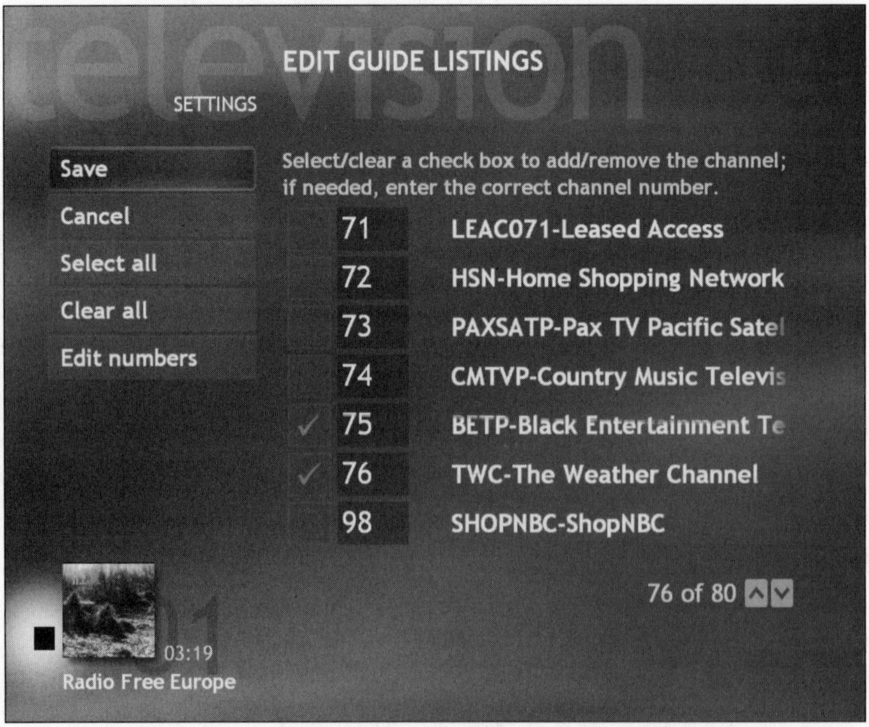

Figure 9-5: Check the channels you want in your guide, and clear the ones you don't want to see.

EDIT GUIDE LISTINGS

SETTINGS

Select/clear a check box to add/remove the channel; if needed, enter the correct channel number.

Save	71	LEAC071-Leased Access
Cancel	72	HSN-Home Shopping Network
Select all	73	PAXSATP-Pax TV Pacific Satel
Clear all	74	CMTVP-Country Music Televis
Edit numbers	✓ 75	BETP-Black Entertainment Te
	✓ 76	TWC-The Weather Channel
	98	SHOPNBC-ShopNBC

76 of 80

03:19
Radio Free Europe

In case it's not obvious from looking at the screen, channels with a check mark next to them *will* appear in your Guide; those without a check mark *will not.*

4. **Select Save when you're finished.**

   You return to the main Guide Settings screen.

5. **If you're missing a channel you expect to be in your Guide, do the following:**

   a. **Select Add missing channels.**

   b. **Select Add channel and follow the on-screen directions.**

   c. **When you're finished, select Done.**

6. **Press the Back button on the remote.**

   You're finished with the Guide for now. The My TV Settings screen appears.

You can manually update your Guide listings from the main Guide Settings screen by selecting Get Guide data.

Customizing TV audio

The next step is to configure your audio settings. My TV not only lets you choose the primary audio program included with a TV show, but also lets you use SAP (or Secondary Audio Program) for listening to programs in a second language and closed captioning (text captioning). Follow these steps to set up your audio preferences:

1. **Press the My TV button on the remote.**

2. **Select Audio.**

   The TV Audio Settings screen appears, as shown in Figure 9-6.

3. **Select your preferred setting for each of the following options by navigating to the setting's plus or minus button and pressing OK on the remote repeatedly:**

   a. **Audio: Select Stereo audio in the primary language of the program or the SAP alternate language.**

   b. **Captioning: Select CC1 or CC2. Most broadcasters use only CC1 (which typically carries verbatim English captioning), but some use CC2 for a second language.**

   c. **Caption display: Select when to display captions. Your options are On (always displayed), Off (never displayed), or On when muted (which displays captioning whenever you mute your MCE PC during TV viewing).**

4. **Select the Save option.**

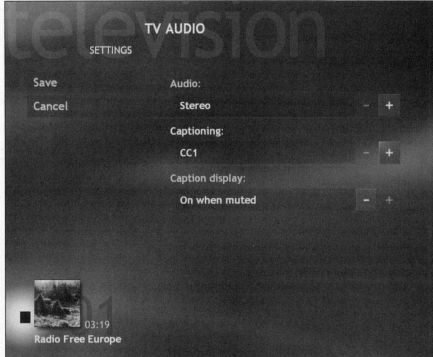

My TV has other settings, but we don't think you'll ever need to use them, so we're not going to walk through the steps here. We will, however, leave you with one last tip.

If you change the monitor or TV that your MCE PC is hooked up to (or just want to recalibrate your TV), the Display Calibration Wizard we talk about in Chapter 7 can be restarted from My TV. Select Settings, and then select Adjust display settings. The wizard starts up and walks you through the process of fine-tuning your monitor or TV.

Using the Guide

The most important interface in My TV is the on-screen Program Guide. From the Guide, you can see what's on TV right now, or you can scroll into the future to see what's coming on in two hours (or two weeks). You can also use the Guide to set up your TV recording schedule.

Going atomic

You can make sure that your PC always displays the correct time using Microsoft XP's Internet Time capability, which synchronizes your computer clock with an atomic-clock time server on the Internet. Here's what you do:

1. **Double-click the time display in your task bar (at the bottom right of your XP desktop).**

   The date is displayed on the screen. Make sure your date setting is correct. The Internet time server won't update the time if the date is wrong.

2. **Click the Time Zone tab.**

3. **If you're in a time zone that observes daylight savings time, click the "Automatically adjust your clock for daylight savings changes" setting.**

4. **Click the Internet Time tab.**

5. **Select the "Automatically synchronize with an Internet time server" check box.**

6. **In the pull-down menu, select the time server you want to use.**

7. **Click OK, and you're finished.**

If you have a personal or network firewall, time synchronization might be blocked. Because so many different firewall programs are on the market, we can't provide the steps for remedying any firewall conflicts you may run into. Call the technical support folks at your firewall vendor for advice.

Guide basics

You can open the Guide in a couple of ways:

- ✔ Press the Guide button on the remote control.
- ✔ In the My TV module, select the Guide menu item on the left side of the screen.

When the Guide first opens, it looks similar to Figure 9-7.

The guide has three *frames,* or sections:

- ✔ **Inset window:** If you're currently playing a TV show or some other media, it appears in a small window in the lower-left corner of the screen.
- ✔ **Channel guide:** The channel guide is across the top two-thirds of the screen — displaying seven channels vertically and up to two hours of programs horizontally. (An extra half hour of programming is displayed if you're using a wide-screen monitor or TV.)

✔ **Details or filters:** Below the Guide is space for detailed information about the selected program or filter options to narrow your Guide choices. (We talk about these shortly.) As you scroll through programs in the Guide, the Details section of the screen changes to reflect the current program.

The Guide can hold up to 14 days' worth of programming information, all downloaded from the Internet, all free of charge. Awesome!

To view what's in your inset window in full-screen mode, just navigate to the inset window using the left arrow button (the window frame turns green) and press the OK button on the remote.

Navigating around the Guide with your remote control is easy. You can move one channel at a time vertically or one program at a time horizontally using the four arrow buttons on the remote. When you find a program that you want to watch or record, just select it. We get into the specifics in the next section, but selecting a program from the Guide performs one of two actions:

✔ If the program is currently being broadcast, pressing OK starts playing the program in full-screen mode immediately.

✔ If the program is in the future, a screen appears so you can tell Media Center to record the program (or the entire series) onto your hard drive.

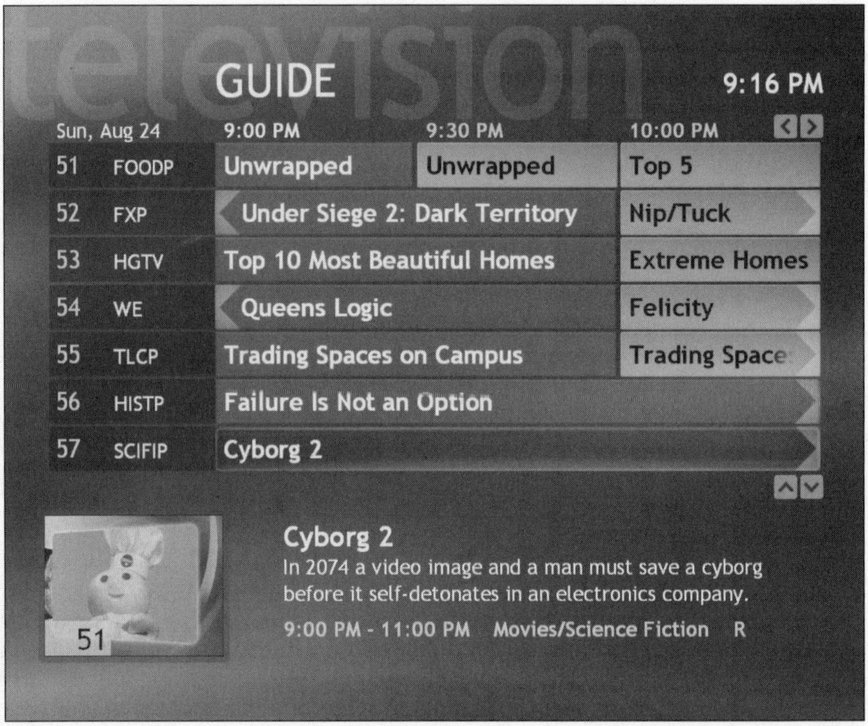

		GUIDE		9:16 PM
Sun, Aug 24	9:00 PM	9:30 PM	10:00 PM	< >
51 FOODP	Unwrapped	Unwrapped	Top 5	
52 FXP	Under Siege 2: Dark Territory		Nip/Tuck	
53 HGTV	Top 10 Most Beautiful Homes		Extreme Homes	
54 WE	Queens Logic		Felicity	
55 TLCP	Trading Spaces on Campus		Trading Space	
56 HISTP	Failure Is Not an Option			
57 SCIFIP	Cyborg 2			

Cyborg 2

In 2074 a video image and a man must save a cyborg before it self-detonates in an electronics company.

9:00 PM - 11:00 PM   Movies/Science Fiction   R

Figure 9-7:
Find the shows you want to watch.

If you want to move through bigger chunks of the Guide (instead of moving one channel at a time vertically or one program at a time horizontally), do the following:

- ✔ To skip 12 hours at a time ahead, press the Skip button on the remote. To go back 12 hours at a time, press the Replay button on the remote.

- ✔ To skip 3 hours at a time ahead, press the Fast Forward button on the remote. To go back 3 hours at a time, press the Rewind button on the remote.

- ✔ To move up and down a *page* (seven channels), press the CH/PG button on the remote.

- ✔ To go to a specific channel in the channel guide, type the channel number using the numeric keypad on your remote control.

To see more detailed information about a program you've selected in the channel guide, press the More Info button on the remote. A new screen appears with detailed program information (such as program rating, actor names, and program length), like the one shown in Figure 9-8. From here, you can play or record the program, using the menu on the left side of the screen. Media Center is nice enough to keep playing your current media in the inset window, so you don't lose track of what you're currently watching. To get back to the Guide, press the Back button on the remote.

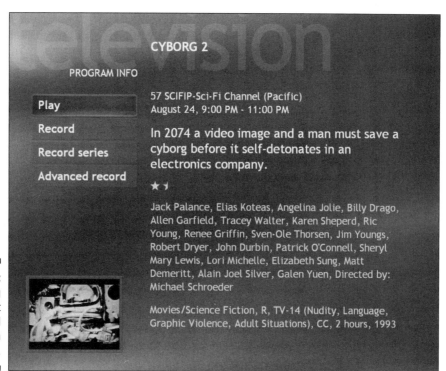

CYBORG 2

PROGRAM INFO

Play

Record

Record series

Advanced record

57 SCIFIP-Sci-Fi Channel (Pacific)
August 24, 9:00 PM - 11:00 PM

In 2074 a video image and a man must save a cyborg before it self-detonates in an electronics company.

★ ♪

Jack Palance, Elias Koteas, Angelina Jolie, Billy Drago, Allen Garfield, Tracey Walter, Karen Sheperd, Ric Young, Renee Griffin, Sven-Ole Thorsen, Jim Youngs, Robert Dryer, John Durbin, Patrick O'Connell, Sheryl Mary Lewis, Lori Michelle, Elizabeth Sung, Matt Demeritt, Alain Joel Silver, Galen Yuen, Directed by: Michael Schroeder

Movies/Science Fiction, R, TV-14 (Nudity, Language, Graphic Violence, Adult Situations), CC, 2 hours, 1993

Figure 9-8:
Checking
out
additional
program
information.

Filtering the guide

You can also filter the Guide so that it shows only certain types of programs. In the main Guide screen, press the remote control's Guide button again. New options fill the bottom of the screen, where the program details were previously listed, as shown in Figure 9-9.

Use the arrow buttons on the remote to navigate to the category filter you want to use (Movies, for example) and press the OK button on the remote. Give Media Center a second to sort your program listings. The Guide reappears, displaying only the channels broadcasting the program category you chose. You can now navigate through this filtered Guide using the same techniques described in the preceding section.

When you want to go back to the full view of all channels and shows, press the Guide button on the remote again.

Figure 9-9:
Filtering
your guide.

Searching the Guide

When you don't feel like browsing through the Guide, you can use Media Center to search the listings in one of three ways:

- ✔ **Categories:** Search for shows based on the category assigned to them in the Guide. For example, you can search for movies, kids shows, or sports.

- ✔ **Title:** You can type part or all of a show's title (using the numeric keypad on the remote or the keyboard).

- ✔ **Keyword:** We think that this search is the coolest. You use the remote control to type a word (such as the name of an actor), and Media Center displays the shows with that word in their description.

Accessing the search function is simple but a bit nonintuitive. You can't get there from the Guide screen. Instead, you need to jump back to the main My TV menu (Figure 9-1). If you're watching TV or are already in the Guide. press the Back button on the remote repeatedly. Or simply press the My TV button on the remote.

Performing the search is easy — and intuitive:

1. **From the My TV main menu, select Search.**

   The Search page appears, as shown in Figure 9-10.

2. **Select the type of search you want to perform.**

   You can select Categories, Title, or Keyword in the menu on the left.

3. **Depending on which search type you've selected, do one of the following:**

   - If you selected a category search, use your remote's arrow buttons to navigate through the category list. Many of the categories have subcategories that you can delve into by pressing the OK button on the remote.

   - If you've selected a title or keyword search, use the numeric entry buttons on your remote to type the title or word you want to search for.

     These keys work just like those on a cell phone. A legend on the screen shows which letters match up to which number buttons. Just press the number corresponding to the letter you want, and remember that you might have to press the number several times to get to the letter you want. Press the Clear button on the remote if you make a mistake. Media Center starts searching based on what you've typed so far — so if you type just *SEI,* for example, it will probably find *Seinfeld.*

   The results of your search appear on the right side of the screen.

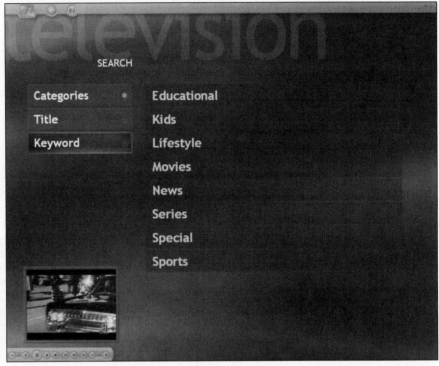

Figure 9-10:
Searching
the Guide by
category,
title, or
keyword.

4. **Scroll through the list of results in the same way you scroll through the listings in the Guide.**

5. **When you find the show you're looking for, press OK on the remote to play or record it.**

Playing with Live TV

If you just want to watch TV, you can get right to it by pressing the Live TV button on the remote. Voila! Live TV takes over the screen and starts playing. When you press Live TV, Media Center (and your cable or satellite set-top box) tunes to and displays the last channel you were watching.

If you're sitting in front of your MCE PC doing some work or Web surfing in the traditional XP interface, you can shrink the full-screen TV display using your mouse and keyboard. Just press the Escape key on your keyboard and you'll have a resizable TV window on your XP desktop. (You can drag the corner of the window to resize it just like any other XP window.)

You change channels just like you would if you were watching a regular TV without a Media Center PC. Press the CH/PG button on the remote to move up and down through the channels. Media Center displays a banner at the bottom of the screen with the channel number, the program name, the air times, and the current time — a nice touch that lets you know where you are and what you're watching even when there's a commercial.

If you want more details about what you're watching, press the More Info button on the remote. This displays another banner across the bottom of your screen with a brief description of the program, including the channel number, title, air times, and part of the Program Guide's description of the program. If you don't do anything, the banner goes away after a few seconds. If you want to see more detail, press the OK button on the remote, and a full-screen description of the program appears, with the program itself in the inset window. (This is the same view shown in Figure 9-8.) Press the Back button on the remote to go back to watching the program.

You can start recording a program from this window using the Record, Record series, or Advanced record menu options, which are shown on the left side of Figure 9-8.

At any time, you can press the Guide button on the remote to display the Program Guide and see what else is on. When you do this, the program you're currently watching continues running in the inset window.

Mastering Your TV Domain

Our favorite feature of My TV is the capability to take charge of your TV experience in two key ways:

- ✔ **Control Live TV:** My TV lets you pause, rewind and fast forward whatever show you're currently watching. You don't have to do anything special — a rolling 30-minute recording session starts whenever you use My TV.

- ✔ **Time shift your TV:** *Time shifting* is the capability to watch the same content aired on TV, but just shifted in time — so you can record a TV show and watch it when you want.

Controlling live TV

My TV *always* records onto your MCE PC's hard drive the up to last 30 minutes of TV you've been watching, so at any time you can rewind up to 30 minutes. The only limitation to My TV's control of live TV is that Media Center supports only a single TV tuner, which means it can control only a single channel (the one you're watching).

My TV records the channel currently on the screen. Whenever you change channels, MCE dumps its buffered content and starts fresh on the new channel. So you can go back only 30 minutes or as long as you've been watching the current channel, whichever is shortest.

Controlling live TV is easy — just use the Pause, Play, FWD, and REW buttons on the remote:

- To pause live TV, press the Pause button on the remote. To resume, press the Play button. If you instead want to go back to real time and see what's currently being broadcast, press the Live TV button.

- To rewind live TV, just press the REW button on the remote. Remember that you can go back up to 30 minutes.

All the tips for using the media playback controls (see Chapter 7) apply here. This means you can control the speed of your rewinding and fast forwarding by pressing the appropriate button more than once. Press the Play button to resume playing.

- To fast-forward TV, press the FWD button on the remote. This fast-forwards your TV show until you reach the current time.

We feel a little silly saying it, but we will anyway. You can't fast forward your TV show past the current time. There's no time warp technology under the hood of Media Center. So if you start watching live TV, pressing the FWD button won't do you any good. But FWD can come in handy if you pause or rewind your live TV program.

Doing the time shift

Controlling Live TV is a great thing. When the phone rings (darn those telemarketers) or the dog has to go out, pausing your favorite program seems like a life saver. But sometimes you want to record entire shows for later playback. No reason to rush home for that vital *Buffy* repeat when your Media Center PC is on the job, ready to record for you.

Media Center offers you many opportunities to record a show whenever you're looking at the Guide or viewing detailed information about a program. We describe the four easiest ways to record a show in My TV. Note that we're talking about individual showings here. We talk about recording a series in the next section.

To record a show, you can

- Browse through the Guide, find a show you want to record, and press OK. By selecting the Record menu item that appears on the screen, you can set up the recording.

✔ Search for a show in the Guide and set up recording.

✔ Manually record (the VCR way!) by entering the channel number and time into Media Center.

✔ One-touch record by navigating to a show in the Guide (or even the show you're currently watching) and pressing the REC button on the remote.

After you've scheduled a few recordings, you can quickly check what Media Center is planning on recording by going to the My TV main menu, selecting Recorded TV, and then selecting Scheduled.

Recording a show from the Guide

To record a show from the Guide, do the following:

1. **Open My TV by pressing the My TV button on the remote.**

2. **Select Recorded TV.**

3. **Select Add recording.**

   The screen shown in Figure 9-11 appears.

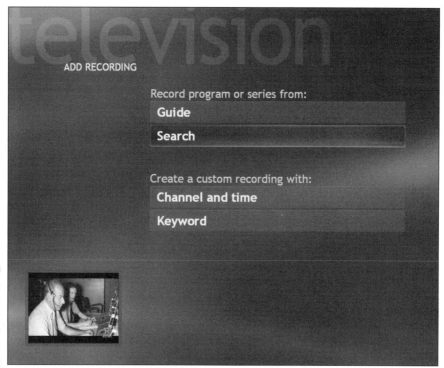

Figure 9-11:
The recording process starts here.

4. **Select Guide.**

   The Guide window appears.

5. **Select the show you want to record.**

   The Program Info screen appears.

6. **Select Record.**

   Media Center saves this recording data in its little computer brain and records the show when it airs.

   In MCE 2002, your MCE PC had to be running or in standby mode — not Hibernate mode — for this to work. Waking from Hibernate mode is now supported in MCE 2004. (Microsoft needed to do this to support notebook computers.) We discuss these modes in Chapter 7.

7. **Press the Back button (or any other Media Center function button on the remote) to get back to what you were previously doing.**

   The program you selected for recording now has a little red dot next to its title in the Guide. You can check that you did things correctly by navigating to the show in the Guide and looking for the dot.

Media Center checks to make sure that you haven't already set up a different recording at the same time. Recall that an MCE PC has only one TV tuner and can record only one program at a time. If you try to make your MCE PC record two things simultaneously, a Conflict screen appears, as shown in Figure 9-12. It's up to you to make a choice — use the remote to select the program you want to record (this is a little bit of TV triage for you). The other program will *not* be recorded.

Searching for shows to record

Just as you don't have to manually scroll through the Guide to find shows to watch, you also don't have to manually scroll through the Guide to set up recordings. With Media Center, you can search for shows to record, as follows:

1. **In My TV, select Recorded TV, and then select Add recording.**

2. **Select Search.**

   The window shown back in Figure 9-10 appears.

3. **Search for the show by category, title, or keyword. When you find the show, select it.**

   For more information on searching, see the "Searching the Guide" section, earlier in the chapter.

4. **When the Program Info screen appears, select Record.**

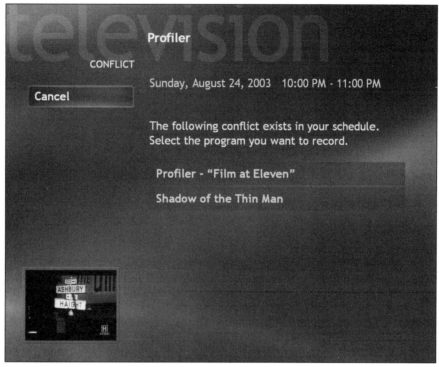

Figure 9-12:
Oops! You
can't record
two shows
at once, so
choose the
one you
want.

Pretending your MCE PC is a VCR

Suppose your favorite show is on a local access channel that doesn't provide programming information in the Guide. To record this show, you have to set up a manual recording on your MCE PC:

1. **In My TV, select Recorded TV, and then select Add recording.**

2. **Select Channel and time.**

   The Manual Record screen appears, as shown in Figure 9-13.

3. **Use the remote's arrow buttons to navigate between the Channel, Frequency, Date, Start time, and Stop time options.**

   Use the numeric entry buttons on the remote to type the channel and times. For the other settings, navigate to the plus or minus button and press OK repeatedly to scroll through the settings.

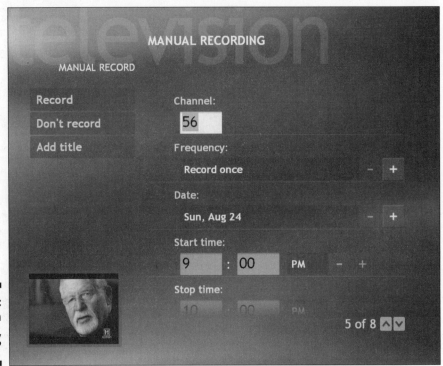

Figure 9-13:
Looks like a
VCR display,
doesn't it?

4. **To add a descriptive title to your manual recording, do the following:**

   a. **Select Add title (on the left side of the screen).**

   b. **In the screen that appears, use the numeric entry keys (or your keyboard) to type a name.**

   c. **Select Save.**

5. **Back in the Manual Record window, select Record.**

The recording settings are saved, and your MCE PC is ready to record for you.

Taking the one-touch approach

The easiest way to set up a recording in My TV is to just use the REC button on the remote. Anytime you have a show actively playing on your screen or selected in the Guide, you can mark it for recording (or start recording it immediately, if it's currently playing) by pressing REC.

Are your kids watching a program on a school night, but it's time for them to go to bed? Press REC, and tell the kids they can finish watching the program tomorrow. Can't get much simpler than that.

Recording your favorite shows

If you have a few shows that you watch all the time, you should set up series recording. *Series recording* is similar to single-episode recording, except Media Center keeps an untiring eye open to the Guide and records episodes of a series each time they're on. You won't miss a single action-packed moment of *This Old House Classics!*

You might hear the term *PVR* (*personal video recorder*) used by some vendors when describing the capability to record TV shows on a computer hard drive. My TV is a PVR on your PC.

The process for setting up a series recording is identical to the one for recording a single show, except instead of selecting Record, you select Record series. (See "Recording a show from the Guide" and "Searching for shows to record" in the preceding section.) Media Center follows the series recording rules you established when you configured My TV's settings (we told you how to do this in Chapter 6), and schedules your recordings.

If you want to sidestep those rules for this particular series recording, select Advanced record instead of Record series. A window appears for configuring custom settings, such as whether you want to record repeat or just first-run episodes. These new modified settings apply only to the individual series — the rest of your recordings adhere to the rules you set up in My TV's settings.

What if you've already selected a show for recording and then decide that you want to record the entire series? No problem. First go to the Scheduled recordings screen (select My TV, then Recorded TV, and then Scheduled). Next, select the show. In the screen that appears, select Record series. You've now switched that show from a single-episode recording to a series recording.

When you select a show for series recording, it has four (overlapping) red dots next to its name in the Guide.

Watching Your Recorded Shows

All these recorded shows don't do you a bit of good if you don't watch them. They just crowd up your hard drive and sit there like the dumb pile of bits and bytes that they are.

Watching your recorded TV on *other* PCs

If you have a home network or a removable media drive such as a DVD burner or a FireWire hard drive, you can share your recorded TV files with another PC if it's a Media Center PC or a Windows XP PC with Service Pack 1 and a DirectShow-compatible media player program (such as Windows Media Player 9).

If the computer on which you want to play your recorded TV show is a Media Center PC, the process is simple. First find the file you want to play. The file name will contain the name of the show you've recorded, and the file will be in the following directory:

```
C:\Documents and Settings\All Users\Shared Documents\Recorded TV
```

Using your network or removable media, copy this file into the same folder location on the other Media Center PC. Now you can open Media Center and My TV and play back the file just as if you had recorded it on that TV.

If you have a regular XP PC, you won't be able to watch the show using the My TV interface, but you're not out of luck. You can watch your shows as long as Windows Media Player 9 is installed, and you download and install Windows XP Service Pack 1 Update from Microsoft's Web site:

```
www.microsoft.com/downloads/details.aspx?FamilyId=FB4C2C2E-60EA-
    4ED9-BC68-E93C9E65C58E&displaylang=en
```

Using your home network or removable media, move the recorded file to your hard drive, and then open it with Windows Media player. It will work like any other media file on your XP computer.

The only potential gotcha — and we don't think that it's currently a problem — is that Microsoft has implemented *CGMS-A* (Copy Generation Management System — Analog) in Media Player 9. This system is one of the many methods that broadcasters and TV and movie studios have developed to try to keep you from watching TV programs when and where you want to. (They want you to be on *their* schedule, not yours.) We don't know of anybody currently using the CGMS-A system, but if a broadcaster or studio started using it, you'd be able to play back your recorded TV shows only on the MCE PC you used to make the recording.

Watching recorded shows is — you guessed it — easy. Follow these steps:

1. **Open My TV by pressing the My TV button on the remote.**

   Your most recently recorded shows are listed below the main viewing window.

2. **If your show is in the list, simply select it and then skip to Step 6. Otherwise, continue with the following steps.**

3. **Select Recorded TV.**

4. **Sort your recorded shows in the fashion you prefer.**

   You can sort by date, name, or category.

5. **Use the arrow buttons on the remote to scroll through the list of shows.**

   If it's a long list, you can jump quickly to the show by typing the first letter of the show's name using the numeric entry keys. Just press the number key corresponding to the first letter in the show's name until that letter appears on the screen.

6. **Select the show.**

   A Program Info screen appears.

7. **To watch the show now, select Play on the screen or press the Play button on the remote.**

While you're playing the recorded show, you can use the Pause, Play, FWD, REW, and Skip buttons to control the playback.

The Skip button jumps forward 29 seconds, which is particularly handy during commercial breaks.

When the show is over, a screen appears, enabling you to choose Restart (start over from the beginning), Delete (erase the show from your hard drive), or Keep (retain the recorded program on your hard drive). If you select Keep, another screen appears where you can determine how long you want to keep the show. We stick with the default Don't change setting, but you might want to use one of the other settings if hard drive space is tight or if it's a show that you *definitely* plan on watching again.

Saving Recorded Programs to DVD

One thing that Media Center is missing is a module that lets you create, or *burn*, your own DVDs. Why would you want to create your own DVDs? Well, we can think of a few reasons:

✓ **You want to create archived copies of your recorded TV shows:** Although MCE PCs have big hard drives, eventually they fill up, and you need to erase some recorded TV shows to make room for new ones. If you want to keep some of those older shows, why not record them to DVD?

✓ **You want to create a DVD of a favorite series:** Perhaps you want to make a *SpongeBob SquarePants* DVD for the kids to watch in the car on that long trip to Disney World. Until they make MCE PCs that will fit in the back of your car, a DVD is your best bet here. (But you know, that Toshiba MCE laptop would fit nicely under the back seat.)

Although Microsoft has not yet provided a way to make DVDs, there *is* a way to burn DVDs in Media Center: using Sonic PrimeTime software (www.sonic. com/primetime). PrimeTime is a DVD-burning application that plugs itself into your Media Center Start menu, so it's easy to access and use with the remote control. You can even find PrimeTime in the Media Center Online Spotlight (Chapter 14). Just open Online Spotlight and navigate to the Downloads section to download a free trial version.

PrimeTime is designed to create DVDs of only your recorded TV content (from My TV). For an all-purpose DVD creation program, you can use Sonic's MYDVD program (see Chapter 13). Many MCE PC vendors include a version of MyDVD with their MCE PCs.

PrimeTime (which retails for $79.95 but is often available less expensively through Net outlets) automatically searches your MCE PC for recorded TV shows and organizes them by name, date recorded, or category — just like My TV does. Using the remote control, you can select the shows you want to burn to DVD and then record them with a single press of a button.

PrimeTime even records *video CDs,* which are similar to DVDs but are on recordable CDs instead of DVD media. Video CDs hold a lot less video, but can be played back on most DVD players and are an option if your MCE PC doesn't have a DVD recorder.

Figure 9-14 shows the PrimeTime interface in MCE. To get to this interface, select Create DVD in the Media Center Start menu.

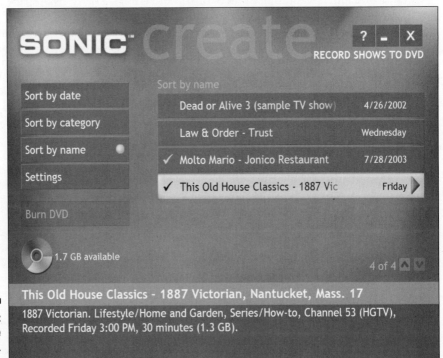

Figure 9-14:
PrimeTime
in action.

PrimeTime is our favorite way of creating DVDs. It has a ton of great features, including the following:

- ✔ You can use DVDs created with PrimeTime in just about any DVD player.

  PrimeTime is also one of the only programs we know of that can convert the files that Media Center uses to record TV (called DVR-MS) to standard MPEG files that a DVD player can display. This is a BIG DEAL!

- ✔ You can insert a *rewritable* DVD (marked RW) into your MCE PC and use PrimeTime to change its contents. You can remove all the programs you recorded and replace them with others, you can remove a few, or you can add more shows if you have room.

- ✔ PrimeTime uses Dolby Digital (AC-3 encoding) to record the audio portion of the DVD. Dolby Digital is a *compressed* audio system (we discuss compression in Chapter 10) that uses about one-tenth the disc space of the uncompressed alternative, PCM. So with PrimeTime (and Dolby Digital) you use up less of the DVD's storage space with audio — leaving room for more TV shows per disc!

  Media Center does not support Dolby Digital 5.1 for My TV, so you get only two-channel (stereo) sound from any recorded TV programs.

- ✔ PrimeTime has a handy "bit-budget" indicator. (See the disc on the left side of Figure 9-14.) As soon as you select a show, the indicator updates the amount of space left on the DVD.

PrimeTime works with all types of recordable DVDs (the blank discs themselves) and makes DVDs that can play in the vast majority of DVD players. You can be pretty darned confident that grandma will be able to play that disc you sent of the grandkids' latest school recital. (For more on DVD discs, see Chapter 17.)

Chapter 10

Listening to Music

· ·

In This Chapter

▶ Reciting the ABCs of MP3s (and WMAs, too!)

▶ Running through the set-up process

▶ Getting your music into MCE PC

▶ Organizing your tunes

▶ Playing music on your MCE PC

▶ Listening to the radio

· ·

*O*f all the features in Media Center, the music ones are our favorites. The way Media Center manages digital music is just outstanding, in our opinion.

Media Center can easily handle just about any type of digital music you might throw at it — Windows Media, audio CDs, MP3 files, and more. And because Media Center is built around Windows Media 9, it can be extended to handle even more types of digital music in the future with just minor — and most likely, automatic — software upgrades.

In this chapter, we discuss the My Music module in Media Center, beginning with some background on the different types of digital music it can handle. Next, you set up My Music. Then it's time to get music into your Media Center PC, organize that music, and finally — the important part — play your music. We wrap up with a discussion of something new to Windows XP MCE 2004 — Radio.

Windows Media Center is an interface that overlays Windows Media 9. That means most of the complicated stuff for Windows MCE is performed by Windows Media 9, and you have to leave the MCE domain and go to XP to do certain tasks, such as transfer music into your system. Windows Media 9 works like a standard Windows program, so you'll rely on your keyboard and mouse. MCE merely makes it easy to use Media 9 from across the room with the remote control. We wanted to emphasize the distinction, so you understood in advance that to exploit My Music in MCE, you have to invest a fair amount of time in XP.

Digital Music 101

Before we delve into the features of My Music, we want to take a moment to discuss the different digital music types, or *formats,* that Media Center can handle. In this section, we give you a little bit of background on the three primary types of audio file formats that MCE supports. That way, when people talk about how they've loaded their MCE hard drive with WMA lossless files, you'll know what the heck they mean.

Digital music files are created by a process called *sampling.* A sound (typically a musical performance, though it could be, say, someone speaking or the sound of a car engine revving) is inherently analog. This analog sound is picked up by a microphone and sent to an *analog-to-digital converter* (ADC), which captures that sound digitally by measuring tiny snippets of the sound (*samples*). Basically the ADC takes a snapshot of that analog sound wave thousands of times per second.

The size of this digital file and the sound quality depend on two factors:

- ✔ The *sampling rate,* which is the number of samples taken in a given period of time
- ✔ The *sampling precision,* which is the amount of data that the ADC uses to "describe" the music in each sample — measured in bits of data

A CD, for example, has 44,100 samples per second, and each sample uses 16 bits of data. So a typical, 74-minute-long CD uses more than 650 *megabytes* of data (remember, a byte is 8 bits). If you want to copy all your CDs to your hard drive, you'll quickly run out of space without some way of making the audio files smaller. That's where compression comes in.

Media Center (and the Windows Media 9 software) uses one of several formats, or codecs, to make audio (and video) files smaller. These smaller files don't crowd your hard drive and are easier to share over a network or the Internet. A *codec* (shorthand for encoder/decoder) uses a special mathematical algorithm to take the extra data out of digital music files without removing too much of the audio quality. When you play the music files on your MCE PC, Media Center *decompresses* these files and then converts the sound from digital computer files to an analog sound wave that your speakers can play.

Many different individual audio codecs are available, but they all fit into one of these two buckets:

- **Lossy:** Most codecs are *lossy,* which means the compression process removes more of the sound than can be replaced when the file is decompressed. These algorithms use something called *psychoacoustics* — a scientific study that determines what parts of the music can be omitted without changing how the users perceive the sound. For most people, a file compressed with one of these codecs sounds just as good as the original, but the music *is not* identical to the original, uncompressed music that began this process.

- **Lossless:** A *lossless* compression system reduces the size of the music file, but it does so in a way that the file, when decompressed, is an identical copy of the original. This is a better way, theoretically, to compress a file, but it's less *efficient* — that it, a lossless-compressed file takes up more room on your hard drive than a lossy-compressed file.

WMA leads the way

The primary digital music codec used by Media Center is *WMA* (Windows Media Audio). This is the built-in, default codec in Windows Media 9. When you turn on your MCE PC, it's set up to use WMA when you copy CDs to your hard drive.

You may be more familiar with the MP3 codec (discussed in the next section). WMA is newer than MP3 and provides higher levels of audio quality for the same file size.

WMA comes in several flavors:

- **Windows Media Audio:** This is the standard WMA codec, using what is called *CBR,* or *constant bit rate.* A CD is compressed using the same number of bits of data per period of time (called the *bit rate*). The advantage of a CBR codec is that it's predictable. You always know beforehand how much drive space will be taken up per song.

  You can select a CBR bit rate ranging from 48 to 192 Kbps (kilobits per second). (We tell you how in the "Setting your CD copying codec" section.) The higher the bit rate, the better the sound quality but also the more hard drive space used to store the file.

- **Windows Media Audio, variable bit rate:** This variant of WMA is a VBR, or *variable bit rate,* codec. This means the codec applies more or less compression depending on the complexity of the digital musical signal.

Compared to CBR files recorded at similar bit rates, VBR files are typically slightly smaller but also sound better. However, you can't predict the size of a VBR file. (The VBR file could end up being larger, depending on the file's characteristics.) You can adjust WMA VBR files (like regular WMA files) to reflect a balance between file size and audio quality. The smallest VBR files use a bit rate between 40 and 75 Kbps, and the largest (but best-sounding) files use a bit rate between 240 and 355 Kbps.

✔ **Windows Media Audio, lossless:** This is the crème de la crème of WMA — a codec that preserves the original file perfectly, without discarding any audio information along the way. As a result, WMA lossless uses the most space on your hard drive: between 470 and 940 Kbps, depending on the music. To put this measurement in perspective, an uncompressed CD uses about 1411 Kbps.

If you have a lot of hard drive space and are serious about your musical fidelity, try the WMA lossless codec. We find, however, that the WMA VBR codec used at one of the highest bit-rate settings is more than good enough for our ears and gives us more space for saving music (and TV programs and other stuff) on our MCE PCs.

MP3 for me

MP3 — which stands for MPEG-2 Layer 3, in case you ever get on a quiz show — is the most commonly used digital music codec. MP3 has spread throughout the computer world as well as the consumer electronics world to become the default language for digital audio. If you download music files from the Internet, they're often in the MP3 format. However, some online music stores are moving to WMA (the default Windows Media 9 codec) because Windows Media 9 has a robust digital rights management (DRM) system that controls the use of downloaded music files. (In other words, the DRM system keeps users from uploading files to a music file-sharing service.)

Media Center (and Windows Media 9) can *play* just about any MP3 file that you've downloaded or transferred onto your MCE PC. But when your MCE comes out of the box, it can't *create* MP3 files. You can install additional codecs in your system that will allow Media Center and Windows Media 9 to create MP3 files. Microsoft has a list of these programs on its Media Player 9 site. To check out the list, go to windowsmedia.com/9series and click the Plug-Ins link.

You might find that you never need to buy an MP3 codec add-on program for your MCE PC. We think the WMA codec is at least as good as MP3. You may, however, need to install an MP3 codec if you have a portable audio player that can't handle WMA files.

CD audio and WAV

Media Center also can play back CD audio files without any conversion or other preliminary steps. Place a CD in your CD/DVD drive, and the Media Center interface will launch, and your CD will start playing (if you followed our suggestion in Chapter 8 to set up CD autoplay).

Media Center can also handle WAV (waveform) files stored on your MCE PC. WAV files are basically uncompressed digital audio and are often recorded with the same sampling rate and sampling precision as CDs. You probably won't have too many WAV music files on your MCE PC because they're used more often for things like system sounds and beeps.

Setting Up My Music

To use My Music, you can just press the My Music button on the remote, and then press the Play button. But that's a bit of an oversimplification. Although you *can* just play music with My Music, you *should* spend a few minutes to set up My Music's preferences the way you want them.

Setting your CD copying codec

If you're like us, the first thing you'll *want* to do with your MCE PC is feed CDs into the disc drive and begin filling up your music library. But we think your first step should be setting up the codec you'll use for copying your CDs to your MCE PC's hard drive. Otherwise, if you decide later to use a higher-quality setting or, on the other hand, save space on your hard drive and use a lower bit-rate setting, you'll have to delete all those music files and start over.

To set up your preferred CD copying codec, just follow these steps in XP:

1. **Choose Start⇨Windows Media Player.**

   Windows Media Player appears.

2. **In the menu bar of Media Player, choose Tools⇨Options.**

   The Options dialog box appears, as shown in Figure 10-1.

3. **Click the Copy Music tab.**

4. **In the Copy settings area, click the arrow to the right of the Format pull-down menu and choose the codec you want to use.**

Figure 10-1:
Get hands-
on with
Media
Player here.

We recommend that you use Windows Media Audio (variable bit rate).

By default, Windows Media Audio (the CBR variety) and 128 Kbps bit rate are selected.

5. **Click the Audio quality slider, and slide it to your desired setting.**

We move the slider all the way to the right (to Best Quality), but you may decide to use a slightly smaller file size (somewhere further to the left) if you need to preserve drive space.

6. **Click OK.**

7. **In the Windows Media Player menu bar, choose File⇨Exit.**

You're finished. Whatever codec you chose is the one My Music will use to record CDs.

Configuring My Music

You've almost completed the setup — just a few more quick steps. You can sit back from the computer now, because you can follow these steps using the remote control (no more of that old-fashioned mouse and keyboard stuff for you).

All that's left to do is to tell My Music how you want it to handle *visualizations.* These are the cool and somewhat psychedelic patterns that flow over your display while music plays. (Visualizations are fractal images generated by the music itself — think of this feature as a built-in lava lamp!)

Just follow these steps:

1. **Open My Music by pressing the My Music button on the remote.**

   The My Music screen and Start menu appear on your display.

2. **Select Settings.**

   The Settings screen appears, as shown in Figure 10-2.

3. **In the Show song information during visualizations section, choose when (or if) you want visualizations to appear when you play music.**

4. **If you choose the Never option, select Save, and you're finished. Otherwise, select the Select Visualizations option.**

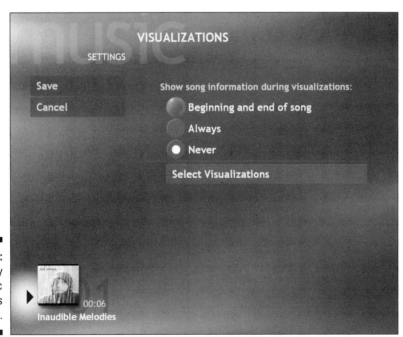

Figure 10-2:
The My
Music
Settings
screen.

5. **Choose which visualizations you want to use as follows:**

   • If you want just a few specific visualizations (maybe you're picky about your psychedelia!), select the Clear all item on the left, and then select the visualizations you want (by navigating to each one and pressing OK).

   • To choose all the visualizations, select the Select all item on the left.

6. **Select the Save button.**

   The screen shown in Figure 10-3 returns.

7. **Select the Save button.**

That's all the settings you have to configure in My Music. Now you're ready to record and play music.

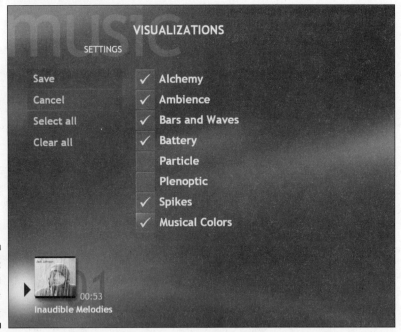

Getting Music into Your Media Center PC

Unless your MCE PC vendor was generous and preloaded your machine with some music files, it comes out of the box with an empty My Music folder. So, before you can play any music on your MCE PC, you have to get some music into it. You can do so in three ways:

> ✔ You can copy your CDs to the hard drive (so you don't need to go find the CD and stick it back in the computer next time).
>
> ✔ You can transfer music files (WMA or MP3 files) from your old computer.
>
> ✔ You can download music files from the Internet.

You'll probably find yourself using each method at different times.

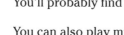

You can also play music directly from CDs without copying them into your My Music folder.

If you're like us, you have boxes of audio tapes as well as LPs or perhaps even 8-track tapes or 45s. So how can you get this music into your system? You need to add *MP3 recorder* or *WMA recorder* software to your system. This software lets you plug your old audio equipment into the Audio In jacks on your sound card and record the analog media as an MP3 or a WMA file. Hundreds of shareware and commercial software products can do this task. We recommend that you go to www.download.com and search under the Audio section for "Rippers and encoders."

If you're trying to record LP records, you *can't* connect the record player directly to your sound card. Instead, run the record player through a receiver that has LP or phono inputs and use one of the Tape Out jacks on the back of the receiver to connect to your MCE PC's sound card.

Getting your CDs into the MCE PC

Every MCE PC includes a CD or DVD drive that can play any CD in your collection. If you've set up CD autoplay (we tell you how in Chapter 8), just open the CD drawer, stick the CD in there, and close the drawer. Media Center and My Music launch, and your CD starts playing. If you don't have autoplay turned on, just select the CD in the listing of albums in My Music and then select the Play option.

You can also select the CD and just press the Play button on the remote control.

Did you select the "Retrieve media information for CDs and DVDs from the Internet" check box back when you were setting your Privacy options for Media Center (discussed in Chapter 8)? Is your MCE PC connected to the Internet? If you answer yes to both, Media Center will connect to a Web service and automatically download the CD's information (title, artist, track names, and even the cover art) and display it on your My Music page. This process might take a few seconds, during which time the My Music screen displays an "Unknown album" message.

When your CD is loaded and the program information has been downloaded, you see a screen like the one shown in Figure 10-4.

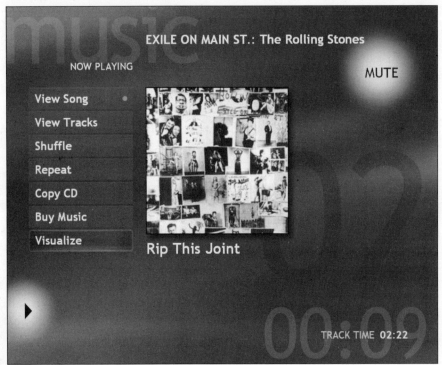

EXILE ON MAIN ST.: The Rolling Stones

NOW PLAYING

MUTE

View Song

View Tracks

Shuffle

Repeat

Copy CD

Buy Music

Visualize

Rip This Joint

00:09

TRACK TIME 02:22

Figure 10-4:
The CD is
loaded and
ready to go!

You can view your CD's information in different ways using the menu at the left. Here's what each option does:

- **View Song:** Shows the CD cover art and the name of the current song. In the background on the right side of the screen, you see the track number, the total time of the track, and the elapsed time (how long the song has been playing).

- **View Tracks:** Lists the songs on your CD in a new screen, as shown in Figure 10-5. You can select particular songs and play them.

- **Shuffle:** Plays the tracks on your CD in a random (or random*ish*) fashion, like the shuffle button on your home CD player.

- **Repeat:** Repeats the music listed in the Now Playing window from the beginning of the list.

- **Copy CD:** Records your CD to your My Music folder (turning the CD into a series of WMA files on your hard drive). After you choose this option, you don't need to put the CD back in your MCE PC again — everything's stored on your hard drive for future use. Cool!

While you're in the middle of listening to a CD, you can copy it. (You might experience a brief pause as the CD begins recording.) You'll see a little spinning disc icon next to the song that's currently recording and check marks next to those that have already been recorded.

✔ **Buy Music:** Takes you to a Web page for the artist, where you can find a discography (listing of the artist's CDs) and find more information about particular albums. You can even click links to buy CDs online.

This element of Media Center has not yet been optimized for remote control use and the 10-foot interface. A warning screen will appear telling you that this Web site may not work as well with your remote. So if you're not sitting in front of your computer with your mouse and keyboard handy, you might want to select the View Later option (it's selected by default). This puts an Internet Explorer shortcut on your desktop, so you can go back to that page at your leisure.

✔ **Visualize:** Activates visualizations, or screen effects (see the "Configuring My Music" section earlier in this chapter). When you want the visualizations to end, press any button on the remote.

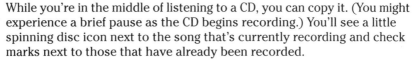

Figure 10-5:
A listing of Pat's favorite Rolling Stones songs.

	EXILE ON MAIN ST.: The Rolling Stones	
NOW PLAYING		
View Song	Loving Cup	4:25
View Tracks	Happy	3:05
Shuffle	Turd on the Run	2:38
Repeat	Ventilator Blues	3:24
Copy CD	I Just Want to See His Face	2:53
Buy Music	Let It Loose	5:18
Visualize	All Down the Line	3:50
	Stop Breaking Down	4:34
	Shine a Light	4:16
	Soul Survivor	3:49
00:10 Ventilator Blues		12 of 18

Getting online music into your MCE PC

You don't have to own CDs to get music into your computer — you probably already know this if you follow the news about the online music services Napster and Kazaa (Napster is extinct, but Kazaa is still around) and RIAA (Record Industry Association of America). These services and dozens like them are often used for peer-to-peer file sharing, where people copy CDs to their hard drives (a process often referred to as ripping), and then share them with others over the Internet. RIAA has sued just about everyone in an effort to stop this file sharing.

We aren't going to describe peer-to-peer file sharing services, but we are going to discuss some for-pay music services popping up online. These services have made deals with record labels and artists, and offer digital music files for download — for a price. Typically you pay a monthly fee of about $10 to get basic access to one of these services, which gives you access to all the songs on its catalog. This access, however, is often just for *streaming* the music files — you can access them on the Internet and play them on demand, but you can't save them to your hard drive. You usually pay a per-song fee of $1 or less to save the files on your hard drive permanently.

The two most prominent services are Napster and Listen.com. Here are the details:

✔ **Napster:** You probably remember Napster — it was the program that launched a thousand lawsuits (well, close to a thousand) back when it seemed that everybody you knew was getting "free" music from the Internet. Well that version of Napster is long gone, but Roxio bought the name and assets of Napster (the company) and is relaunching the service as a new, for-pay online music service. Napster wasn't launched by the time this book was printed, but we got a sneak preview from the folks at Roxio. For a monthly fee (not announced as we go to print), Napster will let you access music files from all the major record labels — directly through Media Center.

Napster will be available through Media Center's Online Spotlight — you can sign up with your remote control and start listening. With Napster, you'll be able to purchase songs and entire CDs, and automatically download them into My Music. The files you've bought can be played back on your MCE PC, or you can burn them to a CD or put them on your portable digital music player. We can't wait for this one to launch — it will be the first online music service available through the Media Center interface.

✔ **Listen.com:** Our other favorite online music service is Listen.com's Rhapsody service. Rhapsody *doesn't* work through the Media Center Interface — at least not yet, though we suspect that Listen.com will eventually provide an MCE experience like the one Napster is launching.

For $9.95 you get unlimited, on-demand access to music from all the major record labels (plus a bunch of independent labels), and you can download songs onto your MCE PC (and into My Music) for $.99 a piece. Listen.com also has a cheaper online radio service for $4.95 a month, with more than 50 commercial-free radio stations — plus you can create your own custom radio stations with your favorite artists. We love Listen.com's service, and are feverishly waiting for an MCE version of Rhapsody.

Both use the WMA file format, for added compatibility with Media Center.

Organizing Your Music

However you get your music into your MCE PC (online services, your own CDs, carrier pigeon . . .), you may at some point decide that you want to organize your music. Perhaps you're sick to death of that latest Euro disco album you downloaded, or maybe you just want to free up some space on the hard drive. Well, it's easy to organize, delete, and add files to your music library in MCE, but these tasks occur in the traditional Windows XP interface, not in the Media Center interface. In other words, this is a job for the mouse, not the remote.

Removing files from Media Library

Your music library is actually part of something called your Media Library, which also contains movies, online radio stations, and other media. To remove files from your Media Library, do the following:

1. **Close or minimize Media Center.**

   Select the close or minimize button, at the top right of the Media Center interface, and press OK on the remote.

2. **Choose Start➪Windows Media Player.**

   Windows Media Player appears, as shown in Figure 10-6.

Figure 10-6:
Organizing
your music
library in
Windows
Media
Player.

3. **Click the Media Library tab, which is on the left side of the Media Player window.**

4. **To delete an album or all the music of a particular artist, do the following:**

   a. **Click the plus sign next to Album or Artist to expand it.**

   b. **Find the album or artist you want to delete, right-click it, and choose Delete.**

   You can also select an individual song for deletion by right-clicking the song's name and choosing Delete. Regardless of what you delete, a confirmation dialog box appears, as shown in Figure 10-7.

   c. **Click the Delete from Media Library and my computer option (unless you want to keep the files on your hard drive, but not see them in Media Center), and then click OK.**

5. **Repeat the process in Step 4 until you've deleted everything you want to clear off your hard drive.**

6. **Choose File➪Exit to close Windows Media Player.**

Figure 10-7:
Confirming a
deletion in
your Media
Library.

Searching for files outside Media Library

You can use Windows Media Player also to search your hard drive (or other hard drives attached to your computer) for additional audio files that aren't in your Media Library and add them. Follow these steps:

1. **In the Media Player window, click the Media Library tab.**

   To get to the Media Player window, close or minimize Media Center and then choose Start➪Windows Media Player.

2. **Choose Add➪By Searching Computer.**

   The dialog box shown in Figure 10-8 appears.

3. **In the Search on pull-down menu, select the Local Drives, minus program folders option.**

   This tells Media Player to search for music files on every hard drive attached to your MCE PC (in case you have more than one).

4. **Click the New files and existing files in library without media information option.**

5. **Click the Search button.**

   Windows Media Player digs into your hard drives and looks for music files to add to your Media Library. When the searching and adding process is over, a Search completed dialog box appears.

6. **Click Close.**

Figure 10-8:
Searching
the hard
drive for
music.

Finding music on your home network

You don't have to keep all your digital music files on the hard drive of your MCE PC. You can have files on other networked computers or even on a *file server* (a computer just for storing files and sending them out to other computers). With My Music, you can play these files on your MCE PC without having to copy them over to the MCE PC's hard drive.

First, your network must be up and running (we tell you how in Chapter 15). Second, you must have file sharing turned on for your music folders on those other computers. Third, follow the process for adding files to your Media Library

described in the "Organizing Your Music" section. The only difference is that instead of choosing the Local Drives, minus program folders option, you choose All Drives. Any networked computers that you have access to will be included in the search, and any music files found will be added to your library. The files themselves are *not* moved, but Media Center knows where they are and can access them.

Please note, as we discuss in Chapter 16, that some wireless networks (particularly those using the slower 802.11b system) may not be fast enough for this process to work well.

By default, Windows automatically searches for new files in your My Music folder (located in the My Documents folder), and adds them to the Media Library for you. If you have other folders that you put music into, you can set up Media Center to automatically search them, too. In Step 2, choose Add⇨By Monitoring Folders. A dialog box appears, and you can put additional folders in this *watch list* of monitored folders. Having a watch list can be useful if you use an online music service that downloads music files to its own folder instead of to your My Music folder.

Playing with Your Music

If you're a bit geeky (like us), setting preferences and organizing digital music libraries can be their own reward. But the fun part comes when you listen to your music files through a good set of speakers.

Playing music stored on your MCE PC with My Music is dead simple — we pretty much described the process when we talked about how to play CDs. In fact, My Music doesn't differentiate much between CDs in your CD/DVD drive and music files on your hard drive — it's all music.

From the main My Music screen, you can find your music by having My Music sort it using the following categories:

✔ **Album titles:** Displays all albums. You can further sort your albums as a text list or by showing the album covers.

✔ **Artist name:** Displays your music according to the artist's name. Select any artist, and that artist's albums appear on the screen.

✔ **Playlist:** Displays your playlists. Using Windows Media Player, you can create playlists of songs (sort of like those mix tapes Danny made back in college to impress the girls). Basically, you mix and match songs in the order you like, save the playlist and then play them back.

Media Center (and Windows Media Player) automatically builds playlists for you — Auto Playlists — based on criteria such as songs you play the most, songs you haven't listened to in a while, and more. You can access these Auto Playlists in My Music by selecting Playlists and then selecting Auto Playlists.

✔ **Songs:** Displays a list of every song in your media library.

✔ **Genre:** Displays a list of musical genres (rock, jazz, hip hop, and so on) in your MCE music collection. Genre information is collected from the Internet when you first put your CDs in the MCE PC and copy them — it's part of the process that finds the cover art and album or song titles.

If you don't have a genre listed for a particular album or disagree with the verdict others have rendered on it (What! Barry Manilow is *not* punk!), you can edit this *tag* (or any of the others — artist, track name, album name, and so on) in Windows Media Player. Just right-click the song in Media Library and choose Advanced Tag Editor. Make your changes, and click OK. Sometimes tags are missing on songs you've downloaded from the Internet or on obscure CDs that haven't made it onto the online databases.

After you select the song or album you want to play — using any of the preceding methods — just press the Play button on the remote control. The Pause, FWD, and REW buttons also work just as you'd expect they would. (In other words, they work just as they do on that CD player in your living room.)

Here are the specifics on what the buttons on your remote do in My Music:

✔ **Play:** Starts playing the selected song or album.

✔ **Pause:** Suspends the song. Press Pause again (or press Play), and the song continues.

✔ **FWD (fast forward):** Press this button once to skip through the song at a slightly increased pace. Press again to move even faster, and press a third time to zip through the song at breakneck speed.

✔ **REW (rewind):** Does the same thing as FWD, but in the opposite direction.

✔ **Replay:** Skips to the beginning of the song and starts playing it again.

✔ **Skip:** Skips to the next song. This button is handy when you just can't stand that one horrible song on an otherwise great album.

Radio

Radio premiered in Windows XP Media Center Edition 2004. With Radio, you can listen to and control FM radio on your Media Center PC.

It its simplest form, Radio puts an FM tuner right into your PC, giving you many of the same capabilities you have in your car stereo, such as preset stations, scanning, and volume controls. However, your Windows XP MCE tuner has one fancy additional feature — the capability to buffer (or store on your hard drive) live radio. This allows you to do two major things:

- ✓ **Pause a station:** Suppose you're listening to a great interview on NPR, and a Girl Scout comes to your door to sell you some of those great mint cookies. You can't simply say, "No!" to such an offer, but you really want to listen to the interview, too. No problem. Just press the Pause button, and you can record the show while you fill out the order form. MCE can buffer up to 30 minutes of radio content.

- ✓ **Enjoy an instant replay:** Did you miss that dial-in phone number for the free concert tickets? Press the Replay button on the remote control to skip back 7 seconds in the broadcast.

Very nice.

You see the Radio option on your MCE Start menu only if your TV card is outfitted with FM tuner capability. An FM-equipped TV tuner card is easy to spot — it has two F (75-ohm cable-style) coaxial connectors, one for the TV cable and the other for the FM cable. If you want to add the Radio feature to your MCE PC, ask your vendor about upgrading to a TV tuner card with an FM input.

MCE 2004 will not show the Radio menu button on the start page if it does not detect a FM tuner installed in the PC when Media Center is started.

When you select Radio from the Start menu, you see two options, Start FM and Settings, as shown in Figure 10-9. Select Start FM to find and play audio content from your favorite FM stations. Select Settings to access some basic options for the Radio experience.

Microsoft kept the FM tuner screen simple. Here's the quick lowdown on what you can do with Radio and how to do it:

- ✓ Use the arrow buttons on the remote control to navigate the screen.

- ✓ To enter numbers, use the numeric keypad on the remote followed by the Enter button. You can enter a station's frequency (for example, 96.5), and press the Enter button on the remote to tell Media Center to tune to that frequency.

✔ To find a specific station, navigate to the Tune option's plus or minus button on the screen, click the button until you reach the specific slot in the FM frequency band that you want, and then press OK.

✔ If you want to scan the available stations in your area, navigate to the plus or minus button in the Seek area, and press OK to move to the next tuned-in station.

✔ There's space for nine *preset stations* — stations that you can select with one-button access. To establish a preset, tune to a station using the plus and minus buttons or by directly entering the numbers, and then select the Save menu option. MCE assigns that station to one of the open presets. From then on, just navigate to the station preset and press OK.

✔ Want to move your presets around? No problem. Use the on-screen up and down buttons to shift the station to another preset. If you want to get rid of a preset station listing, select the on-screen Delete button (it's an X) or use the Delete button on your keyboard.

Overall, the Radio experience in MCE is second only to My DVD in ease of use.

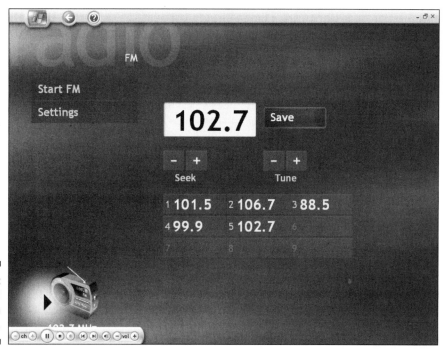

Figure 10-9:
Your FM
Tuner in
Radio.

Chapter 11

Working with Photos

*D*igital cameras have taken the photography world by storm — news articles and market research show that digital cameras now outsell film cameras. Heck, we both have standalone digital cameras, plus digital cameras in our cell phones — Danny even has one built into his camcorder — and we're not even big photography geeks. Regular folks (we're regular, really!) have begun to embrace digital photography. We've even seen an announcement for an $11 disposable digital camera.

Microsoft is full of smart people who know a trend when they see one, so they loaded up the My Pictures module with powerful digital photography features that make it easy to store, organize, view, and print your digital pictures. And an MCE PC combined with a high-quality, big-screen TV is a match made in heaven when it comes to showing pictures of your vacation at Aunt Edna's — this will be one slide show where your friends don't fall asleep or try to sneak out. ("The babysitter — we've got to go relieve the babysitter!")

And even if you don't have a digital camera yet, you can still take advantage of MCE's My Pictures module. We'll tell you about some inexpensive ways you can get your regular film photographs into your MCE PC.

If you don't like to see pictures of two rather homely dogs, try to ignore the figures in this chapter. Pat had to use pictures of something to demonstrate My Pictures, and the dogs didn't complain when having their picture taken. In fact, they liked to ham it up (as long as some biscuits were nearby).

As mentioned in other chapters, when we say you should *select* something, it's shorthand for this: Use the arrow buttons on the remote to move the cursor to that item and then press the OK button on the remote.

Digital Photography Basics

If you've already read Chapter 10, you know how digital music works — an analog musical signal is chopped up into millions of little pieces that can be described by digital 1s and 0s. Digital photography works in a similar way: An analog image (the light going into a camera's lens) is divided into millions of little dots, or *pixels*, which are described by digital 1s and 0s that can be saved on a memory device (such as the hard drive on your MCE PC).

What to look for in a digital camera

Someone already wrote *Digital Cameras For Dummies,* but we want to give you a few quick pointers if you're getting ready to buy a digital camera. Here's what we look for:

✔ **At least 3 megapixels:** Unless you're buying an inexpensive camera for the kids (or to stuff in your pocket for trips to the amusement park), we think 3 megapixels is the minimum to shoot for (pun intended). Below this point, bigger prints (such as 8x10s) don't look good. Prices for digital cameras are dropping like crazy. You can get a really good 3-megapixel digital camera for around $300 (or probably even less by the time you read this).

✔ **Optical zoom:** Some digital cameras use only digital zoom. (Zooming magnifies distant images — like using binoculars with your camera.) Digital zoom doesn't actually magnify your image; instead, it zooms in on a smaller part of the overall image. This reduces your resolution, because your image then consists of a smaller number of pixels. Optical zoom uses a special lens to magnify your image on the CCD, so you get the full resolution.

✔ **USB 2.0:** Most digital cameras connect to the MCE PC using a USB cable (this is how you download the images). USB 2.0 is *much* faster than the older USB 1.1 standard, so you can get your pictures into your computer that much faster. (We discuss the USB standards in Chapter 2.)

Beyond that, it's up to you. In Chapter 17, we list a few of our favorite sites for learning more about digital cameras and comparing the latest and greatest models.

The number of pixels that make up a digital picture determines the *resolution*. Usually a picture is described by the number of pixels measured horizontally (across the picture from left to right) *times* the number of pixels measured vertically. If a digital picture is 1600x1200, for example, it has 1600 pixels horizontally and 1200 pixels vertically. Multiply these numbers, and you find that the picture is made up of 1,920,000 pixels — nearly 2 million!

The more pixels in a digital picture, the better it looks when enlarged (or blown up). As the picture gets big enough, you can begin to see the pixels themselves. For wallet-sized photos, almost any digital photo is fine, but when you start thinking about 8x10 or larger prints, you need a photo with 3 million or more pixels. Most computer monitors are set up to display 1024x768 pixels, so your computer has to shrink this image down a bit to display it on your screen. Media Center shrinks the image automatically.

If you're shopping for a digital camera, you'll hear the term *megapixels,* as in 2.1 megapixel cameras or 3.2 megapixel cameras. In this case, *mega* means a *million.* So that 1600x1200 pixel picture we just described is nearly 2 megapixels.

Digital pictures are usually stored as one of two types of files:

- ✔ **TIFF files:** TIFF (Tag Image File Format) files are *uncompressed* digital pictures (we talked about compression in Chapter 10). Most digital cameras can be set up to take TIFF files, but this format is seldom used because uncompressed files take up a lot of space — with many digital cameras, you can fit ten or more compressed files on the digital "film" for every uncompressed file. Digital picture files using the TIFF format have a .tif suffix.

- ✔ **JPEG files:** JPEG (Joint Picture Experts Group) files are *compressed* versions of TIFF files. The JPEG system looks at the pixels in a picture and uses mathematical algorithms to remove unnecessary data and make the size of the file (the number of bits used to describe the picture) smaller. Digital picture files using the JPEG format have the .jpg or .jpeg suffix.

JPEG files can have different levels of compression — many digital cameras let you adjust a quality setting for this. Files that are more compressed take up less drive space but may look blurry. This is because JPEG is a *lossy* compression algorithm (we discuss this in Chapter 9), and too much compression crosses the line from discarding superfluous data to discarding important data.

A few digital cameras save their uncompressed pictures in the *RAW* format — this format is literally the raw data off the computer chip in the camera that captures the analog image. You'll probably need some special software that comes with your camera to view this format — for the majority of pictures, we recommend that you use JPEG instead.

You can get a digital picture in two ways:

✔ **Use a digital camera:** This is the best way. A digital camera uses a chip called a *charge-coupled device* (CCD) to digitally capture the light coming into the camera's lens. Photos taken on a digital camera are digital all the way — right up to the point where you turn them back to light (on a monitor screen or your TV) or print them on paper.

✔ **Scan analog pictures (either film slides or prints):** A scanner uses its own CCD to create digital picture files by shining a light on existing analog pictures and capturing that image. We talk more about scanners in Chapter 17.

You don't have to buy your own scanner to create digital photos from your existing film pictures. Hundreds of companies (both local and mail order) will scan your photos and send you a CD containing your digital images. Just look in the local phone book or do a Web search for film-scanning services. We talk about one service we like, Shutterfly (www.shutterfly.com), in Chapter 19.

Setting Up My Pictures

Like all the modules in Media Center, My Pictures is a snap to set up. My Pictures automatically searches for picture image files in the My Pictures subfolder of your My Documents folder in your MCE PC. (Yes, we know it's confusing to have a folder and a module with the same name — but the two work together hand-in-hand.) My Pictures finds digital photo files in the My Pictures folder on its own, so you don't have to tell it where to look.

However, you do have to tell My Pictures how you want to display your photos in Media Center. Set seven easy options, and you're ready to play:

1. **Open Media Center by pressing the green button on the remote.**

   You can also use your mouse and choose Start➪Media Center.

2. **Select My Pictures.**

   The main My Pictures screen appears, as shown in Figure 11-1.

3. **Select Settings.**

   The My Pictures Settings screen appears, as shown in Figure 11-2.

4. **In the first group of settings, choose the way you want your pictures to appear on the screen when you use My Pictures to create a slide show:**

   • To display your photos randomly rather than in alphanumeric order (using the pictures' file names), select the Show pictures in random order check box.

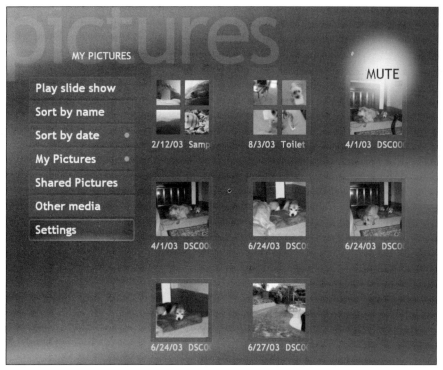

Figure 11-1:
The main
My Pictures
screen.

- If you want the slide show to include pictures in subfolders in your My Pictures folder, select the Show pictures in subfolders check box. If you don't check this box, only photos located in the top level of the My Pictures folder are shown during your slide show.

- To include any captions you entered for your pictures, select the Show captions check box.

5. **In the second group of settings, choose how My Pictures displays information about the music it's playing.**

Media Center's My Music experience can provide background music during your slide shows (you just need to start playing music in My Music before you begin the slide show, as discussed in Chapter 10).

This setting tells My Pictures how you would like to display song information — you'll see an MTV-style overlay at the bottom of your screen. You can display this song information at the beginning and end of the song, always, or never.

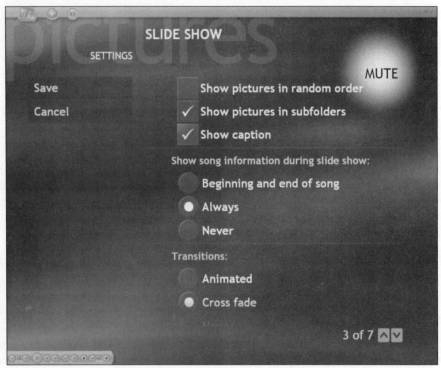

SLIDE SHOW

SETTINGS

MUTE

Save

Cancel

Show pictures in random order

✓ Show pictures in subfolders

✓ Show caption

Show song information during slide show:

Beginning and end of song

● Always

Never

Transitions:

Animated

● Cross fade

3 of 7 ⌃ ⌄

Figure 11-2:
Configuring
My Pictures.

6. **In the next group of settings, choose the effect My Pictures uses during the transition between photos in your slide show.**

   You can choose Animated (My Pictures pans across the picture and then animates the transition to the next picture), Cross fade (the current picture fades out before the next one appears), or None.

7. **In the Transition time setting, decide how long a picture remains on the screen before you move on to the next picture in your slide show.**

   Use the arrow buttons to move to the plus or minus button (shown in Figure 11-3), and then press the OK button as many times as necessary to increase or decrease the time between slides.

8. **In the last setting, choose a background color for your slide-show photos.**

   The final setting, Slide show background color, determines what color appears on your display *outside* the borders of your photos. (When a picture is not the same shape, or aspect ratio, as your screen, you have empty space on the screen, particularly with wide-screen TVs.) Use the arrow buttons to move to the plus or minus button, and then press OK as many times as needed to move between black and white (with shades of gray in-between).

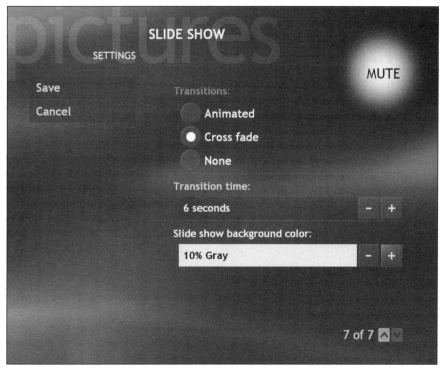

Figure 11-3:
Customizing
slide shows.

9. **Select the Save option (on the left side of the screen).**

   Your settings are saved, and you're returned to the main My Pictures menu.

Is it a camera or a phone?

Another way to take digital pictures is using one of the cool new camera phones offered by the mobile phone companies. For example, Danny just got a cool Sanyo SCP-5300 (you can get one too — Sprint PCS Vision sells them at www. sprintpcs.com). Danny's phone (or is it camera?) can take 640x480 digital pictures with the press of a button. Granted, that resolution is not the same quality you get with a $1500, 8-megapixel digital camera, but who wants to carry an expensive digital camera around all the time? Camera phones are great for the spontaneous snapshot.

The cell phone companies sell camera phones mainly because they'd like you to use their data services to e-mail or SMS (short messaging service) these pictures to your friends. You can also get the pictures off your phone and into your MCE PC at home without using up your minutes. Most camera phones use a USB cable, an IR (Infrared) connection, or Bluetooth wireless technology. As long as your MCE PC is properly equipped with the same connections, you can just "send" the pictures to your XP desktop or right into the My Pictures folder. A cool bit of technology. Don't leave home without one.

Getting Pictures into Your MCE and Moving Them Around

After you've configured My Pictures, it's time to get your pictures into your Media Center PC and put them in the proper location. Media Center can display pictures located in three distinct locations:

- **My Pictures folder:** This folder, located in your My Documents folder on your MCE PC, is the default location for digital photos on your computer. When you use a scanner or plug a digital camera into the USB or FireWire port to download pictures onto your MCE PC, the downloaded pictures end up in your My Pictures folder by default. Photos in the My Pictures folder are available only to the current user. Each logged-in user can see and edit only the pictures in his or her My Pictures folder. (See Chapter 8 for more information about multiple users.)

- **Shared Pictures:** This folder (at C:\Documents and Settings\All Users\Documents\My Pictures) provides a place to store pictures so that they're available to *all* users of the MCE PC. If you have pictures that you want to share with the kids or your spouse, place them here.

- **Other Media:** If you have a 6-in-1 memory card reader, Other Media is for you. My Pictures can read and edit pictures stored on digital "film" (removable flash media) when it's inserted in a memory card reader. This means you don't have to download the pictures to your MCE PC hard drive before viewing or editing them.

Getting pictures from your scanner or digital camera into your My Pictures folder is easy. With most digital cameras (and media card readers), simply plugging the camera into your MCE PC's USB or FireWire port automatically prompts your MCE PC into action.

To get your digital pictures into your MCE PC, just follow these steps:

1. **Attach the camera (or external card reader).**

2. **If you see the screen shown in Figure 11-4, make your selections.**

   This screen appears the first time you download pictures. We recommend that you choose the option titled Copy pictures to a folder on my computer using Microsoft Scanner and Camera Wizard. This screen also appears every time you download pictures, unless you choose the Always to the selected action check box. So, if you want to skip this step in the future, click that check box as well.

3. **Click OK.**

   The Scanner and Camera Wizard appears.

4. **Click Next.**

   You see a series of thumbnail images of the pictures in your camera or memory card.

5. **Use your mouse to check the box next to the pictures you want to download to your MCE PC's hard drive, as shown in Figure 11-5.**

   You can click the Clear All button to deselect all the pictures in your camera or memory card, or click the Select All button to select them all.

6. **Click Next.**

   The screen shown in Figure 11-6 appears.

Figure 11-4: Plugging in your camera or media card reader for the first time.

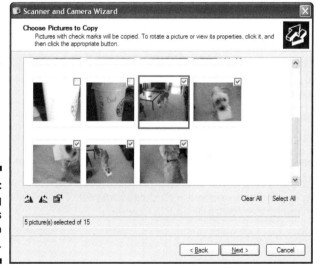

Figure 11-5: Selecting the pictures you want to download.

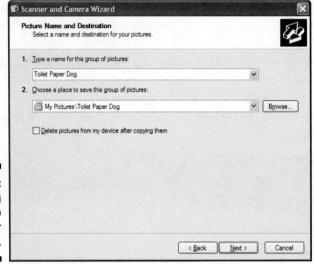

Figure 11-6:
Finding
a place to
put your
pictures.

7. In the first text box, type a name for this group of pictures.

This name is used for a folder that contains all the pictures you're downloading. If you're downloading pictures of your dog running around the house with a newly captured roll of toilet paper, for example, you might want to name the pictures Toilet Paper Dog.

8. In the second text box, change the location, if you want.

By default, the second text box places your pictures in your My Pictures folder, inside a folder with the name you just typed. If you want to put the pictures elsewhere, type that location in the text box or click the Browse button to navigate to another folder on your hard drive.

9. Click Next.

The wizard downloads the pictures to your preferred location, and names the files. (It uses whatever name you chose, and adds a 1, 2, 3, and so on to the end of each file name.)

10. When the download is complete, click Next.

You're offered the options shown in Figure 11-7.

11. Make your selection in the Other Options screen, and then click Next.

Unless you're going to use one of these options, click the option titled Nothing, I'm finished working with these pictures. The Completing the Scanner and Camera Wizard window appears.

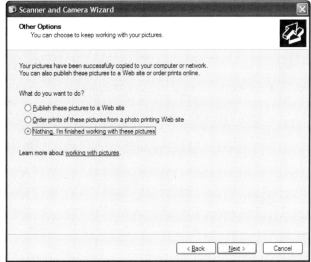

Figure 11-7:
Wrapping
up.

12. **Click Finish.**

The pictures you selected are now in your My Pictures folder (or wherever you told the wizard to put them). Easy as pie.

If you're using a scanner, it should place the scanned photographs in your My Pictures folder by default. If it doesn't, most scanners will let you switch the default folder location by choosing something like Edit➪Options or Edit➪ Preferences.

Making your pictures available to all

If you have pictures in your My Pictures folder that you want to make available to everyone who uses the MCE PC, you need to move them over in the traditional XP interface — you can't use Media Center to change a file's location on the hard drive.

The easiest way to move picture files follows:

1. **Open the My Computer folder in Windows Explorer on your desktop.**

Choose Start➪My Computer.

2. **Press the Ctrl key and double-click My Documents in the My Computer window.**

   The My Documents folder appears in a separate window.

3. **Click the My Computer window to select it and bring it to the front.**

4. **Double-click your hard drive icon (it's probably C:\) and navigate to the following location:**

   ```
   C:\Documents and Settings\All Users\Documents\My Pictures
   ```

5. **Put the two windows next to each other on the desktop.**

   You can move them around by clicking their menu bars and dragging them into place.

6. **Select the files you want to move by Ctrl-clicking each one.**

7. **Copy or move the files as follows:**

   - To copy the files to the Shared Pictures folder (and leave a copy in your My Pictures folder), right-click one of the pictures you've selected and drag it to the Shared Pictures folder. When you release the mouse button, a menu appears. Select Copy Here.

   - To move the pictures to the Shared Pictures folder and not retain a copy, click and drag them to the Shared Pictures folder.

Organizing your pictures

Rearranging the order of your pictures is easy in Media Center. You can arrange the pictures by name or by date, as follows:

1. **Open My Pictures.**

   Press the My Pictures button on the remote control.

2. **Select which group of pictures you want to work with.**

   Select My Pictures, Shared Pictures, or Other Media in the menu on the left. If your pictures are in a subfolder in the My Pictures or Shared Pictures folder, navigate to that folder and press OK.

3. **Select your sorting preference:**

   - To sort your pictures by name, select the Sort by name option.

   - To sort the pictures by date, select the Sort by date option.

Your pictures are displayed on the screen of your MCE PC as a series of *thumbnails,* or small images, so you can see a bunch of them at one time. To see a picture full screen, simply navigate to it and press OK.

Press the OK button again to zoom in on the picture, a third time to zoom in even more, and a fourth time to go back to the full-screen display.

You can press the Back button on the remote to go back to the thumbnail view of your pictures, or press the FWD or REW button to scroll through your pictures full screen, one at a time.

Correcting Your Pictures

Let's face it, most of us are not professional photographers. Even though we have high-quality digital cameras, we still take pictures that don't look quite right. Maybe the flash caused red eye, that evil-looking red reflection from people's retinas. Or perhaps the contrast wasn't right, and the subject of the photo is hidden in the shadows. It happens to all of us.

The great thing about digital pictures is that you're not wasting film (or money) by throwing these pictures away. But sometimes a picture with just one flaw is the best in the batch (maybe you caught Uncle Al asleep in the chaise in the back yard, and you need photographic proof).

My Pictures has tools that automatically help correct your pictures. You don't have to be a Photoshop expert or have the slightest idea of the difference between brightness and gamma.

To edit your photos in My Pictures, follow these steps:

1. **Open My Pictures.**

   Press the My Pictures button on the remote.

2. **Navigate to the picture you want to correct.**

   The picture becomes highlighted by a green border. If the picture isn't in your My Photos folder, you may need to select the Shared Pictures or Other Media option on the left of the screen to find the picture file.

3. **Press the More Info button on the remote.**

The picture appears with a Picture Details menu on the left side of the screen, as shown in Figure 11-8.

4. **If you want to rotate the picture, select the appropriate Rotate menu item.**

You can rotate the picture counterclockwise or clockwise. Press OK as many times as you want; the picture rotates 90 degrees with each press.

5. **If you want to get rid of red eye or adjust the contrast of your picture, do the following:**

   a. **Select Touch up.**

   A Touch Up screen appears, as shown in Figure 11-9.

   b. **Select either Red eye or Contrast.**

   You'll see a spinning "computer working" icon on the desktop of your MCE PC, and then your picture appears with the effect applied.

   c. **If you like the results, select Save. Otherwise, select Cancel.**

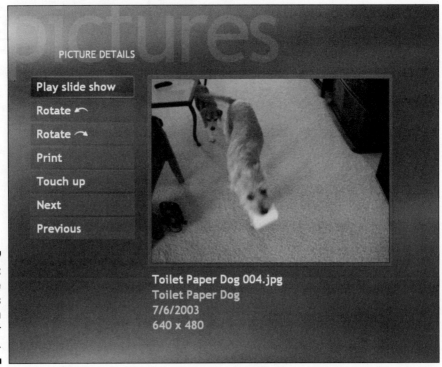

Figure 11-8:
Picture
Details is
where you
edit your
picture.

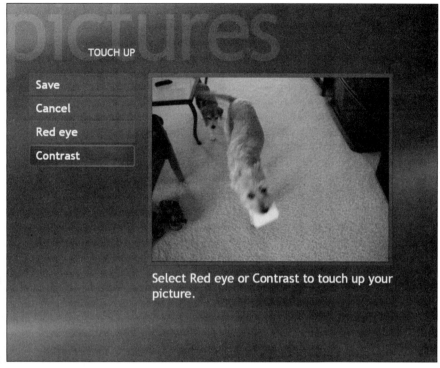

TOUCH UP

Save

Cancel

Red eye

Contrast

Select Red eye or Contrast to touch up your picture.

Figure 11-9:
Touching
up your
pictures.

If you want to edit other pictures, you can select the Next and Previous menu items (shown in Figure 11-8) to scroll through your pictures.

Creating a Slide Show

Looking at thumbnails and scrolling through pictures manually is okay, but when you want to show off your pictures, a slide show is the way to go. Media Center and My Pictures make it easy to run slide shows on your display — if you have a big-screen TV connected to your MCE PC, you can show your pictures in a larger-than-life way!

To run a slide show, follow these steps:

1. **Open My Pictures.**

   Press the My Pictures button on the remote.

2. **Select the source of the pictures you want to use in your slide show.**

Select My Pictures, Shared Pictures, or Other Media in the menu on the left side of the screen. If you have pictures in a subfolder in the My Pictures or Shared Pictures folder, and you want to show only those pictures in your slide show, navigate to that subfolder and press OK.

3. **Select Play slide show.**

   That's it! Your slide show starts.

4. **When you want to quit the slide show, press the Back button on the remote.**

When you're in the middle of the slide show, you can skip back and forth between pictures using the left and right arrow buttons on the remote. If you want to pause on a particular picture, just press the Pause button on the remote.

Printing Your Pictures

Sometimes you want a picture to put in your wallet, on the wall, or in that frame on your desk at work (where your MCE PC is *not* located). Well, MCE makes that easy by letting you print pictures right from My Pictures.

To print a picture, first you need to have a printer attached to your MCE PC and working:

1. **Connect your printer and set it up according to the manufacturer's instructions.**

   Most printers are easy to set up; the XP New Hardware Wizard walks you through the process.

2. **With Media Center closed or minimized, choose Start⇨Printers and Faxes.**

   The Printers and Faxes control panel appears.

3. **Right-click the icon for the printer you want to use with Media Center and choose Properties.**

   The Properties dialog box appears.

4. **Click the General tab, and type** MCE Printer **in the text box containing the printer name.**

5. **Click OK.**

   That printer is now configured to work with Media Center.

Printing the picture is simple:

1. **Open My Pictures.**

   Press the My Pictures button on the remote.

2. **Select the folder containing the picture you want to print (My Pictures, Shared Pictures, or Other Media), and navigate to the picture.**

3. **Press the More Info button on the remote.**

   The Picture Details screen appears (refer to Figure 11-8).

4. **Select Print.**

   A dialog box appears, asking whether you want a full-page printout of the picture you've selected, as shown in Figure 11-10.

5. **Select Print.**

   Media Center sends the picture to your printer.

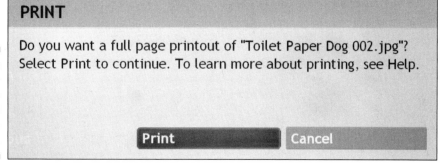

Figure 11-10:
Use your
remote
control
to make
a print.

> **PRINT**
>
> Do you want a full page printout of "Toilet Paper Dog 002.jpg"?
> Select Print to continue. To learn more about printing, see Help.
>
> Print   Cancel

If you really like a picture, consider getting a poster-sized printout from an online vendor, such as Shutterfly (www.shutterfly.com). It's easy, it's cool, and you can really embarrass Uncle Al with that picture of him snoozing through his bachelor party in the back yard.

Chapter 12

Playing DVDs

· ·

· ·

*T*his is the shortest chapter in the book because playing DVDs with Media Center is so easy. (Then again, all the functions in Media Center are pretty easy.) In fact, if you set up DVD autoplay as we explain in Chapter 8, playing a DVD with Media Center is as simple as putting the DVD in the DVD drive tray of your MCE PC and closing the tray. The DVD starts playing automatically, and your MCE PC starts Media Center and goes into full-screen mode. That's it!

A few tips, however, will keep you and your MCE PC on good terms as you become a DVD junkie. In this chapter, you find out how to configure the settings for DVD playback, how to play a DVD with MCE PC, and how to control that DVD when it's playing.

As mentioned in other chapters, when we say you should *select* something, it's shorthand for this: Use the arrow buttons on the remote to move the cursor to that item and then press the OK button on the remote.

Configuring Your MCE PC to Play DVDs Your Way

Before you get started with DVDs on your MCE PC, it's worth spending a few minutes setting your preferences for DVD playback. Just follow these steps:

1. **Open Media Center.**

   Press the green button on the remote. You also can press the start button and select Media Center.

2. **Select Settings.**

3. Select DVD.

The DVD Settings screen appears, as shown in Figure 12-1.

4. Select Language.

The DVD Language Settings screen appears, as shown in Figure 12-2. You use these settings to determine the default language in which you want to view movies.

5. Navigate to the plus or minus button next to each option, and press OK repeatedly to cycle through the alternatives:

- Subtitle: The language in which you want your subtitles (or on-screen text dialogue) to appear. The default is None.

- Audio track: The language in which you want to hear your DVDs. (Many DVDs have audio tracks in multiple languages.) The Title Default option lets your DVD decide which language to use.

- Menu: The language you want to use for the DVD's on-screen menu system. (Again, many DVDs have multiple languages available.)

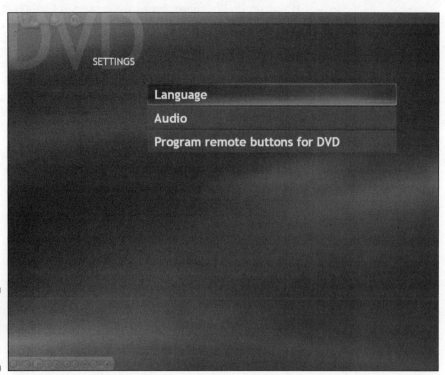

Figure 12-1:
Setting your DVD preferences.

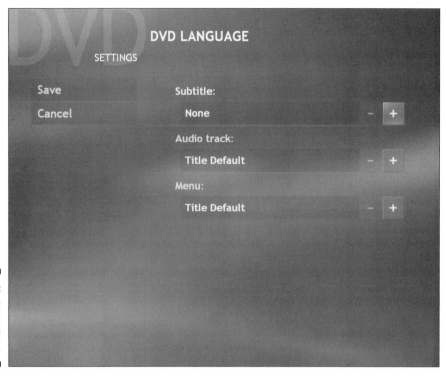

Figure 12-2:
Setting
your DVD
language
defaults.

Most DVDs enable you to adjust the subtitle, audio track, and menu languages from their own DVD menu. These override your system settings when you play the DVD. So you're not stuck with MCE-stored settings — if you're a Kurosawa fan, for example, you can decide halfway through that you want to listen to *Shichinin no samurai (Seven Samurai)* in Japanese, with no subtitles.

If the language you select is not available on the DVD, you get the DVD's default language (usually English).

6. **Select Save.**

You return to the main DVD Settings menu (refer to Figure 12-1).

7. **Select Audio.**

A Windows XP dialog box appears on the screen, similar to the one in Figure 12-3. That figure shows the InterVideo WinDVD used by Pat's Gateway MCE PC. What happens next depends on your MCE PC and your DVD decoder hardware and software.

Figure 12-3:
Setting your
audio up
for DVDs.

8. **Choose the type of audio output you want from your DVD, and then click OK.**

    The options will vary, depending on whether your MCE PC can support digital audio outputs for connecting to a home-theater receiver. Some general advice follows:

    • If two speakers are connected to your MCE PC, click the 2 speaker mode option. Under that option, click Stereo if you have two speakers, or click Dolby Surround Compatible if you don't have digital audio outputs and are planning on connecting to a home-theater receiver with two analog audio-interconnect cables. You'll probably never choose the one speaker option (Mono).

    • Click 4 speaker mode if four-speaker (quad) surround sound is attached to your MCE PC.

    • Click 6 speaker mode (5.1 channel) if a 5.1 surround-sound system is connected to your MCE PC's audio card.

    • Click Enable S/PDIF output if you have a digital audio connection to your home-theater receiver.

    We talk about all these different speaker connections in Chapter 4.

9. **Back in the main DVD Settings screen, select the last option, Program remote buttons for DVD.**

    The Remote Control Settings screen appears, as shown in Figure 12-4.

10. **Select the option you prefer for the Skip and Replay buttons on your remote.**

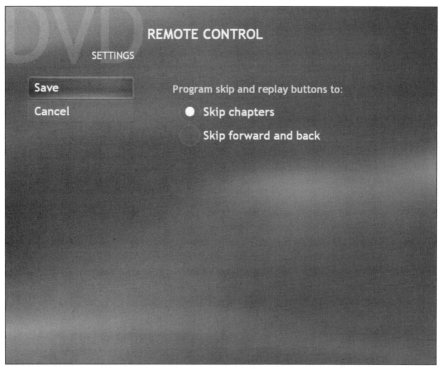

Figure 12-4:
Setting up
your remote
control.

- Select *Skip chapters* if you want these buttons to skip between chapters on the DVD. (*Chapters* are smallish segments of the movie.) We prefer this setting.

- Select *Skip forward and back* if you want these buttons to behave like the REW and FWD buttons on the remote (rewinding and fast forwarding without regard to the chapter structure of the DVD).

11. **Select Save.**

You're finished!

Playing a DVD with Media Center

Well, we already spilled the beans in the introduction to this chapter: If you've set up DVD autoplay, you can play a DVD by simply sticking the DVD in the DVD tray (the cupholder-looking thing) and closing the tray.

Some folks prefer to play a DVD manually. If you haven't turned on autoplay, playing a DVD is pretty darn easy. After inserting the DVD, you encounter one of the following scenarios:

- ✔ **If you're already using Media Center:** A dialog box appears like the one shown in Figure 12-5. Select Yes to play the DVD right away. If you decide not to watch right away (and select No), just go to the Media Center Start menu (press the green button on the remote) and select Play DVD when you're ready.

- ✔ **If you're not using Media Center:** Press the green button on the remote. Media Center launches and starts playing the DVD.

That's almost all there is to it. If you've turned on Parental Controls (we tell you how in Chapter 9) and the DVD exceeds your ratings limit, you see a screen like the one shown in Figure 12-6.

Just press the OK button, and you're be prompted to enter your four-digit code. Type this code using the number buttons on the remote and the movie will start. You don't have to press the OK button in this case — just type the code and watch that adult-oriented movie to your heart's content.

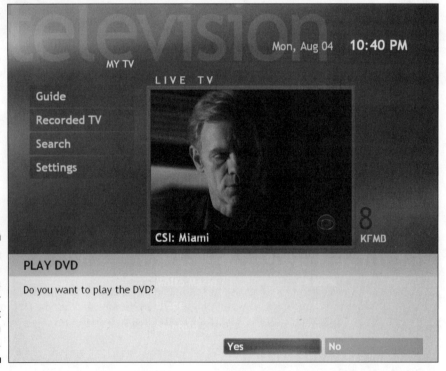

Figure 12-5:
Media
Center asks
you whether
you want
to watch
the DVD.

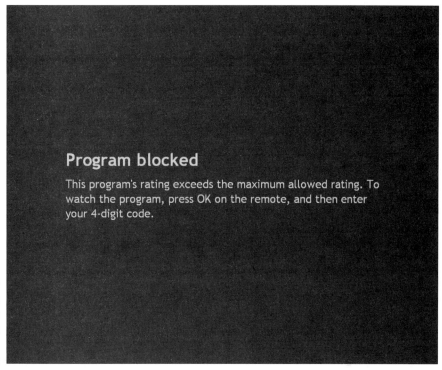

Program blocked

This program's rating exceeds the maximum allowed rating. To watch the program, press OK on the remote, and then enter your 4-digit code.

Figure 12-6:
Uh oh, you
can't watch
this movie!

You can control your DVD with the remote control, just as you would if you were using a regular DVD player in the living room:

- ✔ To pause the DVD, press the Pause button. To resume playing the DVD, press Pause again or press Play.

- ✔ To fast forward or rewind the DVD, press the FWD button or the REW button, respectively.

  - Press the button one time for 3 times the normal speed.

  - Press it again for 40 times the normal speed.

  - Press it a third time for 250 times the normal speed (now that's moving!).

  - Press that button one more time to return to normal play.

- ✔ To stop playing the DVD, press the Stop button.

You can also use the VOL button and the mute button to adjust the audio as you go along.

Getting into DVD Menus

The final piece of the DVD puzzle comes from the DVD itself — the *DVD menu* we've alluded to a few times throughout this chapter. Almost all commercial DVDs have an internal menu that lets you do all sorts of interesting stuff. Depending on the DVD, you can use the DVD menu to

> ✔ Set up the surround-sound format you want to use.
>
> ✔ Select between a wide-screen or normal version of the movie.
>
> ✔ Turn subtitles on and off.
>
> ✔ Select the audio track you want to use (typically you can switch between the native language of the movie and a dubbed version in a different language).

> Some movies also have an alternative audio track with the director's comments interspersed with the dialogue. This is a cool feature if you're seeing a movie for the fifteenth time and want to know why the director did something in that crucial scene!
>
> ✔ Get into special features of the DVD such as "Making of" featurettes, actor biographies, music videos, movie posters, and trailers.
>
> ✔ Find Easter eggs on your DVD. These are special features hidden in the DVD menu — you usually run across them by accident, but you can also cheat and go online to a site such as www.dvdeastereggs.com to find them.

Displaying the DVD menu of the DVD you're playing is a simple one-step process: Press the DVD Menu button on the remote control. After the DVD menu is displayed, use the arrow buttons on the remote to navigate to the different options. The process is a lot like navigating in the Media Center interface.

In this chapter, we talk about *playing* DVDs — because that's what Play DVD does! If you're interested in figuring out how to create your own DVDs, check out Chapters 9 and 13.

Chapter 13

Working with Home Videos

*W*ith your MCE PC, breaking out the home videos when the family visits takes on a whole new meaning. You can transfer, edit, play, and download those special home-video moments that you've captured on your camcorder, and also record live images from your Webcam.

In this chapter, you find out how to capture a video to your MCE PC, edit and play the video, and then offload it to a DVD (so you can play it in your car or at your neighbor's house). Playing your video images on your MCE PC is so easy that we focus on getting images into and out of your PC.

Media Center is well outfitted to help you play your video images (using the My Videos module). However, to accomplish other tasks, such as getting information into and out of your PC and manipulating images, you need to use other programs, which we mention in turn in this chapter.

Anyone who has been taking videos for a while knows that you have to take a lot of extra footage to get those few *America's Funniest Home Videos* shots that make it all worthwhile. The more adept you become at editing your videos, the more you'll enjoy watching them.

We've told you this before, but here we go again. When we say that you should *select* something, it's shorthand for this: Use the arrow buttons on the remote to move the cursor to that item and then press the OK button on the remote.

Getting Ready for My Videos

Unlike the other major areas of Media Center, My Videos doesn't require you to configure any specific settings. So getting prepared to use My Videos is mostly focused on getting your source video equipment connected to your PC.

The primary way to get your videos into the PC is through your camcorder. You can also transfer movies created with a Webcam or stored on old VHS tapes, and you can even download movies from the Internet. If you don't have a camcorder yet, check out the "Camcorder basics" sidebar in this chapter for some tips on purchasing one.

Connecting your camcorder to your PC

You can connect a camcorder to your PC in three main ways:

- ✔ **IEEE 1394 or FireWire port (also called an i.LINK port by some vendors):** This is the most common digital camcorder interface. We talk about FireWire in detail in Chapter 2.

- ✔ **S-video:** If you have an analog camcorder and have a choice between S-video and composite video, use the S-video connection because it delivers higher-quality video and audio.

- ✔ **Composite video:** As described in Chapter 2, composite-video cables have the familiar red, white, and yellow RCA plugs. This type of connection is common for older and low-end camcorders.

A few digital camcorders use USB connectors instead of (or in addition to) FireWire. We think USB is useful only if it's the newer USB 2.0 version. Otherwise, downloading your camcorder videos will take *forever.* MCE PCs support both USB 2.0 and FireWire. If we were buying a new camcorder, we'd go for the FireWire.

If you have an analog camcorder, connect your audio and video cables to your PC's Audio In and Video In ports.

In Chapter 3, we suggest that you consider getting an MCE PC with accessible front panel ports for your FireWire or analog A/V connections. If your PC has these, don't forget to use them when downloading content from your camcorder to your PC.

Connecting other devices to your MCE PC

You can get video images into your PC in other ways than just downloading images from a camcorder:

- ✔ **USB-attached Webcam:** A Webcam can send an image that you can capture to your hard drive using your Webcam manufacturer's software. Most Webcams attach to your PC using a USB connection. Danny uses a QuickCam Pro 4000 from Logitech (www.logitech.com), shown in Figure 13-1. The Pro 4000 ($85 street price) comes with 640-by-480 pixel resolution, a built-in microphone, automatic face tracking (which keeps your face in the middle of the screen), and a range of extra software to help you take advantage of the Webcam. (You can even use the Webcam for video instant-messaging sessions on your PC.) The Pro 4000 transmits at up to 30 frames per second.

- ✔ **Network-enabled Webcam:** A network-capable Webcam, such as D-Link's DCS-1000 (www.dlink.com, $190 street price) or its wireless sibling the DCS-1000W ($280 street price), connects to your home network and allows you to capture video from anywhere in the house. These devices use standard RJ-45 Ethernet connections or wireless interfaces, usually 802.11b. (For details on home networking, see Chapters 15 and 16.) The D-Link DCS-1000W Wireless Internet camera with VGA resolution at 20 frames per second (fps) can be set to stream video from 160-by-120-pixels up to 640-by-480-pixel resolution at 24-bit RGB color.

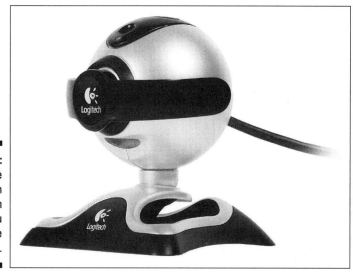

Figure 13-1:
With the
Logitech
QuickCam
4000, you
can capture
live video.

Camcorder basics

The best way to capture great home movies is with a camcorder — more specifically a digital video (DV) camera. We consider a digital video camera a must-have if you own an MCE PC — older analog video systems don't have the same ease-of-transfer and control capabilities that you get with a digital camcorder.

You can use an analog video camera, but we recommend this only if you already own an analog camcorder and aren't yet in the market for a replacement. (You plug the analog video camera into your TV capture card — the same one that you use to connect your television source, such as your cable TV.) Analog camcorders record in formats such as 8mm, Hi–8, VHS, and S–VHS. Using an analog camcorder is inconvenient (particularly if you need to disconnect your TV source to hook up your camcorder) and the video captured this way isn't nearly as good looking as video transferred to your MCE PC digitally.

The first thing to look for in a digital camcorder is an IEEE 1394 or FireWire (or i.LINK) port. We talk about FireWire in detail in Chapter 2. Every Media Center PC has this high-speed port, which makes transferring digital video or audio files from peripheral devices fast and easy.

The other big decision to make when buying a camcorder is the camcorder format. The two most common formats are

✔ **MiniDV:** In consumer-grade camcorders, this is the most common format. MiniDV can provide a high-resolution (though not high definition or HDTV) signal with quality roughly equal to or better than DVD. MiniDV camcorders are usually the top-of-the-line and are slightly smaller than Digital8. MiniDV camcorders use special MiniDV tapes, which cost a bit more than other types of camcorder tapes. Prices vary widely, but you should be able to find a good MiniDV camcorder for under $1000.

✔ **Digital8:** These camcorders provide a DVD-quality picture and use cheaper, standard, 8 mm camcorder tapes (used by many analog camcorders). Digital8 camcorders are usually less expensive than MiniDV models but are also a bit larger and have fewer features. You should be able to find a good Digital8 camcorder for under $600.

From an MCE PC point of view, as long as the camcorder is digital and has a FireWire port, you're good to go. How much you spend depends on what kind of additional features you want. Spending more gets you more optical zoom (see Chapter 11 for why this is good), bigger viewfinder LCD screens, better batteries, a better lens, and other advanced features. Keep in mind that many fancier camcorders also can take digital still pictures and may be able to substitute for a separate digital camera (saving you a few hundred dollars).

For great comparison shopping of available camcorders, check out CNET (www.cnet.com).

You can also find Webcams that connect to your Media Center PC using FireWire instead of USB or a network connection. This type of Webcam costs more but usually gives you a higher-quality picture because FireWire sends much more video data to the PC than the other methods.

In addition to the Webcam installation itself, you typically install *driver* software (which tells your MCE PC how to work with the camera hardware) and as well as programs such as video-conferencing or movie-editing software.

Unless you have a FireWire-connected Webcam, you can't just plug your Webcam into your MCE PC and have movies show up in My Videos. Instead, you need to first capture that video — using either the software that came with your Webcam or Windows Movie Maker (which we describe in the next section). Then you need to save the captured video as a movie file on your hard drive. After that, you can play the movie in My Videos as is, or you can use Windows Movie Maker (or another program, such as the one that may have come with your Webcam) to edit the movie into something more polished.

In addition, your MCE PC can take VHS video input from a composite or S-video signal and convert it to digital data.

In Chapter 5, we discuss how to connect your VCR to your MCE PC. If you want to just temporarily hook up your VCR to your PC to download old movies, you can attach Video Out on your VCR to your the Video In jack on your video capture card, and the Audio Out from your VCR to the Line In jack of your sound card on your PC. Or, if both your VCR and video card provide S-video connections, you can connect them with a single S-video cable to transmit both video and sound. You may have to disconnect some existing connections (such as those coming from your cable box), but you can reconnect them when you're finished transferring the video.

Using your VCR as discussed in the preceding paragraph is a bit of a kludge — recall that Microsoft doesn't have any built-in support for VCRs in MCE. It does work, but occasionally (usually if you're doing something else with your TV tuner card in Media Center), you may get an error on your computer. No big deal, but you might need to reboot your MCE PC to get everything working again.

Be Your Own Director

As we mention at the beginning of the chapter, Media Center doesn't provide a system for *capturing* (downloading to your hard drive) movies from your camcorder, editing your movie clips, and combining them into something professional looking. Instead, Microsoft provides for free an XP program called Windows Movie Maker 2 that gives you a way to download, edit, and save video footage:

```
www.Microsoft.com/windowsxp/moviemaker
```

Movie Maker 2 also has advanced editing features that let you add soundtracks, opening and closing credits, and even titles for different scenes. We think that the best thing about Movie Maker 2 is its extensive automation. Movie Maker 2 provides a simple interface for doing complicated editing work and can perform many tasks on its own (based on answers to some simple questions it asks you in a wizard interface).

We're not going to get into a lot of detail on how to use Movie Maker — we're focused on Media Center here, and Movie Maker 2 is easy to use anyway. However, here's the basic process:

✔ **Capture:** To create a movie file in Movie Maker, you need to feed the program your video clips. Movie Maker provides a handy Capture Wizard that automates the process of downloading movie clips from your digital camcorder, a Webcam, or a movie file on your hard drive. You can also add music files and digital still photographs to your movie.

✔ **Edit:** After all the raw materials are in Movie Maker, it's time to start editing. In this process, you can break video clips into individual pieces (such as the 30 seconds you caught on tape of your kids trying to wash the dog), and then assemble all these pieces in the order in which you want them to appear in your final movie. Movie Maker 2 uses an interface called a *storyboard,* which is a sequential display on your screen of all the elements in the movie. You can drag and drop captured video, music, or pictures onto the storyboard and then move them around until you get the order you want. While editing, you can also add special effects (such as titles and transitions) and create a soundtrack using music files.

✔ **Finish:** When you have all the elements of your movie in place, you can preview your work. When you're happy with it, save the finished work as a movie file. You can choose the file type, such as a Windows Media file or an MPEG file, as well as the file size. (For example, you can trade some quality for a smaller movie that fits on a CD or can be played on a handheld PC.) For a list of supported file types, see Table 13-1.

Table 13-1	MCE Supports These Video File Types
File Format (Type)	*File Name Extensions*
Windows Media video and playlists	.wmv, .asf, .asx, and .wpl
AVI video file	.avi
MPEG video file	.mpeg, .mpg, .mpe, .m1v, .mp2, .mpv2, and .mpa

Movie Maker does *not* support the video streams coming out of the Hauppauge or Emuzed TV tuner cards commonly found in MCE PCs. If you want to try to get video into Movie Maker from your analog camcorder, check the Movie Maker site (www.microsoft.com/windowsxp/moviemaker) to see whether your TV tuner card is supported.

Capturing DV camera images to your PC

You download your digital camcorder videos to your MCE PC using Windows Movie Maker 2's Video Capture Wizard. Follow these steps:

1. **Set the digital video (DV) camera mode to play the recorded video.**

   This mode may be labeled VTR or VCR on a DV camera.

2. **Open Windows Movie Maker 2.**

   Choose Start➪All Programs➪Accessories➪Windows Movie Maker. A screen similar to the one in Figure 13-2 appears.

3. **Choose Movie Tasks➪Capture from Video Device. You can also choose File➪Capture Video.**

   If the Movie Tasks menu isn't visible, click View➪Tasks Pane. Your available video devices appear. You may have more than one, such as a Webcam and your camcorder. In the Available devices window, click the DV camera and then click Next.

4. **Type a file name and location for your captured video, and then click Next.**

   Type a name for your captured video file and then, in the Choose a place to save your captured video pull-down menu, select the location where you want your video to be saved.

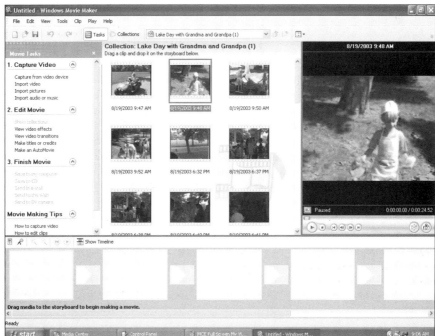

Figure 13-2:
Getting video into your MCE PC.

5. **Choose the video setting you want to use for capturing video and audio, and then select your video quality setting**.

Choosing a quality setting is an important decision. Your choice is a trade-off between storage space and image quality.

For the highest quality, select *Digital device format (DV-AVI)*. However, this choice takes up a lot of space on your computer and is the best option only if you plan on re-archiving the video back to tape or DVD.

If you want to keep the video file on your computer, choose a lower-quality setting that takes up less space. To save hard drive space, we always select *Best quality for playback on my computer (Recommended)*.

You can select other advanced settings in the Other settings category. If you think you want one of these, click the <u>Learn more about video settings</u> link in the middle of the page.

6. **Click Next.**

7. **Select whether to capture the entire tape automatically or just specific parts, and then click Next.**

8. **Watch the Preview window.**

The tape in the DV camera rewinds. The capture process begins automatically when the tape is rewound and ends when the video tape ends. If you don't want the entire tape, you can halt the capture by clicking Stop Capture in the DV Capture in Progress screen (see Figure 13-3), and then clicking Yes in the ensuing dialog box to save the video that has been captured.

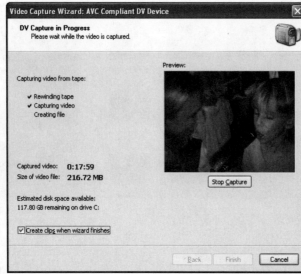

Figure 13-3: Movie Maker 2 updates you on its progress as it captures video.

If you want to separate the video into smaller clips, select the Create clips when wizard finishes check box when the tape is rewinding.

9. **Click Finish to close the Video Capture Wizard.**

Capturing analog video to your PC

Movie Maker doesn't support the use of the most common MCE PC TV tuner cards as analog capture devices. Therefore, you may need to buy and install a separate analog video capture card to perform the steps in this section.

To capture video from an analog source, follow these steps:

1. **Set the digital video (DV) camera mode to play the recorded video.**

2. **Open Windows Movie Maker 2.**

   Choose Start➪All Programs➪Accessories➪Windows Movie Maker.

3. **Select the analog device you want to use to capture video and the settings for where the computer should look for the audio and video signals from that analog device.**

   a. **In the Available devices window, click the analog source device.**

   b. **In the Video input source list, click the input line you want to use.**

   For example, if your analog capture card supports both S-video and composite connections, you'll choose between those input options here, depending on which ports your analog source is hooked up to.

   c. **In the Audio device list, click the audio capture device you want to use.**

   If you have only one audio capture card in your PC, that card is selected automatically for the audio.

   d. **In Audio input source, click the input line you want to use.**

4. **Click Next.**

5. **Name your video, select the place to save it, and click Next.**

6. **Select the video setting to use for capturing video and audio, and then click Next.**

   Again, as discussed in the preceding chapter, select either *Digital video format (DV-AVI)* or *Best quality for playback on my computer (Recommended),* depending on where you intend to store the video.

7. **Select the Create clips when wizard finishes check box to separate the video into smaller clips.**

8. **On your source device, find the portion of the analog video tape you want to record.**

9. In Movie Maker, click Start Capture, and then press the Play button on your analog camera or VCR. When you want to stop capturing, click Stop Capture, and then press the Stop button on your analog camera or VCR.

10. Repeat Steps 8 and 9 for each part of the video tape you want to capture.

11. When you're finished, click Finish to close the Video Capture Wizard.

You can use Movie Maker to capture video directly to your hard drive (that is, without saving the video to tape first). Follow these steps:

1. Set the digital video (DV) camera mode to film live video and audio (usually called Camera mode).

2. Open Windows Movie Maker 2.

3. Select the device you want to use to capture video. If the device is analog, select the settings for where the computer should look for the audio and video signals from that analog device.

4. Click Next.

5. Enter the file name for your video and choose the folder to save your video.

6. Click Next.

7. To begin capturing your images, click Start Capture. When you're ready to stop capturing, click Stop Capture.

8. When you're finished, click Finish to close the Video Capture Wizard.

Capturing video from your Webcam works in a similar fashion. In the Movie Tasks menu, choose Capture from video device, and select your Webcam as your input device. The remaining steps are the same as those for capturing live video from your camcorder.

Editing and finishing your home video

You can stop here. Your video is now available to Media Center to play, as we describe in the next section. However, you might want to consider editing your home video first. Windows Movie Maker 2 makes it easy to edit your movies and then save them to the appropriate format.

We recommend that you visit Microsoft's site for Windows Movie Maker 2 for great step-by-step instructions for editing videos and manipulating images.

After the editing step, which you can skip if you want, you're ready to view, distribute, or otherwise use your video. Movie Maker 2 lets you save your movie, e-mail it, upload it to a Web site, or save it to a CD. Each of these options are available in the Movie Tasks menu on the left of the page or from the File pull-down menu.

Playing Your Movies

You're now ready to launch My Videos and view your masterpieces. You can access My Videos in two ways:

- ✔ Press the My Videos button on the remote
- ✔ Select My Videos from the Media Center Start menu

The My Videos screen appears, as shown in Figure 13-4. Menu options are on the left, and icons representing the available videos are on the right. The icons display the first frame of each video.

Figure 13-4:
Smile, you're on My Videos.

The My Videos module looks for video files in the following three folders:

✔ **My Videos:** This folder, located in your My Documents folder on the PC, is the default location for digital videos on your computer and for any movies imported with Movie Maker 2. When you plug a digital camera into your USB or FireWire port and download videos, this is where they go (unless you indicate otherwise in your capture program).

As described in Chapter 8, each logged-in user can see and edit the videos in his or her own My Videos folder.

✔ **Shared Videos:** This folder provides a spot for storing videos so that they're available to *all* users of the PC. The folder is located in the following directory:

```
C:\Documents and Settings\All Users\Documents\My Videos
```

Videos take up a lot of hard drive space on your PC, so consider placing a shortcut to the video in your Shared Videos folder, instead of copying it there. You can create a shortcut by right-clicking the file in Windows Explorer and choosing Create Shortcut. Then drag-and-drop the shortcut to the Shared Videos folder.

✔ **Other Media:** If you have a FireWire-connected digital camcorder, you'll like Other Media. My Videos can read video content stored on a camcorder, so you don't have to download the video to your MCE PC hard drive before viewing it. Videos stored on removable media (such as FireWire removable hard drives) also appear in the My Videos➪Other media menu option.

The My Videos menu reflects these options with three high-level choices to find your videos, as well as two additional ways to sort the videos after you've found them:

✔ **My Videos:** Accesses video files in the My Videos folder

✔ **Shared Video:** Accesses video files in the My Videos folder

✔ **Other media:** Accesses video on connected devices

✔ **Sort by name:** Sorts the displayed video icons by their file name

✔ **Sort by date:** Sorts the displayed video icons by their creation or modification date

To play a video, simply navigate to it and press the Play or OK button on the remote. You can use all the standard media control buttons on the remote (FWD, REW, Pause, and so on) to control the playback of the video.

Not all videos will support the FWD or REW controls (they're missing an obscure video attribute called I-Frames). In those cases, you'll need to use the Skip and Replay buttons to navigate through the movie.

To watch movies in your Shared Videos folder or on digital devices attached to your Media Center PC, just navigate to the menu on the left side and select the Shared Video option or the Other media option.

The More Info/Details button on the remote control provides information such as the date the file was created and the size of the file. (In My TV, this button displays information about TV shows.)

You can organize your movie files into subfolders in the My Videos or Shared Videos folder. To create a subfolder, you must be in XP. Then open Windows Explorer by right-clicking Start and choosing Explore. Under your My Videos folder, right-click the open folder pane (in the window on the right). Choose New⇨Folder option, name the folder, and move any movies you want into that folder by dragging and dropping. You can do the same with the Shared Videos folder.

When you place a movie in a subfolder, a folder icon appears in My Videos in MCE — select the folder to look inside.

Sharing Your Movies

Unlike your recorded TV shows (which can be shared only with other MCE or XP PCs), the videos you capture and store on your Windows MCE PC can be viewed by other people on just about any PC using Windows Media Player 9 or other multimedia player software.

The biggest issue you'll have is getting the files to them, because video files are huge. Depending on the file format and quality level you selected, your videos could consume more than 700 megabytes *per minute* of video.

As we mentioned, any file in the Shared Videos folder can be accessed from anywhere on your LAN, but in some cases, your network will not have enough bandwidth to play the video file directly from the other computer. You need 6 Mbps throughput to sustain streaming video images, so rather than trying to open the video file over the network, you may have to move the file to a remote computer *before* you try watching it.

To share videos outside your home network, several options are available:

✔ **E-mail the video as an attachment:** You can e-mail a short video to others as an attachment. However, note that many e-mail systems routinely delete e-mail messages with attachments greater than 2 megabytes. If you run into an e-mail account that won't allow your video through, you'll typically get an automated e-mail back from the e-mail system saying that your message could not be delivered.

- ✔ **Upload the video on the Web:** You can upload your movies to a video-hosting provider on the Web. If you don't currently have a hosting provider, you can sign up for one in the wizard.

- ✔ **Download the video to a DV camera:** You can download your movie to your DV camera and then archive the movie on a digital tape.

- ✔ **Copy the video on a CD:** Windows XP offers support for CD burning. You can copy movies created with Windows Movie Maker 2 to CDs, at the full speed of the CD-R or CD-RW drive.

- ✔ **Copy the video on a DVD:** The best option for sharing is a DVD because it has so much space. For more information on this method of sharing videos, read the next section.

Making Your Own DVDs in XP

In Chapter 9, we talk about PrimeTime (www.sonic.com/primetime), a cool program that you can add to your Media Center PC. You can use PrimeTime to create DVDs (and video CDs) of the programs you've recorded in the My TV module in Media Center.

If your MCE PC has a DVD recorder, you probably have the DVD-authoring software you need somewhere on your computer. Although we can't give you step-by-step directions on how to use the software on your machine, we can tell you about the software *we* like to use for this function: MyDVD.

MyDVD is another bit of software from Sonic (the folks who make PrimeTime). The folks at Sonic tell us that about 80 percent of PCs that have DVD recorders installed use some version of MyDVD, so you may already have the program on your MCE PC.

We've had a chance to play around with MyDVD 5 Deluxe, the beta of the next version of MyDVD. (Beta software is the prerelease version that has most of the functionality in place.) With MyDVD, you can create a ton of different customized Hollywood-type effects in your homemade DVDs. The main screen of MyDVD is shown in Figure 13-5.

By the time you read this, the new version will be available at www.mydvd. com. Following are some of the features of MyDVD:

- ✔ Media Center's special DVR-MS files can be translated into standard MPEG files that can be viewed on any DVD player.

- ✔ Cool integrated video-editing functions let you pretend you're a producer. You can create animations, splice scenes, create special effects, and more. You'll have a professional-looking DVD, even if it's just footage of the dogs getting into the kiddy pool again.

✔ You can add *chapter points,* which are the DVD equivalent of song breaks on a CD. Chapter points make it easy to navigate through a DVD.

✔ You can create picture slide shows (with a soundtrack!) on a DVD. You can even put the high-resolution originals on the DVD for reprints and backups.

✔ MyDVD uses Dolby Digital audio (AC-3) to record the audio portion of your DVD. This system uses a *lot* less DVD disc space than the alternative (ten times less, in most cases). Depending on the video quality, you can fit 20 percent to 150 percent more stuff on a single DVD.

MyDVD is not the only program out there for creating your own movie DVDs. We've spent some time using InterVideo's WinDVD creator on our MCE PCs, and we love it! So check out some of these other DVD-creation software systems:

✔ InterVideo WinDVD Creator: www.intervideo.com

✔ Pinnacle Systems Studio Moviebox DVD: www.pinnaclesys.com

✔ Ulead DVD MovieFactory 2: www.ulead.com

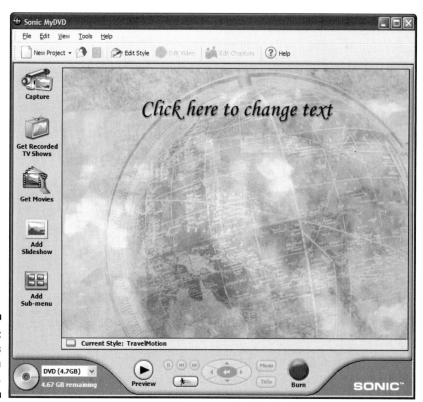

Figure 13-5:
MyDVD's
main
screen.

Some of these programs will install their own video/DVD codec (the bit of software that tells you computer how to decode video files). In a few cases, this new codec may cause problems with Media Center's TV and DVD playing capabilities. If this happens to you, we recommend that you use System Restore to go back to a restore point prior to your installation of the DVD software. If you can, try before you buy with DVD-burning software — download the 30-day free trial (most DVD software vendors provide trials on their Web sties). Install the trial, make sure it works with *your* MCE PC, and then buy the software.

Chapter 14

Working with Third-Party Applications

*A*nyone can take a Mini '03 Cooper S and soup it up with an engine blower, custom 17-inch R85 wheel caps, large-size air intakes, and neon-lighted underworks — to make sure you stand out at night on Rodeo Drive. (Wanna try it yourself? Check out www.miniusa.com/crm/mini_entrance.jsp.)

But what can you do if you want to expand your MCE PC beyond its horizons? Microsoft has provided a mechanism for software developers to create add-ons to the MCE with an active Software Developer's Toolkit (SDK) program. As a result, you can download both authorized and unauthorized software that will make your MCE hum like the three Mini Coops in *Charlie's Angels*.

Buyer Beware

As we write, dozens of add-ins are in development by scores of groups. To find out the latest on these programs, check out the downloads page at The Green Button's Web site (www.thegreenbutton.com).

Because many add-ins for MCE 2004 were not finalized by the time this book went to press, we describe add-ins for the first release of MCE. The screen shots you see here as well as the descriptions may differ slightly from the final release of these programs.

We put almost anything on our PCs because we love to try new software. But most of these programs are not supported by the creators of the program or by Microsoft, even the ones made by Microsoft. Therefore, you install add-ins *at your own risk.* If you're not comfortable dealing with bugs, we suggest that you install an earlier version of an add-in program when possible because the latest beta may not be as stable as an older version. If you're not adept with loading new software onto your machine — in other words, if you live and die by Windows Update and that's it — these programs might not be for you.

Make sure that you have the latest MCE updates installed on your machine before loading any third-party programs. Run Windows Update to get your XP software up-to-date. (To do so, choose Start➪Windows Update and follow the on-screen instructions.)

When installing updated versions of an add-in program, we recommend that you uninstall the prior version first, unless the manufacturer tells you otherwise. You can uninstall any of these programs by choosing Start➪Control Panels➪ Add or Remove Programs, and following the on-screen instructions.

More Programs

With the new 2004 version of Media Center, Microsoft added a special menu item called More Programs on the main Start screen of Media Center. Although Media Center PC makers are not required to install this in their PCs, most will.

More Programs is nothing more than a folder on your MCE PC that can hold third-party software that you can access from the Media Center interface. To access More Programs, just select it from the Media Center Start menu.

MCE PC vendors can configure Media Center so that the Media Center Start menu displays the two most recently used add-on programs (stored in the More Programs folder). This makes access even faster — you don't need to select More Programs and then select the program you want to use. The list is dynamic: Every time you use a different program from More Programs, the list updates itself.

You can remove a More Programs program from the Media Center Start menu by simply highlighting it and pressing the Clear button on your remote. This does *not* delete the program from your computer. It simply removes it from the list of recently used programs in the Media Center Start menu. This is handy if you don't want anyone to know you've been playing games!

If your MCE PC vendor chooses to participate, Microsoft is also providing two free game programs — think of them as a head start on populating your More Programs menu. Both of these games — Otto and Gem Master — are designed for use with the remote control. So if you're lucky enough to have them on your MCE PC, sit back, grab the remote, and play away!

MCE WebGuide

One of the neatest enhancement on the market is Show & Tell's MCE WebGuide:

```
www.showtell.com/mce_webguide/default.asp
```

The concept is simple: WebGuide gives you remote access to your Media Center Program Guide. Figure 14-1 shows WebGuide in action.

With WebGuide, you can

✔ Schedule or cancel individual and series recordings

✔ Manage recorded and scheduled programs

✔ Delete previously recorded shows or cancel individual and series recordings

✔ View your recorded shows over a LAN

✔ Perform a keyword search of Guide listings

Figure 14-1:
WebGuide
lets you
access
MCE over
the Internet.

To view recorded shows over your home network, you must share your Recorded TV folder over the network and have enough bandwidth to stream the files (usually at least 6 to 8 Mbps — exactly how much depends on the size and encoding of the file). An 802.11b Wi-Fi network probably won't cut it, but the faster 802.11a and 802.11g versions should do the job. (Check out Chapter 16 for more information on wireless networks.)

Getting ready for WebGuide

Getting WebGuide into your MCE PC requires a few tricky steps. MCE WebGuide uses Windows XP Internet Information Services (IIS) as a Web server. (A *Web server* handles requests coming from the Web and serves up the content requested.) You can find out more about IIS at

www.microsoft.com/windowsxp/pro/evaluation/overviews/iis.asp

Windows XP Professional, which underlies XP MCE, includes IIS.

To find out whether IIS is installed on your machine, choose Start⇨Control Panel⇨Add/Remove Programs. Click the Add/Remove Windows Programs button. In the Windows Components Wizard, select Internet Information Services (IIS) and then click the Details button. Confirm that everything *except* the Front Page 2000 Server Extensions option is checked. Unless you expect to be using Front Page to create Web pages and manage a local Web site, it's better to leave that feature off your system.

If IIS is not installed on your PC, you can add it from the Details area of your Add/Remove Programs window, as follows:

1. **Insert your Windows XP CD (the one that came with your MCE PC) into the CD drive.**

2. **In the Details area of IIS, select all available options, except the Front Page 2000 Server Extensions option.**

   If you're not already in the Details area, follow the steps in the preceding paragraph to get there.

3. **Click OK.**

4. **Click OK to exit the Add/Remove Programs window.**

   Windows automatically finds the Windows XP CD in your CD drive and adds IIS to your system.

5. **When the installation is finished, restart your computer.**

Sometimes program installations put *older* versions of operating system components in place, so it's a good idea to run the Windows Update program after any installation.

Microsoft's .NET 1.1 (or later) platform must also be installed. Choose Start⇨ Control Panel⇨Add/Remove Programs. Look for .NET in the list of installed applications. If .NET 1.1 isn't installed, you can add it in two ways.

✔ In the Windows Update program, select .NET from the Windows XP options under Pick updates to install.

✔ Choose Start⇨Run and type the following:

```
\Windows\Microsoft.NET\Framework\v1.0.3705\aspnet_regiis.exe -I
```

With these pre-installation steps complete, you can now download the .NET program at

```
www.showtell.com/mce_webguide/download.asp
```

The installation package for WebGuide walks you though the installation process.

TIP

Whoa, my IP address changed!

To access your home network from the Internet (at work, for example), you need to know your IP address. Many cable modem and DSL services, however, don't provide you with a permanent IP address for your home on the Internet, so the address keeps changing.

Consider signing up for a dynamic DNS service, which gives you a static IP address on its system and puts software on your home network to track when the IP address changes. The dynamic DNS service always knows your actual IP address and automatically translates between your current IP address and your fixed address on its server. (Many of these services are free for home users.) With services such as DynIP Software (www.dynip.com/) and Dynamic DNS Services (www.dyndns.org), you can have an address such as dummies. dynip.com that you can *always* use, regardless of your current IP address.

Aside from making it possible to access your WebGuide capability, you may need such an IP translation service if you want to

✔ Set up a home Webcam

✔ Talk over the Internet with voice-conferencing software

✔ Access corporate VPN networks for working from home

✔ Establish a personal Web or FTP server (the home computer, not the ISP, is the server)

✔ Build servers for multiplayer network games or chatting

✔ Run a personal mail server

✔ Connect to friends in a peer-to-peer networking configuration

The lack of a stable address is the result of a shortage of Internet IP addresses. No one expected the Internet to grow this fast. In the next ten years, as the world's Internet providers move to the next generation of IP addressing, called *IPv6*, everyone (and everything attached to the Internet) can have an address of their own, and services like this probably won't be required anymore.

Configuring WebGuide

WebGuide is a Web application, so you open it like a normal Web page (using Internet Explorer), with your machine as a Web server.

To get into WebGuide from another computer, simply type the URL of your MCE PC into your Web browser. For example, you might type `http://12.129.198.128/webguide`, where 12.129.198.128 is the IP address of your Internet access connection. For more information, see the "Whoa, my IP address changed!" sidebar in this chapter. You go straight into the system, or you encounter a login page if a password is set up in the configuration file for WebGuide.

After you install WebGuide, you can change your settings by going to your `\inetpub\wwwroot\webguide` folder and opening web.config in Notepad. You probably don't even need to go to this configuration file, but we mention it here for completeness.

You can configure the following settings:

- ✔ **password:** Your password to get into the application. By default, it's MCE. Leave this setting blank to disable the password capability.

- ✔ **session_timeout:** The number of minutes the system will let you remain idle before requiring you to log on again. The default is 90 minutes.

- ✔ **recorded_tv_share:** The folder to which your recorded TV shows are stored. The directory is created by Media Center (in your All Users folder). This folder is not shared by default, but you must share it to use WebGuide effectively. To share the folder, right-click it and choose Sharing and Security. Choose Share this folder. This enables you to access the folder remotely. Note that you must be an administrator user to create shares.

  When you create a new *resource share,* like a shared folder, Microsoft XP draws the share name from the folder name by default. MCE calls the shared folder for recorded TV shows *Recorded TV* (no big surprise!). As a result, WebGuide's default for recorded_tv_share is Recorded TV. If you change the share name in MCE, you must update the configuration file to reflect that new name in the WebGuide application.

- ✔ **guide_rows:** The number of rows to display in the guide at one time. The default is seven rows.

- ✔ **guide_move_minutes:** The number of minutes to incrementally shift the screen in the Guide when scrolling. The default is 60 minutes.

- ✔ **list_rows:** The number of rows to display in other list pages. The default is seven rows.

- ✔ **use_smart_nav:** A feature of ASP.NET that improves performance. The default is set to On. Change it to Off if you have display problems.

Using WebGuide

When WebGuide launches, the screen shown in Figure 14-1 appears. The options in the main menu — Guide, Recorded TV, and Search — operate much like those in the MCE My TV menu, so we won't go into them in detail. (Check Chapter 8 for a refresher if you need it.) Figure 14-2 shows you the on-screen program guide for WebGuide.

Figure 14-2:
Your on-screen program guide for WebGuide.

When looking around the program guide, you'll see a clock and a calendar page icon at the base of the guide. These show you a hyperlinked 24-hour listing (so you can jump to 7 P.M., for instance) and a hyperlinked calendar (so you can skip ahead to, say, Friday of next week). The links make navigating a lot easier than using the arrow buttons on the remote.

If you want to watch recorded TV, click the file name — just like in the MCE interface — and the file is played from the network location. Windows XP Media Player plays the file from the hard drive of your MCE PC on your network as if it were a local file on the machine you're using. Note: It's impossible to stream a DVR-MS file over the Internet in the file's current form. Shucks. (You can still access your WebGuide over the Internet.)

We think everyone with an MCE PC will want WebGuide. It extends the usefulness of your XP MCE PC from your living room to anywhere in the world.

My Weather

Some things just make sense, such as having today's weather outlook on your screen when you turn on the TV in the morning. We've become fans of our customized www.weather.com pages, especially their hour-by-hour forecasts. But navigating to that site with the MCE PC keyboard and MCE-driven TV display just doesn't work. The text is too small, and you have to leave the MCE interface to go to Internet Explorer.

Along comes My Weather — and we're happy again. My Weather is a program that runs outside the MCE interface but is integrated into the MCE Start menu as, you guessed it, My Weather. My Weather works using the remote control, just like any other Media Center application or module.

To install My Weather, go to www.nacontap.com. Installation is painless; a setup wizard walks you through the process.

To launch My Weather, click it in the MCE Start menu. Although My Weather has many of the same attributes as the MCE user interface (a blue background, green buttons, and remote control), it's a regular XP program outside MCE that's running at the same time as MCE. You're just switching back and forth seamlessly between programs.

The main page displays the weather for your area, as shown in Figure 14-3. You can use the right and left arrows to move forward and back through several days' worth of meteorological prognostications. When you're finished, click the green Exit button, and you're returned to the main Media Center menu. Simple. Works. Useful. We like.

Figure 14-3:
My Weather,
in my MCE.

Nacogdoches, TX (75962)

Sunrise
6:16 AM

72 F (22 C)
1 AM CDT 1

Sunset
8:27 PM

TONIGHT

PARTLY CLOUDY. A SLIGHT
CHANCE OF SHOWERS AND
THUNDERSTORMS. LOWS IN THE
MID 70S. LIGHT WIND. CHANCE OF
RAIN 20 PERCENT.

Exit

Media Center Solitaire?

Microsoft has a page in its Microsoft Windows XP Media Center Edition site where it lists *PowerToys* — programs that Microsoft's developers work on, often for fun, after a product has been released to manufacturing.

For version 1.0 of MCE, only the Solitaire PowerToy was listed. (We guess calling it My Solitaire would be redundant!) This MCE PowerToy enables you to play Solitaire on your Media Center PC from anywhere in the room using the remote control. We expect that Microsoft will add additional PowerToys in the future. We've been told that an Alarm Clock application and a Playlist Maker program for My Music will be added soon.

Downloading and installing any Microsoft PowerToy is easy:

1. **Go to the following page, and click the PowerToy link:**

   `www.microsoft.com/windowsxp/mediacenter/downloads/powertoys.asp`

2. **Do one of the following:**

   - To begin the installation immediately, click Open or click Run this program from its current location.

   - To download the program to your computer for installation later, click Save or click Save this program to disk.

3. **After you've installed the PowerToy, go to its folder (usually located at** `C:\Program Files\PowerToy`**) and view the ReadMe.htm file for more information on how to use the PowerToy.**

Note that PowerToys are no different than many other third-party add-ins. Quoting from Microsoft's site: "Note: We've taken great care to ensure that PowerToys operate as they should, but they are not part of Windows XP Media Center Edition and are not supported by Microsoft. For this reason, Microsoft Technical Support is unable to answer questions about PowerToys. These PowerToys are for Windows XP Media Center Edition only." Enough said.

Other Programs

The programs we've discussed so far in this chapter aren't the only ones available for MCE. Here are some that may apply to MCE 2004. (We say *may* because neither one was optimized for the 2004 edition of Media Center as this book went to press.)

✔ **MCE Sleep Timer:** www.nacontap.com/MyMCE/MCESleepTimer Software.cfm. This program adds a sleep timer (just like the one on your clock radio) to Windows XP Media Center Edition. The software will not put your computer to sleep, but it will close MCE after the period of time specified. With MCE closed, your computer will be able to go into standby mode after the time specified in the power-management options (in the Screen Saver tab of the Displays control panel in XP). Any recordings will continue to record after MCE closes. (See Figure 14-4.) Microsoft has created a similar program called Alarm Clock. We like MCE Sleep Timer better because it lets you use whatever media you like for the sleep timer function, but Alarm Clock can use only your My Music playlists.

✔ **Record TV Button:** www.nacontap.com/MyMCE/MCERecorded TVButton.cfm. This program adds a button to your MCE Start page that takes you directly to Recorded TV (instead of having to go to My TV and then navigate to your recorded programs).

Another one of our favorite MCE programs is Sonic's PrimeTime. PrimeTime lets you organize all your recorded TV programs on your MCE PC and copy them to a DVD — without leaving the Media Center interface. The coolest thing about PrimeTime is that the DVDs you create can be used on any DVD player. Check out Chapter 9 for more information about PrimeTime.

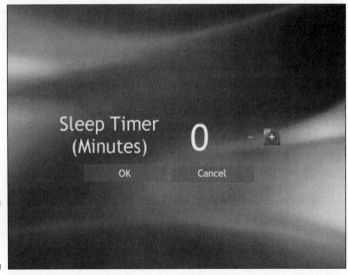

Sleep Timer (Minutes) 0

OK   Cancel

Figure 14-4:
Rock-a-
bye MCE.

Reverting to Stability

Sometimes you load software on your machine and then regret doing so. Using a program called System Restore, you can revert to a prior point in time and reconfigure your PC with those older (but working) settings and programs. This isn't a perfect solution — and it can be drastic — because you get rid of anything else you've added (through, for example, Windows Update) or changed since that previous time (called a *restore point*).

Before you begin, close any open programs and save any open documents. Otherwise, you might lose unsaved data.

To revert, here's what you do:

1. **Choose Start⇨All Programs⇨Accessories⇨System Tools and then click System Restore.**

   The System Restore window (welcoming you to System Restore) appears.

2. **Click Restore my computer to an earlier time, and then click Next.**

   The window changes (it's now labeled Select a Restore Point) and displays a calendar, as shown in Figure 14-5.

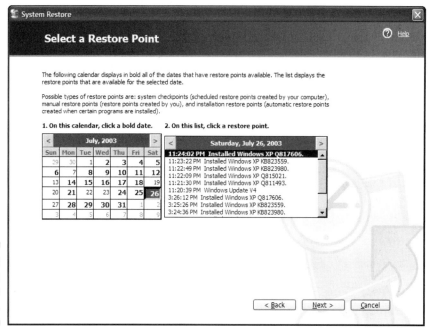

Figure 14-5:
Select a
Restore
Point here.

3. **On the left, click a date (before you began experiencing difficulties). On the right, click a Restore Point.**

4. **Click Next.**

   The window asks you to confirm your selection.

5. **Verify that you selected the right date in Step 3, and then click Next.**

   Your computer performs the restore and then restarts. When the reboot is completed, you see a Restoration Complete window.

6. **Click OK to close the window.**

After you do a restoration, it's a good idea to run Windows Update again, in case you deleted any critical Windows updates during the restore process.

Using Online Spotlight

With the launch of Windows XP Media Center Edition 2004, Microsoft has created its own online guide for third-party software and content for Media Center: Online Spotlight. You can access Online Spotlight from the main Media Center Start menu using your remote. Online Spotlight is just what its name implies — an online service. You need a working Internet connection (preferably a broadband connection) to use the service.

Microsoft controls Online Spotlight, but most of the content (software and digital media) available in the Online Spotlight is provided by third-party companies that have become part of Microsoft's software development program for MCE.

Online Spotlight was just being launched as we finished this book, and only a handful of the more than 100 companies who were developing for Online Spotlight had working content. Much more will be added to Online Spotlight over time.

The content in Online Spotlight is divided into five categories:

✔ **Music:** Online music (and music video) providers like Napster will use Online

Spotlight to offer music download and online radio services.

✔ **Movies:** Movie download providers such as Movielink and CinemaNow will allow remote-controlled movie purchases and downloads.

✔ **News:** Microsoft has customized its MSN TV online channel for Media Center — you can both read text articles and also access MSNBC TV using your remote.

✔ **Tips:** Microsoft also provides an online compendium of tips for using Media Center more efficiently.

✔ **Software:** This is our favorite part of Online Spotlight — you can access interesting third-party Media Center software and download it from Media Center. For example, Sonic's PrimeTime software is available here, as are Microsoft's Media Center PowerToys software offers. We expect to see a lot more programs here, as more Microsoft partners develop their Media Center software.

Part IV

Connecting to the Rest of Your House

By Rich Tennant

"Now, when someone rings my doorbell, the current goes to a scanner that digitizes the audio impulses and sends the image to the PC where it's converted to a Pict file. The image is then animated, compressed, and sent via high-speed modem to an automated phone service that sends an e-mail message back to tell me someone was at my door 40 minutes ago."

In this part . . .

Mama never told you about stuff like this. Well, not unless she's a network administrator. In this part, we get into the detail of using your MCE PC as a major cog in your whole-home entertainment system. By spending a few dollars and fiddling with a few pieces of software, you can create a whole-home network that links your computers (MCE or not) and your entertainment systems. The MCE PC can play a powerful role as one of your centralized repositories of digital media. Heck, Danny even has his powering his outdoor "drive-in" theater.

We start by walking you through the basics of building a home network — we even get down to the level of defining the term home network. You find out what pieces and parts you need. (MCE PCs already come with a few of these, thanks to built-in Ethernet and easy file sharing in Windows XP). Then we discover some other devices (besides your MCE PC) that you can connect to a home network.

We also spend some time — an entire chapter, actually — discussing the hottest thing in home networking since . . . well, ever. Wireless networking! We explain the different systems and how to connect an MCE PC wirelessly. We also talk about another hot topic: *convergence* equipment that bridges the computer and the audio/video worlds in the home.

Chapter 15

Building a Home Network

In This Chapter

▶ Divining your optimal home networking solution

▶ Working with hubs, switches, and routers, oh my!

▶ Configuring and connecting to your network

▶ Introducing your network to the Internet

*Y*our Media Center PC is a powerhouse of audio, video, and home-computing information. Properly set up, your Media Center PC is connected to your stereo system, your Internet connection, and your TV set, making it a power-house of audio, video, and home-computing information.

As complete as that sounds, it's nothing compared to what you can do with a home network. Imagine being able to play a DVD on any TV set in the house, or play CDs through speakers in the kitchen or even by the pool.

A home network can be as big or as small as you want. You can pipe signals all over the house or limit the network to extending audio to another room. Adding a home network simply makes sense. You spend a lot of money on entertainment and computer equipment around the house, so it makes sense to be able to access it outside its location.

In this chapter, you are introduced to the main concepts behind putting a home network in place. We advocate a whole-home view of home networking — that is, an approach that yields broad coverage all over house — instead of doing it haphazardly on a room-by-room basis. You save a lot of money, and it's far more functional.

This chapter condenses an entire book that we wrote on the topic, *Smart Homes For Dummies* (published by Wiley Publishing, Inc.). We highly recommend it because we're sure you'll find lots of stuff in there worth thinking about. Also check out its companion site, www.smarthomesbook.com.

What's a Home Network?

In a home network, your MCE PC can act as a massive central *server* with which you communicate all over your home. The devices you connect to your MCE PC become *shared resources* among many computers.

In computer parlance, you are going to be installing a full-fledged computer *local area network (LAN)*. A home LAN provides a high-speed data connection among all the computers in your home, allowing them to share files, share networked peripherals (such as printers), play networked games, and more. Multiple computers can easily share high-speed Internet access devices, such as DSL or cable modems, over a LAN. Your MCE 2004 PC is the center of all this, providing content not only to TVs and audio systems but also to computers throughout your house.

Following are the ways you can connect networked devices:

- ✔ LAN cables running between machines (and under rugs, and around corners, and so on)
- ✔ In-wall LAN cabling (especially when building a new home)
- ✔ Existing in-wall telephone cabling enhanced with data connectors
- ✔ Existing in-wall electrical lines (yes electrical!) enhanced with data connectors
- ✔ Wireless LAN connections (various types)
- ✔ Combination of the previous methods

We'll focus on the first two methods in this chapter. In the next chapter, we describe the other methods, which are alternatives to the wired LAN solutions.

Our bias is toward building a structured wiring solution in the home, complemented with wireless endpoints to create a whole-home wired and wireless backbone. This approach gives you a high-speed backbone with flexibly located on-ramps to your content from anywhere in your house.

The exact networking solutions you use in your home will be based on how you use your home network. Simplistically, the more data you need to send over your network, the narrower your options. Windows XP MCE 2004 deals with large files, such as video files and recorded TV files. Big files need big bandwidth. And most of the home-networking solutions you buy off the shelf today were designed to facilitate getting computers onto Internet access pipes that typically are not more than 1.5 Mbps, for applications such as checking e-mail and browsing Web sites. They don't have enough bandwidth to carry the MCE video file content fast enough to give a quality picture, even if you're just moving it down the hallway.

How much you plan to use your home network matters, too. Look at the Briere household around 7 o'clock any weekend night. Danny has four kids playing multiplayer games, instant messaging, surfing the Web, playing videos from Yahoo! Launch, watching stored recorded TV episodes, and printing color pictures. Dad and Mom are likewise entertained: editing home videos, creating photo albums, and potentially streaming some recorded TV on their own. That requires a lot of bandwidth.

Hence our bias toward wired and very-high-bandwidth wireless solutions. In-wall data wiring (its special data-conditioned cable called *CAT-5e*, short for *Category 5e*) is capable of very high speeds, at least 100 Mbps. The latest wireless solutions can carry traffic at speeds greater than 20 Mbps (although vendors advertise much higher speeds). If you have a small place, you might get better performance if you run cabling under the rug rather than using a wireless option.

The bottleneck may not be your souped-up MCE PC — it could very well be the weak points in your network.

Components of a Home Network

Building a LAN is easier than ever before, thanks to cool home-networking wizards in Windows XP and off-the-shelf network equipment packages at stores such as CompUSA and Staples.

If you're building a new home, you'll probably use more of a wired solution for most connections. A structured wiring solution can be added to your house for probably $2000 to $3000, which is a small price to pay for such a huge benefit. Structured wiring solutions are available from companies such as Leviton (www.leviton.com), Siemon (www.siemon.com), and ChannelPlus (www.multiplextechnology.com/channelplus/).

If you have an existing home, some of the options in Chapter 16 — wireless, home-phone line, and home-powerline networking — will play a larger role, with point-to-point data wiring for specific key links.

With the exception of most structured wiring solutions, which are best installed by professionals, most home-networking solutions involve plugging in adapters and running some cable, or merely plugging devices into electrical outlets (really, the data runs through the electrical cabling). It's pretty easy.

Nearly all LAN technologies share a few basic building blocks:

> ✔ **A network protocol, such as Ethernet:** The network protocol is a language of sorts that controls access to the network, allows individual devices on the network to find and identify each other, and determines when each

device can transmit and receive data. Ethernet, which we describe in more detail in the following section, is the most common protocol for home network.

✔ **Network interface cards (NICs):** You must have *NICs* (pronounced like the New York basketball team) — in each device that connects to the network. NICs generally work with only one kind of network, such as an Ethernet NIC for Ethernet-based networks. Many computers and home-entertainment devices today are shipped with Ethernet NICs already installed — all you see is the RJ-45 port on the back or side. If one of your PCs doesn't have one, it's easy to install. Just pop the cover off your computer and slide a card into an empty PCI slot inside, leaving the RJ-45 jack part sticking out of the back of the computer.

✔ **Cables:** Unless you have a totally wireless network, cables will provide the connection between at least some of your networked devices. Most LAN wiring is *unshielded twisted pair (UTP) cabling*. Like telephone networks, computer LANs utilize a common connector on the ends of this UTP cabling, the RJ-45 (see Figure 15-1). The standard jack and plug for all UTP computer LANs, RJ-45 connectors look like the familiar (old-fashioned) telephone jacks called RJ-11s, only wider. RJ-45 connectors terminate all four pairs of wire found in typical CAT-5e UTP cables.

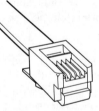

Figure 15-1:
The RJ-45 connector, your path to the promised LAN.

Ethernet: Your home language

Ethernet is the most common LAN for the home or small office (and in any size business for that matter). Scores of Ethernet variations are available, based on the total bandwidth and type of cable, but you need to consider only the following options:

✔ **10BaseT:** 10 Mbps over twisted-pair cable

✔ **100BaseT:** 100 Mbps over twisted-pair cable — often called Fast Ethernet

✔ **1000BaseT:** 1000 Mbps over twisted-pair cable — often called Gigabit Ethernet, or Gig-E

The first number in each of these names stands for the maximum bandwidth of the system in megabits per second, so 10BaseT is a 10-Mbps connection. The last number or letter tells you the kind of cable that it goes over; for example, _T_ means twisted pair.

Hubs, switches, routers, and more

Twisted-pair Ethernet LANs (such as 10BaseT or 100BaseT) use a network architecture called a star. In a _star configuration,_ all hardware connects to a central device called a _hub_ or a _switch._

The hub transmits the data from each incoming cable to every other cable that attaches to the hub — and, therefore, to each device that attaches to the far end of those cables.

Hubs and switches do basically the same thing. They are the central point to which each run of CAT-5e UTP cabling connects back to, and they allow data to flow down different legs of the network to get from device to device. However, a switch uses internal intelligence to figure out which legs of the network the data needs to flow over, but a hub just sends the data (called _packets_) down every leg of the network simultaneously. If only two computers are talking to each other, the difference between these approaches isn't significant. But as more devices start to talk to each other, a switch can make things much faster. We talk about only switches from here on out because they're the superior way to go and don't cost much more.

Physically, the switch is a small electronic box with a number of RJ-45 connectors (called _ports_) across the front. Inside the switch is a circuit board that electrically connects all these RJ-45 connectors to each other in the proper way. The _proper way_ means that the wire carrying outgoing data from one computer connects to the wires carrying incoming data to all other computers connected to the switch.

The _uplink port_ (also sometimes called a _WAN port_), which is a special RJ-45 port, is another feature of a typical switch. Unlike the other ports, the uplink port doesn't cross the incoming and outgoing data signals. Instead, it sends them straight through (incoming to incoming, outgoing to outgoing). This capability becomes useful if, for example, you want to connect two switches or you have an Internet connection device, such as a cable modem, that you want to connect to all computers in the network. In these cases, you use the uplink port instead of a standard port.

Some Ethernet switches and hubs don't have a dedicated uplink port. Instead, they have a switch (a button, in other words) next to one of the regular ports that lets you configure the port to act as an uplink port.

You might be thinking, "Well, where do home-network routers fit in?" Most home routers have built-in Ethernet switches. So you don't need to buy a router _and_ a switch. Just go shopping for a home-network router, and you'll be set. We talk more about routers in a few pages. For now, if you're buying just a switch, get one with at least eight ports, each of which supports at least 100 Mbps.

Figure 15-2 shows a network using these components and built using a star architecture.

Need to add another device to the network? Just run another length of network cabling and connect it to the switch. Someone drive a nail through one of your network cables? Your whole network doesn't go down — just the affected segment.

You can easily expand a star network by hooking up a switch at one of the endpoints. So if you have a single Ethernet outlet in a bedroom and need to connect two or three devices to it, you can just plug a switch into the outlet, and then connect those devices to the switch. All computers connected to this remote switch will be able to "see" the rest of your network — just as if they were connected to one of your Ethernet jacks.

We recommend that you have a central point somewhere in your house for all your wiring. It's generally in a closet or in the basement. Your home LAN's *central node* — the place from which all your cabling runs start — goes here. A key piece is a device called a *patch panel* or *punchdown block* mounted in your central wiring closet that serves as a place to manage all the wiring going in and out of the closet. The punchdown block needs to be CAT-5e rated to allow high-speed data transmissions.

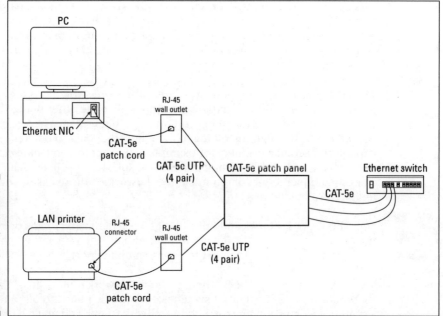

Figure 15-2:
A typical
in-wall
10BaseT
network
with a
network
printer.

The shortest Ethernet primer in computerdom

Ethernet in its traditional form is a shared network. All computers and other connected, networked devices share the 10 (or 100 or 1000) Mbps of bandwidth available on the network. Ethernet uses a protocol called *CSMA/CD (Carrier-Sense Multiple Access with Collision Detection)* to divide access to the network. Basically, CSMA/CD means that all devices on the network listen for a free moment on the network before sending data. When the coast is clear, the data goes out. If two devices happen to choose the same moment to send data, a collision occurs. The devices then each wait a random amount of time before resending their data.

Newer versions of Ethernet hardware systems are *switched.* These Ethernet networks use a sophisticated device — the switch, of course — to direct data throughout the network. Instead of sharing 10 or 100 Mbps, each device has that amount of bandwidth dedicated to it at all times. The switch basically keeps each segment of the Ethernet network separate from the others — directing data between the devices that are talking and keeping data off the wires running to other devices, instead of sending the data to every device. This process can reduce the number of collisions and make the overall network faster as more and more devices are connected to it.

Other home-network components

With cables and connectors, patch panels, NICs, and hubs, you're 90 percent of the way toward putting together a home LAN. The final piece of the puzzle is another set of CAT-5e cables called *patch cables.* Patch cables fill the gap between wall outlets and computers. They also connect the patch panel to your Ethernet switch or home-network router.

Just like all the other components in your network, your patch cables should be rated CAT-5e. Most are, but some of the cheaper ones are rated CAT-3 or even unrated. You don't want these — they're a false economy that may keep your network from reaching its maximum speed or working reliably.

Configuring Your Home Network

Probably the most difficult task is configuring all the network protocols and software on each of your home's PCs and other devices. This job used to be the domain of hard-core networking experts, but it has become less onerous with each successive release of Windows software.

In XP, choose Start⇨My Network Places. On the left, click Set up a home or small office network. You are guided through the process of setting up your XP MCE PC as well as any other attached XP PCs.

For non-XP PCs, no specific Windows Networking Wizard walks you through the paces like the one in XP. Setting up your network is more complex than we can cover in one chapter, but here are some resources for networking info:

- ✔ Microsoft "Insider Home Networking" site (`www.microsoft.com/insider/networking/`)
- ✔ Cnet's Networking & Wireless site (`reviews.cnet.com/Networking/2001-3243_7-0.html?tag=cnetfd.dir`)
- ✔ World of Windows Networking site (`www.wown.com`)

Home-entertainment and consumer devices typically have their own network-enablement process. For example, Danny has an AudioRequest music server (`www.request.com`) that contains his 600 audio-CD collection. The AudioRequest unit has a settings screen that allows him to set up his Ethernet configurations. Many consumer electronics do not even have this much, defaulting to common Ethernet settings and self-discovery capabilities to get on the LAN.

Getting Your Network on the Internet

The home network we've been discussing deals with moving data among computers across your LAN. But what about getting data to and from the Internet? That's where the home-network router fits in. A router's main purpose (besides switching local LAN traffic) is to send data between your Internet connection and the computers and devices on your LAN.

A switch is a device that connects multiple PCs on a LAN. A router connects the computers on a LAN to a wide area network (such as the Internet). Although we said that most home routers have a built-in switch, not all switches are also routers.

The router handles its role as a traffic cop by creating its own *subnet* (or private IP network) within the home. The router then assigns private IP addresses to each computer connected it. When the router connects to the Internet, it is assigned a public IP address (one that other computers on the Internet can send data to and from) and then figures out which packets of data go to which Ethernet device in the subnet.

The first time you set up your router (or when you change the configuration of your network by adding or removing computers), you have to use network configuration software to get things organized, but most routers have easy-to-understand, wizard-style programs to lead you through the process. Figure 15-3 shows how you might set up a router in your home network.

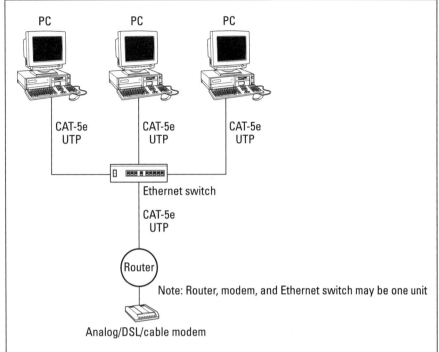

Figure 15-3:
Using a
router to
share a
modem
across the
network.

The types of technology that make your home router work are called NAT (Network Address Translation) and DHCP (Dynamic Host Control Protocol). NAT *translates* between the private IP addresses of the computers on your network and the public IP address that they all share and is smart enough to make sure everything ends up in the right place. DHCP hands out those private IP addresses to the computers on your network.

Many home-network routers use your Internet browser as the software to configure the system. The configuration software is written as *HyperText Markup Language* (HTML) files — the language of Web pages. To set things up, you simply open your Web browser software, type the Web address of your router (it's usually a number, such as 192.168.1.1), and open these HTML files. Fill in a few blanks, answer a few questions, and click a few buttons, and your router is ready to go.

Home-network routers range in price depending on what kind of modem is included (if one is included at all) and how many computers they can work with. The majority of home-network routers work with only cable or DSL broadband connections. So, if you're still stuck on dial-up, you'll have to shop around to find a model that works for you. (A few models are available with a built-in analog modem, but they're getting scarce.) Other features that influence the price of a home-network router include the following:

- **Firewalls:** Although NAT itself provides some network security functions, many home-network routers also contain sophisticated firewalls, which keep hackers out of your computer.

- **Wireless LAN support:** The wireless networks we talk about in Chapter 16 are often supported by a home-network router. Many have built-in wireless access point functionality, so you can support both your wired and unwired computers from a single device.

- **Other home-networking support:** Besides the wireless systems just mentioned, many home-networking routers also include support for connecting PCs to your network using existing telephone lines or even electrical power lines. We talk about these systems in Chapter 16 as well.

- **Support for VPN:** Many businesses use VPNs (Virtual Private Networks) to allow their employees to securely connect their computers from remote locations back into the corporate network. Not all home-network routers will let you connect in this way. (VPNs have special protocols that not all routers will pass through to the Internet.)

The cheapest home-network routers start at about $100 (these boxes were at least $500 just three years ago). The major vendors of home-network routers and router-modem combos include the following:

- Linksys: (www.linksys.com)
- NetGear (www.netgear.com)
- D-Link (www.dlink.com)
- Siemens SpeedStream (www.speedstream.com)
- 2Wire (www.2wire.com)

Although you can buy your own home-network router directly from the manufacturer or from online and other retailers, you may also have the option of getting one directly from your Internet service provider. DSL providers such as BellSouth, SBC, and Earthlink will provide you with a home-network router, usually for a monthly fee. Although you might end up paying more for such a solution over time than just buying the router yourself, you do have the advantage of having someone to call if you run into any problems.

Routers are the hardware-based way of sharing an Internet connection. Given their low price, we think they're also the best way. The software-based alternative is to install a *proxy server* program on one of your networked PCs. This program performs a similar function as a router — that is, it distributes Internet data packets from a single connection to multiple PCs on a network. However, a proxy server program puts extra processing stress on your PC, which is why we prefer routers instead.

Chapter 16

Using a Wireless Home-Networking System

· ·

In This Chapter

▶ Understanding the basics

▶ Buying wireless network equipment

▶ Making wireless and wired networks get along

▶ Getting other devices on your wireless LAN

▶ Looking at the alternatives

· ·

Your Media Center Edition PC makes a great centerpiece of a whole-home entertainment network — a network that lets you centralize the storage and management of nearly all your digital content (pictures, movies, and music), and share this content between MCE PCs, regular PCs and other devices, such as home theaters and networked audio/video systems.

For many people, however, running the CAT-5e wire required for a traditional wired home network (or LAN) throughout a home or apartment is often too difficult and time consuming. For those who rent a house or apartment, running wires inside walls is simply not allowed. And some homes, no matter who owns them, present insurmountable obstacles to running new wiring.

You can take heart, though, because the hottest new technology in home networking is the wireless LAN, which uses radio waves, not wires, to connect computers. In this chapter, you find out about these exciting wireless LAN technologies and get advice on how to choose a wireless LAN for your MCE PC (and the rest of your PCs). You also discover how to use wireless LANs to connect other devices in your home (such as audio/video systems). And finally, you read about some other "no new wires" networking technologies that you can use to augment a wireless LAN.

Wireless Networking 101

Wireless LANs aren't that difficult to understand — essentially, they're a lot like cordless phones (note that we said cordless, not cellular). Just as a cordless phone system has a *base station* that connects the wired and wireless worlds, so wireless LANs have base stations, known as *access points,* that do the same thing. And just as cordless phones have the wireless devices themselves (cordless handsets), wireless LANs have wireless devices known as *wireless network adapters.*

In a wireless LAN, the access point connects to your Ethernet LAN (which we discuss in Chapter 15), and the wireless network adapters go inside (or connect to) your MCE PC and other PCs and devices. All the data that would have traveled over wires in a traditional home network is now converted to radio waves (just as your voice is converted to radio waves in a cordless phone system), and transmitted around your house.

Figure 16-1 shows a typical wireless LAN setup, with an access point connected to a wired LAN (and the Internet), and PCs connected using wireless LAN network adapters.

Wireless networks are based on an international standard known as *802.11.* The 802.11 standard ensures that different pieces of wireless LAN equipment based on the standard will work together, regardless of which company built a particular device.

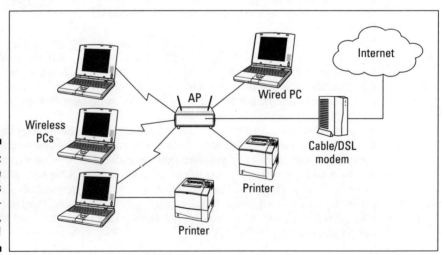

Figure 16-1:
A simple wireless network — look Ma, no wires!

Introducing wireless LAN standards

The 802.11 standard is actually a group of wireless LAN standards. Each one is identified by an additional letter at the end of the name, such as 802.11a or 802.11b. These different standards identify the speed and radio frequency of wireless LAN equipment.

The standards operate in *unlicensed frequencies,* a set of frequencies set aside by the government that anyone can use without having a license. Some frequencies are more crowded than others. Common household items such as microwave ovens and wireless electronic gear can interfere with your wireless LAN signals, degrading their network performance. The two major frequency bands used by wireless LAN networks are in the 2.4 GHz and 5 GHz range, with most household items, including most cordless phone systems, residing in the 2.4 GHz band.

The three groups of 802.11 wireless LAN equipment available today follow:

- ✔ **802.11b:** This is the most common wireless LAN equipment. 802.11b wireless LAN equipment operates at a radio frequency of 2.4 GHz and has a maximum speed of 11 Mbps. In practice, however, most home networks based on 802.11b are limited to speeds of about 4 to 5 Mbps — not blazingly fast, but fast enough for general file-sharing network applications and to share streaming music files over a network.

    802.11b *is not* fast enough for sending *streaming* video files over a wireless network. In other words, 802.11b is fine for sending files back and forth between computers but not for watching video files stored on other computers. Since so much of MCE is based on video content, we don't recommend that you install an 802.11b network. Luckily, 802.11g is quickly replacing 802.11b in most stores.

- ✔ **802.11a:** Despite the fact that *a* comes before *b* in the alphabet, 802.11a is a newer wireless LAN standard than is 802.11b. 802.11a is a faster system than 802.11b, with a maximum speed of 54 Mbps, and a "real world" speed of about 20 to 30 Mbps. This speed is more than fast enough for most video applications. 802.11a uses a different set of radio frequencies (in the 5 GHz range, instead of the more crowded 2.4 range), so you can't use 802.11a equipment with 802.11b equipment.

- ✔ **802.11g:** The newest wireless LAN standard, 802.11g was approved in mid-2003. 802.11g uses the same 2.4 GHz radio frequencies of 802.11b, but operates at the same high speed as 802.11a (54 Mbps maximum, real world speeds above 20 to 30 Mbps). The biggest advantage of 802.11g is that it is fully *backwards compatible* with 802.11b, so older 802.11b wireless

LAN devices can communicate on the same network with 802.11g devices, although at the lower 11 Mbps speed of 802.11b. And any 802.11g device can connect to an existing 802.11b network — which is good news if your MCE PC is a laptop and you take it to work or to use on other wireless LAN networks.

Wi-Fi is a limited-range technology — you can't go a mile from your access point and stay within radio range. Nominally, the range of Wi-Fi systems can be as long as 300 feet, but in the real world, with walls and bookcases and filing cabinets in the way, you can expect to be able to roam 60 to 100 feet from your access point and still get good reception.

In case you're wondering, Wi-Fi stands for *Wireless Fidelity,* which means — well it really doesn't mean anything, it's just nice marketing-speak.

Table 16-1 summarizes the three major wireless LAN systems and their uses in a home network.

Table 16-1	Comparing Wireless LAN Systems			
Technology	*Frequency*	*Speed*	*Compatibility*	*Usage*
802.11b (Wi-Fi)	2.4 GHz	11 Mbps	802.11 g	File sharing, music
802.11a (Wi-Fi5)	5 GHz	54 Mbps	none	File sharing, music, video
802.11g	2.4 GHz	54 Mbps	802.11b (at 11 Mbps)	File sharing, music, video

Moving forward, we think that 802.11b, a, and g will all be supported by the majority of wireless LAN equipment. Just like most radios are AM/FM (meaning they can pick up different kinds of signals in different frequency ranges), we think that *dual band* (*2.4* and *5 GHz*), tri mode (a, b, g) wireless LAN gear is just inevitable. Already, all the wireless equipment manufacturers we know (and we know a lot of them) are working on developing inexpensive computer chips that can automatically tune into the different frequencies used by the different wireless LANs — so a single computer chip could be the basis of a wireless LAN network adapter that could handle any wireless LAN. So increasingly, you'll see gear that supports all three standards, giving you flexibility to decide which standard you want to use at home.

The Wi-Fi Alliance (www.wi-fi.com), a group of wireless LAN equipment makers and developers, gives wireless LAN equipment the all-important *Wi-Fi certification* that ensures that equipment from different vendors has been tested to be *interoperable* (in other words, the equipment plays nicely with others). If two pieces of wireless LAN gear both sport a Wi-Fi certification on the box (and if they're using the same 802.11 standard), you can rest assured that they'll work together, no matter who made them. Look for this certification when buying any Wi-Fi gear.

Wireless LAN pieces and parts

As we showed you back in Figure 16-1, wireless LANs consist of two major parts: the access point and the wireless network adapter.

The *access point,* or *AP,* connects to your wired home network or directly to your broadband (cable or DSL) modem if you don't have a wired LAN. The access point acts as the base station of your wireless network and performs several functions:

✔ It directs data between different computers on your wireless LAN. Just as an Ethernet hub or switch directs traffic on a wired network (see Chapter 15 for a refresher), an access point sends data to and from each computer attached to the network, and helps ensure that the data you send gets to the right computer.

It's possible to create what's known as a *peer-to-peer wireless network,* where computers talk directly to each other, without going through an access point. We think that this is not the best approach, particularly since you can buy an access point for well under $80 these days. The setup of a peer-to-peer network is considerably harder, and the performance tends to be not as good.

✔ It acts as a *bridge* between your wireless and wired networks. The access point sends data between wirelessly networked computers and devices and can also direct communications among wired and wireless computers on your network. So if your MCE PC is on the wired part of your network and your laptop is wireless, your access point makes sure the two computers can talk to each other.

✔ It can act as a home-network router. Like the routers we discuss in Chapter 15, most access points can provide routing functionality such as NAT (also discussed in Chapter 15) that lets all the computers on your network share a single Internet connection and IP address.

If you think you'll eventually have both wired and wireless computers on your network, it's a good idea to just buy a home-networking router with an access point built in. Most of the vendors we discuss in Chapter 15 (such as Linksys, NETGEAR, Microsoft, and D-Link) make home-networking routers with built-in access points.

The second major component of a wireless LAN is the *wireless network adapter,* which is the wireless equivalent of the NIC (or network interface card) we talk about in Chapter 15. Every computer connected to your network must have a wireless network adapter of some sort attached to it. Many types of wireless network adapters are available, but the most common are the following:

- ✔ **PC Card:** Most commonly found in laptop computers, PC cards are small (credit-card-sized) cards that fit into the PC (or, as many computer old-timers call them, PCMCIA) card slots on the side of the computer. PC Card wireless network adapters include a small antenna attached to the end of the card (the antenna typically sticks out of the side of your laptop an inch or so). PC cards also can be used in some handheld computer devices.

- ✔ **PCI Card adapter:** Desktop computers that don't have a PC Card, can use a wireless LAN card that fits into an internal PCI slot (the same slots used for many wired Ethernet NICs or for video cards). If you use a PCI Card NIC, you still need to have an external antenna (which will come in the package), so everything won't be all neat and hidden inside your PC. Most MCE PCs do *not* have a PC card slot, but many (except for laptop MCE PCs) have a PCI slot inside that can use this kind of adapter.

- ✔ **USB external adapter:** A better alternative for desktop MCE PCs is an external NIC that connects through a USB port. Every MCE PC has a *bunch* of USB ports, and the external NIC requires no real installation — just plug it in and load the software driver. The only problem with USB adapters is that most still use the older USB 1.0 standard, not the higher-speed USB 2.0 standard. For an 802.11b network, this is not an issue, because USB 1.0's maximum speed of 12 Mbps is faster than 802.11b's maximum speed. But for the faster 802.11a and g networks, USB 1.0's maximum speed is well below the maximum wireless LAN speed — so you'll be leaving some speed on the table. Figure 16-2 shows the wireless USB adapter that Pat uses, NETGEAR's MA111. It fits right in your pocket (it's smaller than a marker pen and very cool).

If you're using 802.11g or 802.11a, and you want to use a USB wireless network adapter, make sure it supports USB 2.0, and connect it to one of your MCE PC's USB 2.0 ports.

- ✔ **Wireless Ethernet bridge:** The wireless Ethernet bridge is a relative newcomer to the wireless LAN world. On one side of a wireless Ethernet bridge is an antenna and radio system for 802.11b, g or a; on the other is a standard Ethernet port. Using a wireless Ethernet bridge, you can connect *any* device with an Ethernet port (meaning every MCE PC ever made) to a wireless network without installing any additional equipment (or even doing any special software configuration) — the MCE PC "sees" a standard Ethernet connection and doesn't even know that it's connected to a wireless network.

Wireless Ethernet bridges are also handy for connecting non-computer devices to your wireless network. For example, they're great for hooking gaming consoles (such as Microsoft's Xbox) and networked audio systems (such as Philips' Streamium system) to the wireless network. Basically, if the device has an Ethernet port (heck, even some refrigerators have them now), it can connect to a wireless Ethernet bridge.

Figure 16-2:
NETGEAR's
MA111
802.11b
wireless
USB
adapter.

Choosing Wireless Network Equipment

Now that we've talked about the different pieces and parts, it's time to choose which wireless LAN equipment is best for you. The first decision to make — before you even start looking at different vendors and specific pieces of equipment — is which of the 802.11 standards to use. We mentioned earlier that we think all wireless LAN gear will eventually be able to work with both 802.11b and g (remember, these two standards already work together) and 802.11a.

Let's look at your choices again:

✔ **802.11b:** This is the cheapest solution. (802.11b network adapters can cost as little as $40, and 802.11b access points are under $80.) It's the most common, so if you take your wireless LAN-equipped computer elsewhere (such as to a public hot spot), it should work. On the downside, it's slow — too slow to let you share video content in real time on your network. If you want to send video between devices on an 802.11b network, you need to move the file from computer to computer ahead of time, and then watch it. We prefer to *not* have to move the files around between computers in advance — we just want to play them when we want to play them. For that reason, we think 802.11b is not the best wireless network to use for your MCE PC.

✔ **802.11a:** This is faster than 802.11b and is the least likely to be bothered by interference from other wireless devices in your home. Is this a home run then? Actually, no, because 802.11a gear is the most expensive (more than $150 for an adapter and more than $250 for an access point). So far, it seems 802.11a is being marketed as a business-network solution, not a home-network solution. Over time, prices will plummet, and consumer-grade options will emerge.

✔ **802.11g:** This is as fast as 802.11a but doesn't cost as much as 802.11a equipment (around $100 for an adapter, and about $150 for an access point). It's completely compatible (at lower speeds) with 802.11b. Sounds like a winner, doesn't it? We think so.

In the end, though, we'll let you make up your own mind about what to buy, based on your budget and your needs. If you can afford it, we highly recommend that you skip 802.11b and go right to 802.11g. If you're a bit of a risk taker and not at all price sensitive, you might want to use 802.11a — the fact that it has much less chance of interference disrupting your network is a good thing if you live in a crowded area. If you're really loose with the cash, get an a/g/b tri-mode access point. If you just want to be able to transfer files between your computers, don't overlook 802.11b. It's cheap, and getting cheaper.

The price of just about every piece of computer equipment tends to drop like a stone over time. Wireless LANs are no exception — so don't be surprised when you go shopping if our prices seem high.

After you've made your technology decision, it's time to start shopping for wireless LAN gear. A lot of good Wi-Fi gear is out there, and we recommend that you look online (at places like Amazon.com) for the best price. Among our favorite vendors of Wi-Fi gear are the following:

✔ **NETGEAR:** www.netgear.com

✔ **D-Link:** www.dlink.com

✔ **Linksys:** www.Linksys.com

✔ **SMC Networks:** www.smc.com

✔ **Speedstream:** www.speedstream.com

✔ **Microsoft:** www.Microsoft.com/hardware/broadbandnetworking

When you're looking at Wi-Fi equipment, particularly the network adapters, check the box (or online) to see whether the equipment has been certified to work with Windows XP (note that we said XP, not MCE). You can usually still use gear that's not certified, but it's a lot more difficult.

Your shopping list should consist of the following:

✔ An access point, or AP

✔ A network adapter for your MCE PC

✔ Network adapters for your other PCs

✔ Optional: Network adapters (Ethernet bridges are best for this purpose) for your Xbox or Playstation 2 and any other Ethernet-enabled home-entertainment equipment (such as Internet radios)

Consider an outdoor access point if you have a pool or other outdoor area where you spend a lot of time. Many of the vendors listed previously have environmentally-hardened units for that purpose.

Also, try to buy all your gear from one vendor, because you'll have fewer problems. Although all the different vendors' gear is made to be interoperable, nothing beats the performance of a single vendor's devices working together.

Integrating Wireless with a Wired Network

Your wireless LAN can work well with a wired network (like the ones we discuss in Chapter 15). In fact, when you're building a whole-home network, this might be the best approach due to the range limitations of Wi-Fi. (Remember, it can reach less than 100 feet in typical conditions.)

Combining a wired and wireless network is simple. Depending on what kind of access point you've purchased, the process may be as simple as plugging wired Ethernet connections into the *switch* ports on your access point. (For more on switches, see Chapter 15.) Here's the lowdown:

✔ If you're starting from scratch for both your wired and wireless networks, buy an AP that has both wireless connections *and* a built-in home-network router and Ethernet switch. Most vendors call these *wireless DSL/cable modem routers*. Use Ethernet cabling to plug any wired network connections into the switch ports on the router, and use the wireless network adapters to connect other devices to the router's internal AP wirelessly.

✔ If you already have a wired network (with a router or an Ethernet switch or both), just plug the access point into one of the switch ports on your router. In this case, your AP acts as a network *bridge* connecting the wired network (and your broadband modem) to the wireless PCs on your network.

Figure 16-3 shows a mixed wired and wireless network.

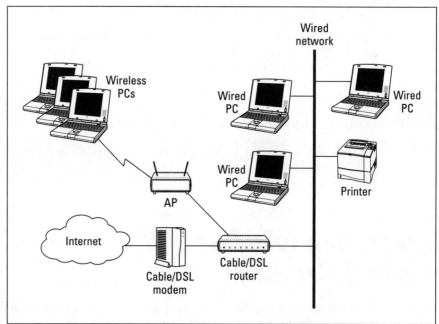

Figure 16-3:
Mixing your
networks.

Other Devices that You Can Connect to a Wireless Network

Your MCE PC (and other PCs) aren't the only devices that can connect to a wireless LAN. An increasing number of computer peripherals and home-entertainment devices are being made with built-in wireless LAN capabilities — so they can easily connect to your network without running cables.

Following are some examples of wireless stuff:

✔ **Printers:** Many inkjet and laser-printer manufacturers have begun offering 802.11b cards or adapters that attach to their home printers. With a wireless printer adapter, you can stick that printer in some out-of-the-way corner and still gain access to it for printing photos in Media Center (or whatever printing job you might have). If you use a wireless printer, you'll need to have the *driver* software (that lets your MCE PC use the printer's services) installed on each computer you want to print from.

If you already have a printer, consider a wireless DSL/cable modem router with a built-in *print server*. This feature lets you connect a standard wired printer directly to the router and access it from any computer on the network (wired or wireless).

✔ **Webcams:** Danny has a D-Link (www.dlink.com) DCS-1000W wireless Webcam on his network, and he loves it. These cameras will send video or still images to any computer on the network and even to remote viewers on the Internet, without any wires. Most wireless Webcams have a built-in Web server, so you don't need *any* software on your PCs, besides Internet Explorer, to view them. D-Link's DCS-2000 adds motion detection and surveillance options.

✔ **Digital cameras:** These are new on the market (announced but not yet shipped) and are very cool. Digital cameras with built-in Wi-Fi network adapters can download their pictures to your MCE PC without any need to find that darned cable hidden in your desk drawer.

✔ **Internet radios:** Philips Streamium is our favorite example of this product — a mini stereo system (complete with CD player, AM/FM radio, and speakers) that can also connect to your network and play Internet radio stations. Check out audio.philips.com/streamium/product.asp for more information.

Check out Chapter 18 for our predictions about some future products that will perform a very similar function, wirelessly, *and* work directly with Media Center.

✔ **Cordless phones:** For the home market, cordless phones don't work with Wi-Fi — in fact they work against it, as many cordless phones use the same radio frequencies as Wi-Fi and cause interference. In the business market, however, we're starting to see a lot of Wi-Fi cordless phones that connect to your access point (and can let you make inexpensive phone calls over the Internet to boot). We expect that in just a few years, most cordless phones will work with a Wi-Fi network.

Any device that has an Ethernet port on the back — game consoles, printers, whatever — can connect to a wireless network using one of the wireless Ethernet bridges we discussed earlier in the chapter (in the "Wireless LAN pieces and parts" section).

Phone and Power Line Alternatives

Although wireless networks have been the most prominent and popular home-networking technology, a couple of other technologies fit into the same "no new wires" category (in other words, technologies that don't require you to run networking cables inside your walls).

These systems use either your existing telephone lines or your electrical power lines:

- ✔ **HomePNA:** PNA stands for Phoneline Networking Association — the industry group that sets the standard for this equipment. This system uses the phone lines already in your walls to communicate. HomePNA is currently on its second iteration (called HomePNA 2.0) and allows communications at speeds up to 10 Mbps between any phone jacks in the house. (A newer version in development, HPNA 3.0, will allow up to 100 Mbps speeds!) HomePNA is built into many home routers (such as those from NetGear, Linksys, and 2Wire), so if you think you might want to use HomePNA, choose your router accordingly. To install HPNA in your home, you plug HPNA adapters into your wall phone-jack outlets; these adapters enable you to plug your phone and Ethernet cables into the same outlet. At the phone jack nearest to your Internet router, you run the Ethernet patch cable into that router — and your network is connected to the Internet.

- ✔ **HomePlug:** This is the electrical powerline alternative to HomePNA. HomePlug network adapters can "talk" to each other at speeds of up to 14 Mbps (although speeds are much slower in practice). It operates in a similar fashion to HPNA. You plug HomePlug adapters into your electrical outlets, and they communicate over the higher frequencies available on your electrical lines. At least one vendor sells a HomePlug adapter that includes an 802.11b access point — plug this into an outlet, and you have an instant 802.11b network. This is great for big homes where the main AP is too far away from the computers in the distant corners of the house. The leading providers of routers also sport HomePlug options, so you can connect to your network by simply powering up your router.

The coolest HomePlug gear we've seen comes from Speedstream (www.speedstream.com), which makes home-network routers and access points with HomePlug built in. To add an AP to a Speedstream network, you just plug the HomePlug-enabled AP into a wall outlet — no other wiring is necessary. Pretty simple and easy to use.

We prefer high-speed wireless over either of these systems for all the bandwidth reasons previously mentioned. However, these other systems have their place, especially as a way to extend a wireless network in a larger house. Between the two systems, HomePlug is more popular.

Part V
The Part of Tens

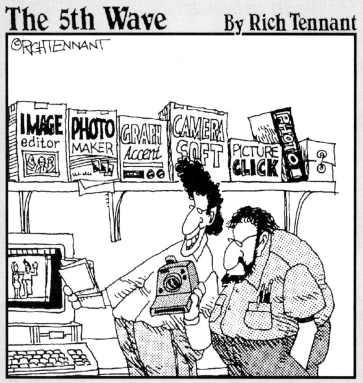

The 5th Wave — By Rich Tennant

"...and here's me with Cindy Crawford. And this is me with Madonna and Celine Dion..."

In this part . . .

We've written several *For Dummies* books, and this is the part we always have the most fun writing. This is where we get to cut loose with some fun facts and interesting tidbits about Windows XP Media Center. We've tried to come up with lists that will amuse and edify. We sure hope we were right!

We start off by telling you about cool accessories you can buy for your MCE PC. (We're typical gadget guys that way — we love the neat little tchotchkes that go along with our computer gear.) Following that, we dust off the old crystal ball and tell you where we think MCE is going and predict the new features on the horizon. Finally, we talk about ten online sites that will be just plain fun to surf to with your MCE PC.

Chapter 17

Ten Cool Accessories for Your Media Center PC

Compared to the average off-the-shelf PC, Media Center Edition PCs come loaded with features. Depending on which MCE PC you bought, your unit might have tons of gizmos and gadgets (such as a remote control and PVR software) that would be on the extras list of your average PC — if you could get those features at all. But after you become an MCE PC pro (and find yourself spending every non-working, non-eating, and non-sleeping hour of the day in front of your MCE PC), you'll probably want a few extra toys, to make using your MCE PC more convenient and more fun.

In this chapter, we give you our list of must-have accessories. Note that some items are standard with some MCE PCs or can be ordered when you configure your machine.

Making Digital Picture-Taking Easier

The My Photo function of MCE is a great way to store, edit, view, and share your digital pictures. My Photo takes a great hobby — digital photography — and makes it even better. With MCE helping us out, we take (and keep) even more digital photographs than we did before!

We love the concept of digital photographs: We can snap pictures of whatever we want without worrying about buying, developing, and printing film. But digital photography requires that you have a way of creating digital photographs. So our first MCE accessory recommendation (first three recommendations, actually) is to get yourself equipped to enter the digital photography era.

Going digital

For all the pictures you're going to take, we highly recommend that you put that old film camera on the back shelf. Following are our favorite sites for purchasing a digital camera:

- **Digital Photography Review (DPR) at** `www.dpr.com`: This site is loaded with news, information, and reviews of hundreds of the latest and greatest digital cameras in all price ranges.

- **Digital Camera Resource Page (DCRS) at** `www.dcresource.com`: Another great site that's similar in scope and function to DPR. We've been looking at sites by the creator of this one (Jeff Keller is his name) for years. We don't know him, but we trust his sites — and we think you'll feel the same way after you visit this one.

- **CNET's digital camera page at** `www.cnet.com`: Click the camera icon at the top of the page. CNET's reviewing and news-hounding capabilities are at the top of the heap as far as we're concerned — of all the big-name online news sites, we go here first. It has a lot of reviews, articles, comparisons, and links to online shopping sites. You can conduct your research and then buy the camera you want online at a great price, all in one fell swoop.

Some of the newest models of digital cameras have USB 2.0 connections instead of the slower USB 1.0 system. (We discuss these connections in Chapter 1.) All MCE PCs come with USB 2.0 ports, and using this port will allow you to spend *much* less time getting your pictures from the camera to the MCE PC.

Wow, what a bonus. Two tips. If you've purchased a digital camcorder in the past few years and never read the manual, you might find that you have a digital still camera on board! But if your camcorder is bulky, replace it — the small shape and price of today's digital camcorders make it likely that you'll want to upgrade.

Don't forget to call your cell phone company and see what camera-outfitted phones it offers. You'll want one of these, too. For more information, see the "Is it a camera or a phone?" sidebar in Chapter 11.

Salvaging your analog

The second digital photography item we recommend is for your *existing* photographs. If you're like us, you have shoeboxes (or albums, or archival-quality, acid-free photo storage systems, if you're the fussy type) with thousands of pictures of you and your family when you were all younger, thinner, and more beautiful. Don't let those pictures miss out on your MCE adventure: Scan them!

Buy a digital scanner, and you can turn existing photos, slides, and negatives into digital photo files for less than you think. You have two main choices to make when looking at scanners:

- ✔ **Flat-bed scanners:** These scanners, as the name implies, have a flat bed, or glass screen, that looks like the one on your office copier. You can place any document (such as a photo print, printed document, or magazine) on the bed for scanning. Flat-bed scanners are versatile, work well, and are available for under $100.

- ✔ **Film or slide scanners:** These are more specialized devices that can accept 35 mm film negatives or color slides or both. A film or slide scanner usually gives you better results — mainly because film negatives and slides have a higher *resolution* (or more dots making up the picture) than a print does. You have to pay more for a film or slide scanner — at least $200, and the price rises rapidly — and you can't use these scanners for more general-purpose scanning.

If you're going to work with a lot of photos, we think you should go with a purpose-built film scanner, which is optimized for pictures. Again, we recommend that you go to the CNET site (www.cnet.com) for reviews and links to online stores selling scanners.

If you're not ready to buy your own scanner, a good interim solution is to use one of the many film-scanning services. They have the MOAS (mother of all scanners) and are ready to use it on your pictures and negatives, for a few dollars per print (more or less, depending on the resolution of the scan and the size of the print).

A digital camera jackknife

We have one other must-have photo-related accessory for you: the 6-in-1 card reader. (Many MCE PCs already have this accessory.) Digital cameras use removable digital memory cards as their digital "film." The default way to get your pictures from this memory card to your MCE PC is to plug the camera into the computer (usually using a USB or USB 2.0 cable) and use software to download the pictures to your hard drive. There's nothing wrong with this approach, but it's cumbersome, particularly if you have multiple devices that require downloads. An easier way is to just pop that digital film (the memory card) out of the camera and into a dedicated card reader that's always attached to your PC. This gives you more flexibility (you can, for example, pop a fresh memory card in the camera and keep shooting pictures while the others download) and requires less juggling around with wires and cables.

You can buy an inexpensive, single-function card reader, which reads only the type of card in your camera. However, for less than $40, you can buy a 6-in-1 card reader, which reads the most common types of memory cards and will probably still be useful when you upgrade to a new card.

Here are those six different *media* (or memory card) types:

- ✔ Compact Flash (Type I/II)
- ✔ SmartMedia
- ✔ Secure Digital (SD)
- ✔ MultiMediaCard (MMC)
- ✔ Memory Stick
- ✔ IBM Microdrive

A 6-in-1 card reader can come in handy for more than just digital cameras. These memory cards are showing up in portable MP3 audio players, handheld PCs (such as PocketPCs and Palms), and even cell phones. The card reader itself plugs into the USB port. Some models can even be mounted internally in your MCE PC, if you have an available 3.5-inch drive bay (where an extra optical disc drive might be mounted).

Upgrading Your Remote

The remote control that comes standard with all MCE PCs is a handy device that enables you to use your MCE PC the way it's designed to be used: from ten feet away. But the standard remote is not at the top of the remote-control food chain. If you want a does-it-all remote control for your MCE PC — and the rest of the devices connected to your MCE PC, such as your TV — you need to do some shopping.

Luckily, the MCE PC uses a relatively standard *IR* (or infrared) remote control that uses invisible light beams to do its business. This is lucky because it's exactly what 99 percent of the universal remotes out there use. These universal remotes are so-named because they can be programmed to control just about anything and everything that has a remote — including your MCE PC.

If you're feeling rich, look into a *touchscreen* remote control, like those offered by Philips in the Pronto product line (www.pronto.philps.com). These devices, which can cost well over $1000, have a large, touch-sensitive LCD screen. Instead of limiting yourself to a fixed number of buttons, you can create *soft buttons* on the screen by programming the remote.

At $200 to $300, the programmable remotes offered by companies such as Harmony (www.harmonyremote.com) are cheaper and almost as capable. These remotes include a small LCD screen and an array of programmable buttons that you can customize to control functions on your MCE PC, TV, home-theater receiver, and more. You can also create remote-control programs (called *macros*) that link a bunch of functions. So instead of turning on the TV, setting your receiver to Video, and navigating through MCE to the Record TV section, a Harmony remote can crunch those steps down to one efficient Record TV button that you can create on your PC and load into the remote through a USB connection.

If you want to spend about $150, check out the Gyration Media Center remote (www.gyration.com/mcr.htm). This cool remote dispenses with most of the buttons found on similarly priced remotes and instead uses an internal gyroscope that tracks the motion of your hand (and the remote) in the air. So you can navigate through the MCE interface as if you were sitting at a desk with a mouse. The included GyroTools software lets you assign certain MCE functions to specific hand motions or gestures. So, for example, a flip of the hand up and to the right could switch channels or turn on your TV. It takes some getting used to, but it's very cool if you can master it.

If you want to get really high tech, check out Nevo software at www.mynevo.com). Nevo software runs on Pocket PCs and Microsoft Smart Displays, such as ViewSonic's airPanel V110 and V150. Note, however, that only the Smart Displays (which are special wireless touch screens that connect to your MCE PC) can control MCE PC in the current version.

Nevo is sort of like Media Center — you can't buy it and install it yourself. Instead, you buy a Smart Display that comes preinstalled with the software. Check out the Nevo Web site for an up-to-date list of Nevo-equipped Smart Displays.

Nevo software (made by a company called UEI — Universal Electronics, Inc.) is a whole-home control and automation solution. With a Nevo-enhanced Smart Display (such as the ViewSonic shown in Figure 17-1), you can control an unlimited number of home-entertainment devices (including your MCE PC) and also control any automated devices in your home (such as lighting systems and motorized drapes). The Nevo interface lets you create macros and automatically saves your most frequently used controls in its activity center.

For some good information on the latest in remote controls, visit the following Web site: www.remotecentral.com.

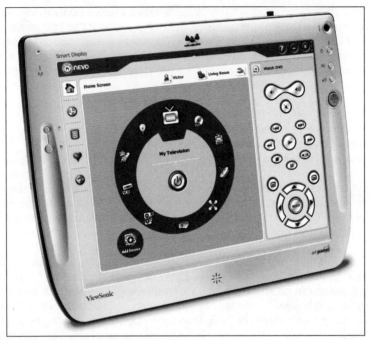

Figure 17-1:
Going high
tech with
Nevo.

Going Wireless

In Chapter 15, we talk in detail about creating wireless home networks using a system called Wi-Fi or 802.11. This is a whole-home wireless system that connects computers and computer-like devices (such as game consoles or servers) at relatively high speeds. Another wireless networking system, Bluetooth, is designed for shorter distances (30 feet instead of 300 feet) and different uses, including replacing short-run cables that connect peripherals (for example, the mouse or keyboard.) to your MCE PC.

Adding Bluetooth to your MCE PC is a great way to "cut the cord" for all sorts of devices. Imagine downloading movies from your camcorder without plugging in a FireWire connection, or transferring digital pictures without using a USB cord. Well, Bluetooth can do that. Even more importantly, Bluetooth can make your keyboard and mouse wireless as well — so you can sit back on the sofa and still use these more traditional input devices with your MCE PC. No more getting off the couch when you need to switch out of the MCE interface and send an e-mail.

To get Bluetooth working on your MCE PC, you need two things:

✔ **A Bluetooth adapter for your MCE PC:** These small devices (about the size of a pack of gum), plug directly into one of the USB ports on your MCE PC and contain a Bluetooth *transceiver* that can send and receive Bluetooth radio signals. You don't need to plug the adapter into a wall outlet — it gets its power from the USB port. You can buy a Bluetooth adapter from Belkin (www.belkin.com) or D-Link (www.dlink.com) for under $100.

Microsoft sells a cool Wireless Optical Desktop kit (www.microsoft.com/hardware/keyboard/wodbt_info.asp) for about $160 that includes not only a Bluetooth adapter but also a Bluetooth wireless keyboard and mouse.

✔ **Bluetooth-enabled devices:** You also need Bluetooth in the devices you want to connect wirelessly to your MCE PC. As Bluetooth becomes more popular, you'll be able to find it built into almost every accessory or peripheral device for your MCE PC. As this time, Bluetooth-enabled keyboards, mice, printers, digital cameras, cell phones, handheld computers (PocketPC or Palm), and even video cameras are available.

You *can* buy wireless keyboards and mice that don't use Bluetooth. These systems have their own proprietary radio systems. We've used these over the years, and we've loved them. But if we were buying a new wireless keyboard and mouse system today, we'd probably spend a little bit more and get a Bluetooth system. Although the proprietary systems work well, they're limited — you can't use the same system for other devices. Bluetooth lets you use a single adapter to connect *any* Bluetooth device to your MCE PC. So you could, for example, carry your Bluetooth keyboard from PC to PC if you needed to.

Enjoying the Great Outdoors

Ever go to the drive-in movies when you were a kid? Fun, wasn't it? Well, drive-ins have pretty much gone the way of the dodo, but with a few (relatively) inexpensive pieces and parts, you can create your own outdoor theater.

Danny has created an outdoor home-theatre-in-a-box solution that is easy to set up and has a high "fun quotient." Here's what he came up with:

✔ **A projector:** Unless you're going to bring a direct-view, big-screen TV outside (we think you shouldn't do this), you'll want to use a front-projection video system for your outdoor theater. An LCD or DLP projector (see Chapter 4 for details) works best outdoors, because it can put out brighter pictures than CRT projectors. Danny recommends InFocus SP-4800 ($1300, www.infocus.com) in both indoor and outdoor theaters — it's portable and easy to set up quickly in both environments. The screen quality and features are great. And the price point is about the lowest you can get for such a high-quality device.

✔ **An outdoor screen:** The screen you use for your projector indoors is too expensive, too fragile, and probably too small for an outdoor theater. You don't need to get too fancy (or spend too much money) here — white sheets sewn into a frame work well. If you want something more permanent, consider using professionally-mounted, white, vinyl tarps. Danny got a great 10-foot-by-20-foot white tarp for $25, complete with grommets and wonderful bungee cords, from www.partytentcity.com. That's about the size of the movie screen you see in many multiplex theaters! WAAAAAY cool.

If you have problems with wrinkles, consider ironing the vinyl tarp. Place a cloth sheet over the plastic, and iron on low heat. Be careful so you don't melt the plastic.

✔ **An outdoor frame:** You need to mount the screen to something. Danny called www.partytentcity.com and asked them to create a special, outdoor-home-theater product based on the same principles of a party tent — lots of strong rods bundled together with special joints. The result: An outdoor home-theater framing system that you can put up anywhere. Check out www.smarthomesbook.com/outdoor.shtml for details. With shipping, the joints should run around $200. You can get the rods (1-inch EMT pipe) at any Home Depot or Lowe's for about $100.

An early evening dew on a humid night can coat everything with a serious amount of moisture. Keep a regular bed sheet over your electronics until you're ready to use them.

The next part of the equation — audio and video signals to power the stuff in the preceding list — is more difficult because it depends on your situation, equipment, and desires.

A big part of your home-theater equation will be about sound. Unless you're into silent movies, you'll want at least full 5.1 surround-sound capability, presuming your source content (DVD, video) can accommodate that.

Hooking up your audio to your PC will entail some tradeoffs. Before you start connecting everything, you must decide what to use as a source device. You can get audio and video signals from a source file and into your outdoor home theater in a number of ways:

✔ **Run cables from your MCE PC:** You can run a fairly long set of cables out to your outdoor home theater to power your content in the system. (You can also disconnect your system from your TV and locate it right near the outdoor theater, too.)

If you're using cables from your MCE PC, InFocus can connect to your MCE through the S-Video port or through the VGA monitor cables. We found that the VGA monitor cables were the better way to go because the quality of Danny's screen-resolution driver is better than that of the S-video driver in his laptop. Danny bought three 10-foot VGA "extension cords" from Radio Shack (www.radioshack.com) so that he could place the InFocus 4800 30 feet away. This distance produces a 10-foot-by-20-foot image on the screen. Danny also got 100-foot long speaker cables (be sure to get 12 or 14 gauge for that long a distance) for the rear speakers in the system. (More on speakers in a second.)

✔ **Run cables from a portable (laptop) PC:** If you bought a desktop PC for your MCE, you might want to create a DVD (as shown in Chapter 12), and play it on a laptop. This approach can be easier than reinstalling all the cables on the MCE when you're finished using it for an outdoor theater. (In fact, Danny is craving a Toshiba MCE laptop with multiple docking stations for that reason!)

You need a Windows XP computer (with all the latest Windows XP service packs installed) to play your MCE PC's special DVR-MS recorded TV files. Emerging programs will convert MCE-based DVR-MS files to MPEG2 and other formats, so you might try one of those to make your saved movies portable from one machine to another. Also, some material may be encoded so that you can't play it on other PCs (to prevent file sharing) — this is rare, but it can happen.

✔ **Transmit content wirelessly:** You can send the signal from your PC to your projector and speakers with wireless options. Most of these systems are based on two main approaches. The first is a wireless bridge with an Ethernet or USB connection in one transmitting device and RCA plugs in the other receiving device. You plug your speakers and projector into this receiving device. The second approach is to use wireless speakers. If you don't want to bring your nice surround-sound speakers outdoors, consider buying inexpensive wireless speakers designed for portable use. (Radio Shack sells some good wireless outdoor speakers for about $200.) If you want to get fancy, install permanent outdoor speakers, like those from Stereostone (www.stereostone.com, starting at $300 a pair). These speakers look like rocks in your garden — and they rock in the musical sense, too. Video cue: Pink Floyd's *Dark Side of the Moon* DVD!

Some high-quality wireless bridges are flooding the market as we write. Most of this gear transmits signals using proprietary signaling — not Bluetooth or 802.11. As a result, the signals are mostly point-to-point. Some 802.11b products coming on the market enable any compatible device in range to pick up the signals, making your entertainment center more accessible by lots of devices, from your PC to the audio server in a car. Get an 802.11-based product if you have the choice.

Following are some places to look for these wireless units:

- The RCA Model RD 900W Lyra Wireless (www.rca.com, $99) device plugs into your PC's USB jack on one end and the entertainment center's RCA jacks on the other. Unfortunately, as of this printing, the Lyra uses 900-MHz technology, not standardized 802.11 chips.

- Jensen's Matrix Internet Audio Transmitter (www.jensen.com) Model JW901 works the same way: a 900-MHz connection between the PC and stereo.

- X10's Entertainment Anywhere (www.x10.com) uses a proprietary 2.4-MHz signal.

- Linksys's (www.linksys.com; $199) Wireless Digital Media Adapter is an 802.11b-based transmitter. Instead of connecting to an Ethernet port like a normal AP, the device is equipped with audio/video connectors.

- SMC Networks' (www.smc.com, $210) EZ-Stream line of home-entertainment networking products includes a Universal Wireless Multimedia Receiver, the SMCWMR-AG, which can wirelessly distribute entertainment media — audio, pictures, and streaming video — throughout the home.

Now, you may think that an outdoor theater is a bit much. But on a warm August night, nothing's better than sitting outside with your family watching your favorite movies. It's well worth the effort. Check out our site at www.smarthomesbook.com for additional information.

For more detail on hooking up your home theater and ensuring you have sur-round sound enabled in your system, check out our *Home Theater For Dummies* (published by Wiley Publishing, Inc.).

Making Movies

The MCE is a great tool for watching movies. You can play DVDs, TV movies, downloaded movies, and more. But you can do more than just watch movies on an MCE PC: You can make them, too.

You need two MCE PC accessories to create your own movies on your MCE PC:

- ✔ A digital video camera for filming your new artistic creations
- ✔ A DVD recorder to turn those films into DVDs that you and your friends and family can watch

Being a film auteur

You can use one of the newer digital video cameras (using the Digital8 and MiniDVD formats) and feed video into your MCE PC for editing and display. These digital cameras have a higher *resolution* (meaning sharper pictures) than analog video cameras, and connect directly to your MCE PC using the IEEE 1394 or FireWire port (discussed in Chapter 2).

Build your own drive-in

Sadly, one of the cultural icons of the twentieth century is disappearing from our roadsides: the drive-in theater. You can do your bit for americana by building your own drive-in — it's not hard at all. If you live some place where the houses are pretty much jammed together, you might not be able to even fathom a home drive-in. If you have some land, however, it is *really* cool.

Your gear for the outdoor theater works well, but you need one more item: an FM transmitter to broadcast the sound to all the cars. A range of low-cost ($60–$250) FM transmitter devices rebroadcast audio from portable CD players, portable cassette players, or computer audio to an unoccupied channel on the FM broadcast band. The range of the units varies from 50 feet to ¼ mile, so check the fine print.

Most of these units use a stereo miniplug connection between the external sound source and the FM transmitting unit. To decide which FM frequency to use, you must find an unoccupied FM frequency by listening to the FM channels at your location. You then tune the FM transmitter to an unused channel from 88 to 108 MHz, and start transmitting.

Warning: Causing interference to existing FM broadcasts is prohibited by FCC Part 15 regulations, so be sure to choose that spare channel carefully. As long as you use the FM transmitter unit in accordance with manufacturer instructions, you'll be in compliance with FCC Part 15 rules and regulations.

We like the FM25B unit from Ramsey Electronics (www.ramseyelectronics.com). It has great range, great performance, and a reasonable price ($270). It connects directly to the line output from your CD player/changer or to one of the tape-out connections on your receiver. Simple as that.

You're not going to get surround sound out of one of these FM transmitters — just like you don't get it at a real drive-in.

 If you're buying your first video camera or need to upgrade, go for one of the digital camcorder models that use the FireWire connection. You'll be able to download movies to your MCE PC more easily and faster, and the picture is far better.

Burn baby, burn!

Many MCE PCs come with a built-in DVD recorder, or burner. If your MCE PC does, you're in luck! Edit your movies in Windows Movie Maker (discussed in Chapter 13) or your favorite movie-editing program, and you'll have a professional-looking DVD to send to grandma.

If your MCE PC didn't come with a built-in DVD recorder, you'll have to go to your favorite electronics store and buy one. Unfortunately, the manufacturers of DVD recorders haven't agreed on a standard for recordable DVD formats, so you can't play any home-recorded DVD in any DVD player. (We know this is just plain stupid, but we aren't in charge of the DVD industry.) The three DVD recording formats on the market are

- ✔ DVD-R/RW
- ✔ DVD-RAM
- ✔ DVD+R/RW

When you see R/RW in an optical format (such as DVD-R/RW or CD-R/RW), you're actually seeing two related formats. The *R,* or recordable, format refers to optical discs that can be recorded once — record your data on the disc, and it's there permanently. *RW,* or rewritable, discs can be recorded multiple times. DVD-R/RW systems are considered the most compatible with existing DVD players. (However, even with DVD-R/RW, some DVD players won't be able to play your homemade DVDs.) The DVD-RAM format is the least compatible. DVD+R/RW is somewhere in the middle — slightly less compatible with standard DVD players than DVD-R/RW but more compatible than DVD-RAM.

Expect to pay between $3 and $8 for a blank, recordable DVD disc.

You'll always get the best results if you use high-quality, brand-name blank DVD discs in your recorder (from companies such as Verbatim). Whatever you do, make sure that the blank disc you're using, the burner you have installed, and the system you're running are tested for the speed you want to burn at. For example, if you have a 4x DVD burner, make sure the blank disc you use has been tested at that speed (check the label).

Gaming Galore

Although few games are currently available for the MCE PC, its fast processor, copious memory, and kick-butt video card make it an excellent PC gaming platform. (See Chapter 18 for some prognosticating about the future direction of MCE and gaming.)

Hook up an MCE PC to a fast Internet connection, load the latest and greatest RPG (role-playing game), and you'll be blowing away your friends in record time. But to play games well, you need something better than a plain old mouse and keyboard. Luckily, MCE PCs are loaded with USB ports, which you can use to connect a variety of joysticks and controllers that make game playing more fun.

You can buy a controller that replicates a WRC rally car steering wheel and controls, or a controller that gives you the stick on an F-14 (turn and burn!). You can also buy specialized controllers for specific games. (We've even seen game controllers that include a pad that you put on the floor so you can dance along with a game.) If you're a gamer, go to www.gamespot.com and check out the reviews.

Beefing Up Your Infrastructure

Our final set of accessories aren't as sexy as the ones we've mentioned so far — nor are they as far out there as an outdoor home theater (which really is pretty cool, trust us). In this section, we talk about the underpinnings, or infrastructure, of your MCE system. Except for us geeks, most people don't find this exciting.

Suppose that you just spent a lot of money on some fancy new W speed-rated high-performance tires. You're anticipating the fun and exciting driving you'll soon be experiencing. However, those tires won't do you much good if the road (the infrastructure) is a wreck. So too with your MCE PC. It's exciting and fun, but it won't perform the way you want if it doesn't have a solid infrastructure.

Here's our infrastructure road map for your MCE PC:

✔ **Clean power:** Electrical power is ugly. Between lightning bolts, bad drivers hitting electrical poles, and a thousand air conditioners being turned on at once during the heat of summer, the nice clean electrical sine waves that leave the power plant are not so nice and clean when they get to your home. Surges occur when the voltage drops and then rises beyond normal limits. During a surge, electronic devices get zapped. So buy a good surge suppressor and use it. Keep your MCE safe, sound, and protected. You can't go wrong with any of the power protection from www.monstercable.com.

✔ **Staying power:** Beyond cleaning up your power supply with a surge suppressor, you might consider keeping your power on, even when the lights go out. Pat's from Southern California, where brownouts and the infamous "rolling blackout" have become a fact of summertime life. A *UPS* (uninterruptible power supply) is just the ticket. These devices go between your MCE PC and the wall outlet and have a built-in battery that can keep your MCE PC running throughout a short blackout or at least give you enough time to save open files and shut down properly.

Most types of UPS include a built-in surge suppressor. Check out www.apc.com for some solid power supplies.

✔ **Fatter pipes:** No, we're not talking about a plumbing upgrade here. Instead, we're talking about your pipe to the Internet. We feel that broadband (if you can get it) is a must with an MCE PC, especially if you want to play online video and movies. As more and more content for your MCE PC becomes available on the Internet, you'll find that much of it is accessible only to broadband users. So, if you can, consider moving up to DSL or cable modem service. If you have DSL or cable, but only the lowest-priced (slowest) service, consider bumping up to a faster speed.

Chapter 18

Ten Future Features of Media Center PCs

*W*e think Windows XP MCE is plain cool. We use it all the time. Even our kids are hooked. But there's always room for improvement, and we can always find something to wish for.

Over the next couple of years, we expect Microsoft to improve the MCE platform to further refine its role as a centralized server of all content in the home. Media Center PCs will be able to wirelessly connect to more parts of the home and draw in more content from remote sources. Future versions of Media Center will allow you to do more things at once, such as watch one TV show while recording another, and provide access to more applications and media types. It will get slimmer, sleeker, and more powerful — sort of like Demi Moore in *Charlie's Angels*.

Wireless Connectivity between TVs and Other Devices

As we discussed in Chapter 16, your Windows XP MCE PC is a great thing, but why bottle it up in one corner of the house with one TV set? Why not share the wealth? The most logical improvement in MCE is the expansion of its domain in the home using wireless technologies to get from room to room, TV to TV.

A Media Center TV *client* could distribute all the great digital media experiences and the simple user interface of a Microsoft Windows XP MCE PC to any room in the house that has a display. You could listen to music, record TV programs, or watch photo slide shows on a television or PC display in the living room, even if your Media Center PC was in the bedroom.

An MCE TV client would be a hardware device (not just software), most likely driven by 802.11a, 54-Mbps wireless technology. The goal would be to extend the MCE experience to other places, through a device that could decode content and decrypt the user interface on another TV or set of speakers located elsewhere in the house. So you'd see the same interface on every TV and hear the sound as if you were using the TV located with the MCE PC device.

What's required to do create this MCE TV client? You'd need network access and a powerful graphics chip. You'd need an OS designed for non-PC hardware, such as Windows CE. This means the MCE TV client is likely to be a small box about the size of a paperback book — something that can fit unobtrusively in your living room.

Multituners

If you want to drive multiple TVs in the home, you have to be able to tune into more than one show simultaneously. That means your PC must support multiple TV tuner cards (multituners), each capable of outputting a different channel. This gives you the ability to watch different shows on different TVs, or to record one show while watching another.

This way, Mom and Dad could watch *Alias* on the TV upstairs, while the kids watch *Star Trek* downstairs — driven by one MCE PC. It would also enable you to watch something else on TV while you're recording a favorite movie.

Today, you're limited to one stream, one tuner, one movie. Argh. You can, however, watch a recorded show while Media Center is recording another show. This requires the use of a single live TV stream, because the show you've recorded is stored on disc.

Although you can add additional tuners to your MCE PC now, it's not clear how multiple tuners will work with MCE. People who have tried to use more than one TV tuner card have reported only limited success. It's best to wait for Microsoft to fully support multituners on your MCE PC, we think.

Support for Remote Content and Servers

One of the problems with the current version of MCE is that it's almost totally focused on local content. (The exception is Online Spotlight, which extends the MCE experience to a Web page on the Internet for content providers who partner with Microsoft.) Windows XP MCE is designed to work with content stored on local hard drives. If your CDs are stored on a CD server or your videos are stored on a video server, why should you have to copy them to the MCE PC if you have a decent home network in place? (You can use your network for some parts of Media Center today, but it's not as easy or intuitive as it should be.) Why not support better software pointers around your home network, enabling you to create a whole-home storage array?

Microsoft has announced a plan to develop Content Directory Services (CDS), which is a fancy name for a home server that will enable hardware manufacturers to easily develop devices that are better at storing and playing PC media files over home networks. The concept is based on the Universal Plug and Play (UPnP) Forum A/V Working Group (www.upnp.org) specifications, which call for different devices to be able to access user-specified music, picture, and video files anywhere on a local network. The Content Directory Service will allow compatible devices to access both the files and the metadata (such as the name of a song or an album cover picture) associated with this media. This means you could have non-MCE-driven electronic devices in your house that store media files, and those files could be accessed by other compatible hardware devices, such as your MCE PC.

Suppose you have a wireless-enabled picture frame (an LCD display that looks like a regular picture frame but displays digital pictures) that's storing a hundred pictures of your kids. Why duplicate those pictures on the MCE just to display them in My Pictures on your TV, too? Under this new initiative, you wouldn't have to duplicate the content — you could point to those pictures, and your MCE would "see" them just as if they were on your MCE hard drive.

What effect does CDS have on today's MCE owners? You'll be able to buy networked media devices and integrate them into your home network without having to upgrade the hardware, install additional software, or follow complicated setup instructions. (Your system would have to support network connectivity, presumably wireless connectivity, to take advantage of this new OS service.) As you add CDS-supporting devices in your house, they'd appear on the network, and future versions of MCE would be able to find and catalog their content.

Better Support for Network Content

Online Spotlight was just taking off when we wrote this book. Online Spotlight allows third-party content (and Web pages) to be accessible from the MCE interface. This will become really cool when you can do things such as true interactive TV. Imagine watching the Discovery channel on your MCE PC, and when the little "for more information" text box pops up on the screen, just having to click it to go to the Discovery channel Web site. Well, in the future, we think Media Center will have that kind of seamless integration with network content.

Right now, MCE is local-disk-drive-centric. Opening Media Center up to the Internet just makes sense.

Better Support for Gaming

Something conspicuous is missing from the menu of your Media Center Edition software: My Xbox — or at least My Games. Well, what's really missing is support for any types of computer gaming platforms or PC games.

Microsoft is already moving towards better game support with Media Center. Some MCE PC vendors install two cool games integrated into the 2004 version of Media Center. You can play these games on your big screen, using your remote control.

Millions of Xbox, Nintendo, Sony, and other gaming devices are connected directly to the TV set (like your MCE PC). Those users also have wired and wireless devices to control the action on the screen (like your MCE PC). And many people are using leading-edge, plasma-screen displays or other sophisticated displays for viewing (like possibly your MCE PC).

And that's just the gaming platform (such as Xbox) market. What about the PC gaming market? Kids have tons of PC games. How will these fit into the MCE architecture?

We think a good model for the future is to look at what's on the market today. Danny uses a program called Virtual CD (`www.virtualcd-online.com/default_e.htm`) to put a semblance of organization into four kids fighting over gaming discs. Virtual CD allows Danny to load each PC game onto the gaming server connected to his home network. The server makes a copy of the game CD, and when the kids want to play the game, they double-click a shortcut on their machine, and the game starts playing over the home network. The game can be accessed from any PC on the network, and the original discs sit in a box in the attic.

We think this game server concept fits well into an MCE and home-server environment, where the point is to serve up and control access to copyrighted content.

We also think that Microsoft's Xbox gaming console system will probably become more tightly integrated into a home network with the MCE PC. The Xbox is just a powerful PC specially configured and optimized for gaming. The connection between the MCE PC and the Xbox would be a marriage made in heaven — the Xbox is capable of dealing with digital music and video stored on the MCE PC, and every Xbox is ready to connect to an Ethernet network and the Internet.

Totally off-topic: Want to read a good book about why and how the Xbox came about? Check out Dean Takahashi's *Opening the Xbox: Inside Microsoft's Plan to Unleash an Entertainment Revolution* (published by Prima Lifestyles).

Better Video — HDTV Support, Too!

The current generation of MCE PCs are great for watching video on computer monitors (such as the LCD monitors that come standard with many MCE PCs), regular analog TVs (traditional TVs, in other words) and digital TV monitors (such as plasma and front-projection TVs). But, unfortunately, MCE PCs can't display true HDTV.

HDTV, or *high-definition television,* is the new generation of television signals that that use digital *encoding* (a technique in which video is transformed from analog pictures into a electronic signal) and digital *transmission* (where the television signal is sent over the airwaves, or through a cable system) to provide a more detailed picture on your display.

HDTV video is distinguished from conventional video primarily by its *resolution,* or number of distinct points that make up a video image. HDTV pictures using the 720p system consist of 720 distinct lines. (The 1080i system uses 1080 lines.) Each line contains hundreds of individual points, or *pixels*, like the display on your MCE PC's computer monitor. By comparison, regular analog TV (also called *NTSC*) and even high-quality DVD video contains a maximum of only 480 lines of resolution.

Because of the limitations of both software and hardware, MCE PCs can handle only 480-line resolution for displaying TV, recording TV video, and playing DVDs. So even if you have a fancy, megabuck HDTV television set hooked up to your MCE PC, you won't get real HDTV.

Most HDTVs use a technique called *upsampling* to display lower-resolution 480-line content on their high-resolutions screens. Special computer chips inside the HDTV guess what the video picture would look like if it had 720 or 1080 lines of resolution. This approach usually improves your picture, but it's *not* HDTV.

In future versions of MCE (and in future MCE PCs), we expect that Microsoft and its vendor partners will jump aboard the HDTV bandwagon by adding software, TV tuner cards, and other hardware that will allow you to receive, record, and watch HDTV through your MCE PC. The hardware that can handle HDTV on the PC is already available (for example, many high-end video-graphics cards already handle HDTV) and Microsoft already has versions of HDTV working internally, so it's only a matter of time before MCE PCs can be full-fledged members of an HDTV system.

Better Audio

For listening to audio CDs and computer audio files (such as Windows Media and MP3 files), MCE PC is about as good as it gets, unless your budget stretches to high-end audio equipment costing thousands of dollars. And because the MCE can handle digital surround formats, it's also great for playing the audio tracks that accompany DVD movies.

But the MCE PC isn't perfect — yet. It should have the following audio features:

- **5.1 surround sound for TV:** MCE doesn't support surround sound for television programming that you watch and record — even though digital cable and satellite TV systems are beginning to support digital surround-sound formats. (MCE does supports surround sound with DVD movies.) We think Microsoft will add this functionality soon.

✔ **Support for new high-resolution music discs:** The audio world has seen the arrival of two new *optical* music formats that use optical discs such as CDs and DVDs. The formats, known as SACD (Super Audio CD) and DVD-Audio (or DVD-A), use higher bit rates, or sampling frequencies, or both to provide better-sounding audio. (Check out Chapter 9 for more on bit rates and sampling.) Today's MCE PCs can't handle these new optical discs, but we think future versions of MCE PC will, as audio cards and optical disc drives mature.

Microsoft and Intel are cooking up some new audio system specifications in their labs that we think will help support for these high-end audio systems and bring even better audio support to MCE. Universal Audio Architecture (UAA) is a Microsoft-led initiative that will provide built-in drivers on Windows-based PCs to raise the bar in PC audio quality. With UAA, Microsoft plans to deliver a new set of Windows audio drivers for USB, IEEE 1394, and Azalia, the code name for Intel Corp.'s next-generation, PC-audio specification.

Support for Portable Devices

Portable devices present hardware designers with a tough line to walk between maximum functionality and maximum portability. The last five years have seen incredible miniaturization of devices — portable video players are now the size of a deck of cards.

But portable devices have only recently started getting the attention they deserve from the designers of the operating systems that reign over the content to be transferred to the device. Microsoft is working hard to open up its media systems and ease the flow of media to these portable devices. One approach to this improved portability of content depends on Microsoft's Media Transport Protocol (MTP), which improves the transfer and management of digital media between the PC and portable media players.

MTP enables devices to synchronize and manage playlists, and helps the MCE PC figure out what kind of content goes on what device. Devices that use MTP as their connection protocol can be installed on the home network without additional software.

MTP is not the only approach that Microsoft is taking for portable media content. For example, Microsoft has said it will continue to work on specific, optimized transport protocols with individual vendors. Microsoft and Matsushita Electric Industrial Co. Ltd. (Panasonic) have demonstrated their High-Performance Media Access Technology (HighMAT), which improves interoperability for digital-media content between PCs and popular electronic devices, such as CD players, car stereos, and DVD devices. HighMAT also dramatically improves startup times for devices by providing a consistent, easily-navigated method of storing, arranging, and playing back digital photo, music, and video collections on recordable discs such as CD-RW and DVD media.

If you want to create a digital media collection on CDs or other physical formats today, you'd discover that CD and DVD players read this data in different ways. Each device has a different interface for finding media and viewable information such as playlists, music metadata (the who, what, where information about songs and artists), and folders containing photos and videos. This can make finding content confusing. In addition, with large collections of music and videos, it can sometimes take several minutes for the DVD or CD player to "read" what music or video is available.

HighMAT solves these problems by creating a standard way for PCs to structure digital media on physical formats and for consumer devices to read those discs. This approach will make startup times for data CDs and other physical formats faster and give consumers a consistent, easy navigation experience across a broad range of consumer electronic devices — especially the portable devices that consumers crave.

Cooler Cases

We often joke about how everything should come in a black matte finish to match our stereo systems. But with MCE, it's not a joke. MCE, and Windows-CE based variants, are moving in next to your stereo and TV.

Right now the Media Center PC typically uses a standard tower-style desktop computer — a big box that looks just right in the office but not so good in the living room or home theater. A few vendors have begun selling MCE PCs that come in cool *form factors* (case designs) that look like pieces of stereo equipment.

We think that Media Center will move further down this road over time. More and more Media Center PCs will look not like a PC but instead more like a DVD player or TV set-top box. We also think that there will be MCE PCs designed for particular purposes or locations, such as home-theater MCE PCs and bedroom MCE PCs.

We also expect that the MCE PC will become more socially acceptable in the living room by staying out of that room entirely. With new generations of wireless devices that provide an extension of the Media Center interface (and content) on your TV screen, you can leave the big tower PC hidden away and still get the Media Center experience in your living room.

Remotes with a Power Button!

As Pat says, "Danny won't let this one go!" Danny is peeved that he has to retain his DirecTV remote just to turn his MCE-driven TV on and off. The MCE reference design for its MCE remote control doesn't include a universal remote functionality that can control *all* your other electronic gear.

Universal remote controls are generic remote controls that you configure to match your particular brands of remote-control-driven devices. We discuss a number of universal remote controls in Chapter 17. But these are third-party remotes, not Microsoft remotes.

Microsoft, in its quest to simplify the 10-foot experience (the experience of the user 10 feet away from the PC), will enhance the design of the remote control so that it can control all the new features being added to Media Center PCs. And any of the high-end, home-theater remote-control companies could create a killer MCE remote, if they wanted to. The remote will also be upgraded to control MCE-accessible devices and other Microsoft products in the home. It makes sense that more functional remote controls have to come down the road soon.

Does this mean that the remote will get a lot more complex? No, but we do expect that you'll see some additional buttons. And one of those buttons had better be one that Danny can press to turn off his TV set!

Chapter 19

Ten Great Places to Visit with Your Media Center PC

*Y*our MCE PC is all set up, everything is working great, you've tested the functions, and now you're ready to take it for a spin on the Internet. The only question is, "Where to go?"

In this chapter, we put together our top-ten sites to go to with your newly christened MCE PC to really put it through its paces. We describe each site briefly, but seeing and hearing is believing.

The easiest (and best) way to get to online content from *within* the Media Center interface is to select Online Spotlight from the Media Center Start menu. Online Spotlight provides the Media Center 10-foot interface, and lets you surf to specially configured music, video, game, and software download sites from within Media Center, using only your remote control.

Microsoft Windows XP Media Center Edition Home Page

We find out something new each time we visit the Media Center Edition home page, which is at the following address:

```
www.microsoft.com/windowsxp/mediacenter/default.asp
```

Microsoft does a great job of consolidating a lot of information into one place and keeping it fresh and up-to-date each time you go there. You can find the latest news and software reviews, as well as tips for doing cool stuff with your MCE PC.

In the Expert Zone, you can join chats with Microsoft product management about its programs. (Here's your chance to ask why the MCE remote doesn't have a Power button for your TV!)

Of particular significance is the Windows XP MCE newsgroup, where people log in to answer questions about installation and operations issues. The newsgroup is accessible at the following:

```
http://communities.microsoft.com/Newsgroups/default.asp?ICP=
        windowsxp&sLCID=US&newsgroup=microsoft.public.
        windows.mediacenter
```

This is the place to post your "Help!" questions when you're desperate for a solution.

You can also use your MCE PC's Outlook Express e-mail program to view and post to this newsgroup. Follow the instructions at the following URL to set this up in Outlook Express:

```
http://www.microsoft.com/windowsxp/expertzone/newsgroups/
        setup.asp
```

Media Center FAQ Sites

We've found not just one but several useful FAQ (frequently asked question) sites to recommend, all under the same topic — solving problems in your Media Center PC. Microsoft and some of the more established Media Center PC manufacturers provide tips about your Media Center PC. Here are the present FAQ sites for the Media Center PCs and operating system:

- **Microsoft:** www.microsoft.com/windowsxp/mediacenter/evaluation/faq.asp

- **Gateway:** www.gateway.com/dw/home/mediacenter_faq.shtml)

- **HP:** (h20015.www2.hp.com/en/document.jhtml?lc=en&docName=bph08021#P9_1037)

You can also find out a lot by reading user manuals from other manufacturers. For example, Pat helped Danny solve a question about his Viewsonic by looking up the way that Gateway handled it in its configuration. If you don't find the answer in this book nor in your PC maker's manual, check out these online sources of user guides for the Media Center PCs:

- **Cyberpower PC:** www.cyberpowersystem.com/wrv_oemMANUAL.DOC

- **Gateway:** support.gateway.com/support/manlib/Appliances/mediacenter.shtml

- **HP:** h20015.www2.hp.com/content/common/manuals/bph07860/bph07860.pdf

- **Northgate Innovations:** support.lan-plus.com/support/tech_notes/MediaCenter.asp

Web sites change a lot so if these URLs are not correct, check out www.smarthomesbook.com, where we keep a current listing of all these URLs.

Media Center Fan Sites

MCE users are MCE fans. Two great sites have Media Center-specific forums and help areas that can make your MCE experience even more exciting.

The Green Button (aptly named for the Windows MCE button on your MCE remote control) is found at www.thegreenbutton.com. This site focuses heavily on its message groups, where you can ask questions, review other people's dilemmas, and track down that one bit of information you were hoping you'd find somewhere. It also has a download area where you can find unsupported third-party software to supplement your MCE programming. And the news area is a good place for finding out what's happening in the realm of MCEs and for researching your MCE PC purchase.

Our favorite area is the Windows XP MCE Mother of All Wish Lists (MOAWL) Forum, where people vote on what they'd like to see in the next version of MCE:

```
thegreenbutton.infopop.cc/6/ubb.x?a=tpc&s=9476092391&f=465604
          2591&m=8246050043
```

Another great fan site is `www.xpmce.com`. This site, which was under development when we last visited it, has FAQs, download areas, forums, articles, and more.

Although third-party downloads are available on both The Green Button and XPMCE.com, third-party software is not directly supported by Microsoft. In addition, if a program you install causes problems with your MCE, your MCE PC vendor won't be too helpful because you might have a maligned version of the OS now. So, download these third-party programs at your own risk.

Yahoo! Music Videos

Yahoo! says it has the most videos on the Web at its Launch site (`launch.yahoo.com/`), and we don't doubt it. Pop, rock, electronic dance, R&B, you name it, there's something there for everyone. You can set up your own video station made up of all your favorite videos (plus the ones Yahoo! thinks you'll like), and play them on your TV display. You want your MTV? You got it.

From your Internet Explorer browser, go to `www.yahoo.com`, and click the Launch Music on Yahoo! link. You go directly to the Launch site.

If you click View Top 100 Videos, they begin playing automatically. When you watch a video, you can rate it; your highly-rated videos are what populates your video list in the Play My Video Station area. Your ratings also enable Yahoo! to match you up with other songs based on other people's similar ratings. This will be a big hit at parties, where you can not only play the music but watch it, too.

NetFlix

We're thrilled with the no-hassles NetFlix service. It's simple: NetFlix subscribers can rent as many DVDs as they want, with three (or more) movies out at a time. There are no due dates and no late fees. DVDs are delivered directly to the subscriber's address by first-class mail — with a postage-paid return envelope — from shipping centers throughout the United States. When you're finished watching a movie, just drop it in your mailbox (using that prepaid envelope), and when it arrives in NetFlix's mailbox, it sends you the next movie on your list (you maintain a queue of movies you want to rent on the NetFlix site).

Pricing is fixed, based on how many you want to rent a month and how many titles are out at a time:

✔ $13.95: Four DVDs a month, two titles out at a time

✔ $19.95: Unlimited DVDs, three titles out at a time

✔ $29.95: Unlimited DVDs, five titles out at a time

✔ $39.95: Unlimited DVDs, eight titles out at a time

NetFlix has more than 15,000 titles spanning 300 genres. Blockbuster and other rental chains are launching similar services, but we've found NetFlix to be the easiest.

MovieLink.com

Another way to watch movies is through a movies-on-demand service, which you might be familiar with if you have a cable or satellite hookup. A new kid in town is competing with the cable and satellite folks: a group of major Hollywood studios and their Movielink Web site (www.movielink.com).

We didn't get to see this in action before the book was printed, but we've been told that Movielink will be part of Online Spotlight — so you can access Movielink directly from the Media Center interface.

Movielink is an online movie download service that offers U.S. broadband customers a decent selection of feature films including new releases, classics, and foreign films. The service enables customers to rent movies for a limited time on a per-movie (versus subscription) basis and legally download them to their computer. Movielink generally offers new movies about 45 days after the DVD release date, at the same time as other video-on-demand services. You can view a trailer of any movie it has on the site for free, without downloading it.

After you download a movie from Movielink, you have 30 days to watch it — after 30 days it self-destructs in *Mission Impossible* fashion. When you start playing the movie, you have 24 hours in which to view it (and you can stop and start it anytime within that period). This is far better than the traditional pay-per-view on satellite channels. You can watch the movie as many times as you like within this 24-hour period. Prices ranges from $2.95 to $4.99 per movie.

You can download a free two-minute preview from the Web site. The first time you visit the site, you need to install Movielink Manager. Click Download Movie, follow the on-screen installation prompts, and the movie begins to download automatically. You can even pause and then resume the download if you want. An average download (not the preview) takes about 80 minutes over a broadband connection. The average downloaded movie takes up 500MB to 600MB on your PC.

To play the movie, simply double-click the Movielink Manager icon on your desktop and select the Play Movie tab.

At the end of the 24-hour viewing period or rental period (whichever comes first), Movielink deletes the file to restore your hard drive space, so you don't have to worry about doing it yourself. Movielink sends you an e-mail to remind you of your last day to download and watch each movie.

Although it takes more than an hour to download a movie, this is a great service. And an hour or so is not so bad, compared with the time it takes to go to the rental store and back. In addition, you have tons of choices online. So we say, "Two thumbs up!"

Shutterfly

In Chapter 11, we talk about getting pictures from your digital camera straight into your Media Center PC. We also talk about the various ways you can scan pictures and have your own slide show. Sometimes, however, you want someone else to do all the hard work for you. Shutterfly (www.shutterfly.com) is a Web-based photo service that expands the world of possibilities for you and your camera.

After you upload pictures from your digital camera to Shutterfly or send in your film to be developed by them, you can use Shutterfly's online photo editing tools to correct red eye, adjust the colors if they're a bit off, crop the picture to make sure your intended subject is the center of attention, and even attach fun creative borders to make it extra special for the one you love. It'll even bind a personal picture album for you. Now that's service!

Then, with the click of your mouse, you can order top-quality prints for yourself, friends, and family or share your online albums with anyone you choose.

Pricing is reasonable, but not as cheap as discount-store processing. But with Shutterfly, you're buying access to a range of services and flexibility.

When you put your pictures on the Shutterfly Web site, you can't download full-sized versions of them back onto your MCE PC. If you store your pictures only on Shutterfly and then want your own digital copies of the pictures, you'll have to order a CD from Shutterfly. So you should keep your original files on a Zip disk, CD-ROM, or other storage format as a backup unless you want to buy Shutterfly-supplied CDs.

Atom Films

What better way to break in your new Media Center PC than to check some content previously available only on PCs — and watch it on your TV set. Atom Films, which was bought by Shockwave, specializes in creating and buying all sorts of animated and live-action independent film shorts and making them available on its site. You can find it at

```
atomfilms.shockwave.com/af/home/
```

Under each section, you can find the top five shorts for that genre. Be sure to check out the comedy section. The most popular comedy when we visited was "What's Wrong With This Picture?" This live-action short of a 4-year-old boy and his purple crayon stickman is universally funny.

To view these on your Media-Center-powered TV, simply surf to the Web site and use your cursor to select the movies you want to watch. Windows Media Player will launch automatically, and you can sit back and enjoy the films. Visit this site — you'll be glad you did.

Galleries Galore

One of the nice developments in the growth of the Internet has been the degree to which artists all over the world have embraced the new distribution medium. We found a lot of galleries on the Web, including many that showcase traditional art, such as the Metropolitan Museum of Art, at www.metmuseum.org, and those that display new computer-generated and digital art, such as the International Digital Arts Awards site at www.digitalart.org. If you find something you like, you can contact the artist and see about getting a full-sized print for your home or office.

Another neat site to visit is the Fine Arts Museums of San Francisco Virtual Museum:

```
www.thinker.org/fam/about/imagebase/subpage.asp?subpagekey=76
```

You can create your own virtual gallery from the 82,000 images found in the museum's archives. Then have an opening and invite your friends to view your selections.

Kodak's Picture of the Day

You can find hundreds of other digital image sites. One of our favorites is the Kodak Picture of the Day site. You can see amateur pictures at their best, arranged in a neat matrix photoquilt:

```
picturespots.kodak.com/cgi-bin/potdQuiltAsCgi.pl?app=
              photoquilt
```

You can't help but smile when looking through these pictures. Now if they'd only make them into a slide show, we'd be even happier!

Appendix

Connecting Your MCE PC to Your Home-Entertainment System

S etting up your Media Center PC entails a fair amount of discussion of ports, cards, cables, amplifiers, connectors, and the like. But nothing beats a picture.

In this appendix, we provide drawings of potential MCE setup configurations. We show the most common entertainment gear — VCRs, cable and satellite set-top boxes, receivers, monitors, and speakers — and how you would run cables to and from this gear to your MCE PC, in different possible situations.

Your particular situation may be a combination of two diagrams. If so, follow the appropriate parts of each diagram to accomplish your goal of setting up your MCE PC so that it works perfectly.

When putting together a system, it's easy to make a mistake. So make sure you read the specific warnings and tips in Parts I and II pertaining to putting your system together.

We present seven likely scenarios here, each in increasing order of complexity. We start with just a TV set. Then we add a VCR, a set-top box (with different types of cable connections), and a stereo system (with two-channel and 5.1 surround-sound connections).

Each scenario is presented in a before-and-after view — on facing pages — so you can match your present situation as best as possible to the seven options, and then plot your best course for connecting your MCE PC.

Before

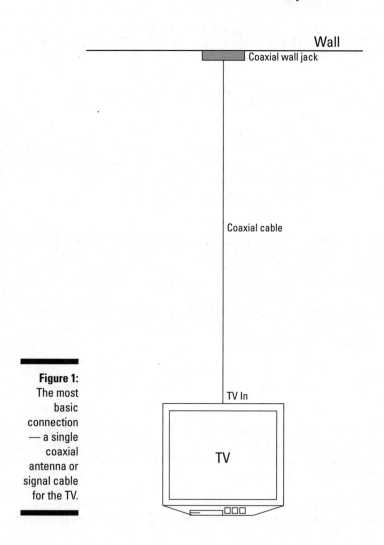

Figure 1:
The most
basic
connection
— a single
coaxial
antenna or
signal cable
for the TV.

After

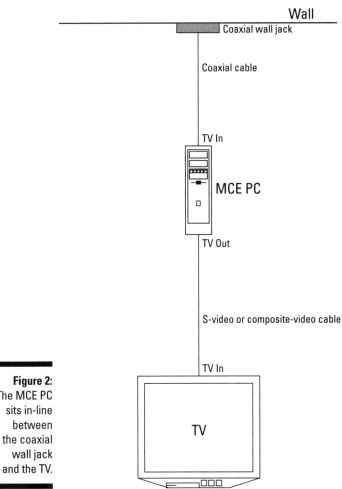

Wall

Coaxial wall jack

Coaxial cable

TV In

MCE PC

TV Out

S-video or composite-video cable

TV In

TV

Figure 2:
The MCE PC
sits in-line
between
the coaxial
wall jack
and the TV.

Before

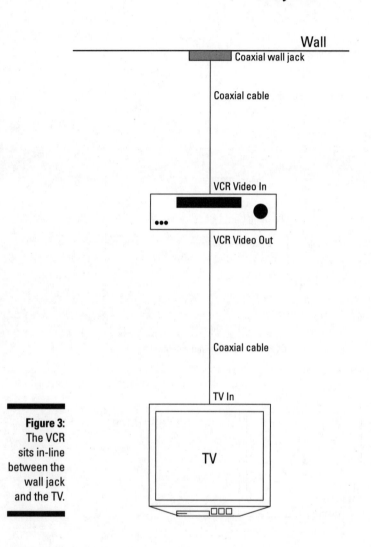

Wall

Coaxial wall jack

Coaxial cable

VCR Video In

VCR Video Out

Coaxial cable

TV In

TV

Figure 3:
The VCR
sits in-line
between the
wall jack
and the TV.

After

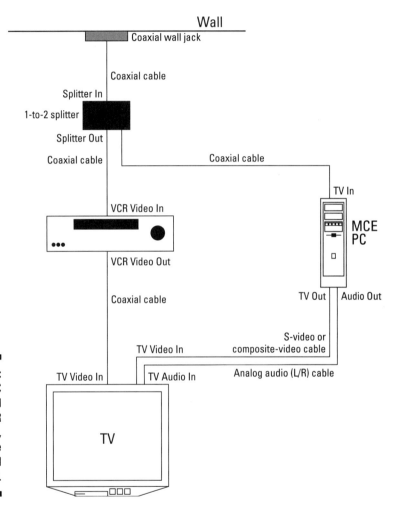

Figure 4:
The MCE PC
runs parallel
to the VCR
connection,
sharing the
inbound
signal.

Before

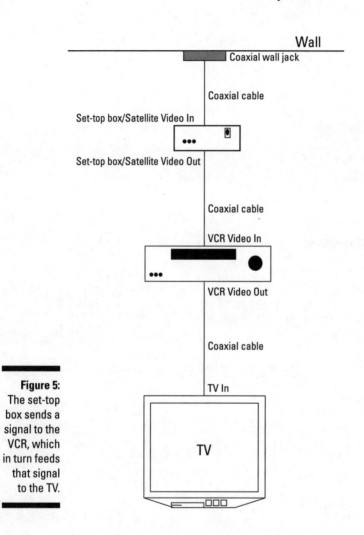

Wall

Coaxial wall jack

Coaxial cable

Set-top box/Satellite Video In

Set-top box/Satellite Video Out

Coaxial cable

VCR Video In

VCR Video Out

Coaxial cable

TV In

TV

Figure 5:
The set-top
box sends a
signal to the
VCR, which
in turn feeds
that signal
to the TV.

After

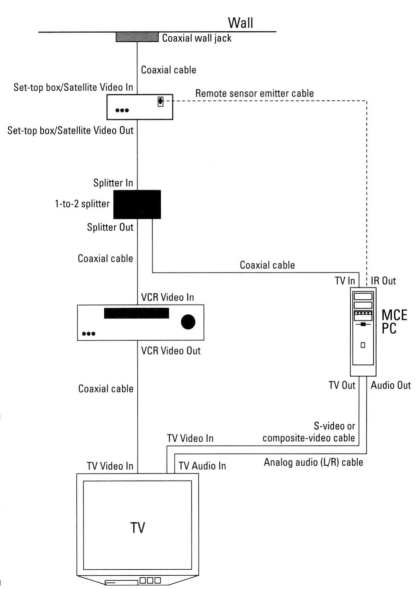

Wall

Coaxial wall jack

Coaxial cable

Set-top box/Satellite Video In

Remote sensor emitter cable

Set-top box/Satellite Video Out

Splitter In

1-to-2 splitter

Splitter Out

Coaxial cable

Coaxial cable

TV In   IR Out

VCR Video In

MCE PC

VCR Video Out

Coaxial cable

TV Out   Audio Out

S-video or composite-video cable

TV Video In

Analog audio (L/R) cable

TV Video In   TV Audio In

TV

Figure 6:
The MCE PC sits parallel to the VCR, with an IR emitter cable running to the set-top box.

Before

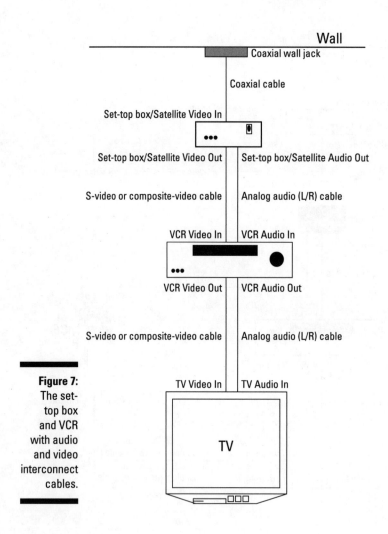

Wall

Coaxial wall jack

Coaxial cable

Set-top box/Satellite Video In

Set-top box/Satellite Video Out | Set-top box/Satellite Audio Out

S-video or composite-video cable | Analog audio (L/R) cable

VCR Video In | VCR Audio In

VCR Video Out | VCR Audio Out

S-video or composite-video cable | Analog audio (L/R) cable

TV Video In | TV Audio In

TV

Figure 7:
The set-
top box
and VCR
with audio
and video
interconnect
cables.

After

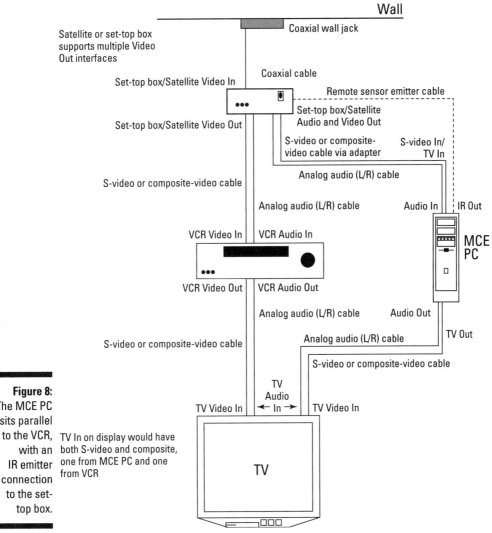

Figure 8:
The MCE PC sits parallel to the VCR, with an IR emitter connection to the set-top box.

Before

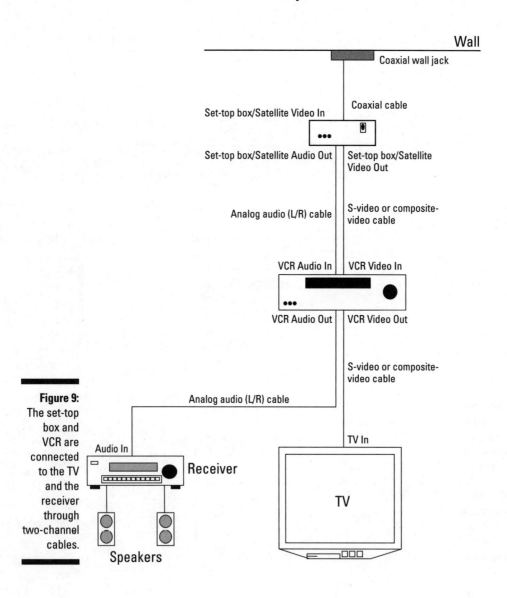

Wall

Coaxial wall jack

Coaxial cable

Set-top box/Satellite Video In

Set-top box/Satellite Audio Out | Set-top box/Satellite Video Out

Analog audio (L/R) cable | S-video or composite-video cable

VCR Audio In | VCR Video In

VCR Audio Out | VCR Video Out

S-video or composite-video cable

Analog audio (L/R) cable

TV In

Audio In

Receiver

Speakers

TV

Figure 9:
The set-top box and VCR are connected to the TV and the receiver through two-channel cables.

After

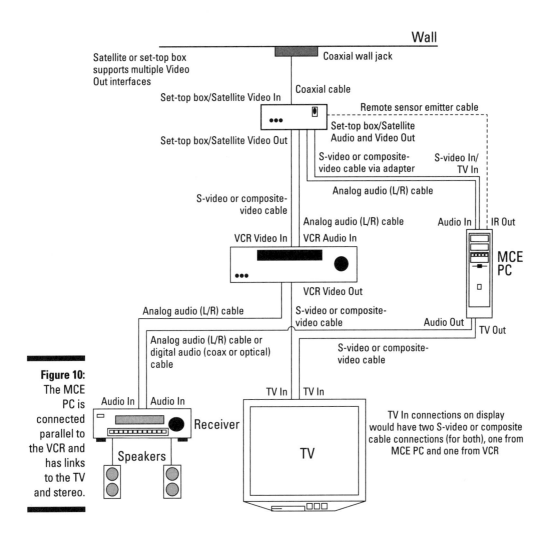

Wall

Satellite or set-top box
supports multiple Video
Out interfaces

Coaxial wall jack

Set-top box/Satellite Video In

Coaxial cable

Remote sensor emitter cable

Set-top box/Satellite
Audio and Video Out

Set-top box/Satellite Video Out

S-video or composite-
video cable via adapter

S-video In/
TV In

Analog audio (L/R) cable

S-video or composite-
video cable

Analog audio (L/R) cable

Audio In   IR Out

VCR Video In   VCR Audio In

MCE
PC

VCR Video Out

Analog audio (L/R) cable

S-video or composite-
video cable

Audio Out

TV Out

Analog audio (L/R) cable or
digital audio (coax or optical)
cable

S-video or composite-
video cable

Figure 10:
The MCE
PC is
connected
parallel to
the VCR and
has links
to the TV
and stereo.

Audio In   Audio In

TV In   TV In

Receiver

TV In connections on display
would have two S-video or composite
cable connections (for both), one from
MCE PC and one from VCR

Speakers

TV

Before

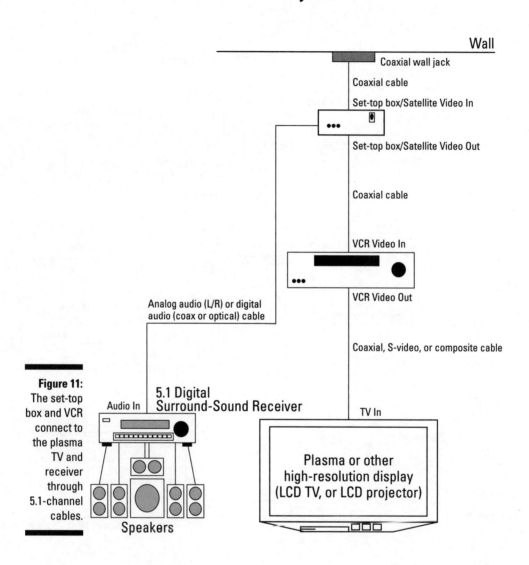

Figure 11: The set-top box and VCR connect to the plasma TV and receiver through 5.1-channel cables.

After

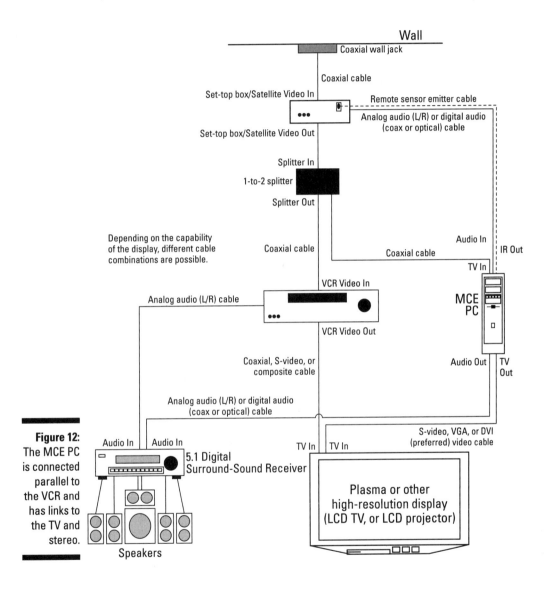

Wall

Coaxial wall jack

Coaxial cable

Set-top box/Satellite Video In

Remote sensor emitter cable

Analog audio (L/R) or digital audio
(coax or optical) cable

Set-top box/Satellite Video Out

Splitter In

1-to-2 splitter

Splitter Out

Depending on the capability
of the display, different cable
combinations are possible.

Coaxial cable

Coaxial cable

Audio In

IR Out

TV In

VCR Video In

MCE
PC

Analog audio (L/R) cable

VCR Video Out

Coaxial, S-video, or
composite cable

Audio Out   TV
              Out

Analog audio (L/R) or digital audio
(coax or optical) cable

S-video, VGA, or DVI
(preferred) video cable

Figure 12:
The MCE PC
is connected
parallel to
the VCR and
has links to
the TV and
stereo.

Audio In   Audio In

5.1 Digital
Surround-Sound Receiver

TV In   TV In

Plasma or other
high-resolution display
(LCD TV, or LCD projector)

Speakers

Before

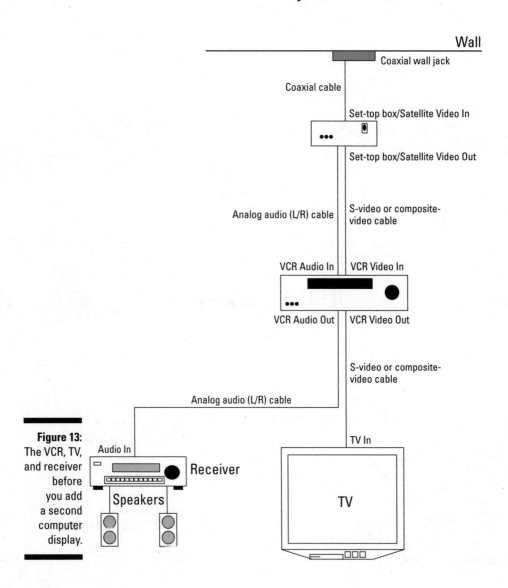

Wall

Coaxial wall jack

Coaxial cable

Set-top box/Satellite Video In

Set-top box/Satellite Video Out

Analog audio (L/R) cable   S-video or composite-video cable

VCR Audio In   VCR Video In

VCR Audio Out   VCR Video Out

S-video or composite-video cable

Analog audio (L/R) cable

Figure 13:
The VCR, TV,
and receiver
before
you add
a second
computer
display.

Audio In

Receiver

Speakers

TV In

TV

After

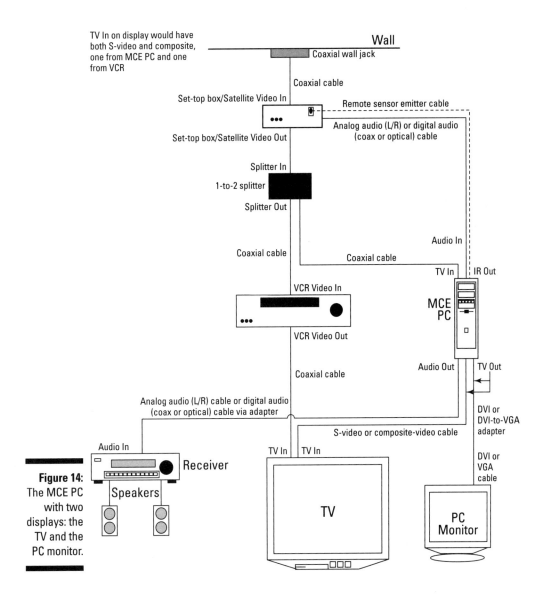

TV In on display would have both S-video and composite, one from MCE PC and one from VCR

Wall

Coaxial wall jack

Coaxial cable

Set-top box/Satellite Video In

Remote sensor emitter cable

Analog audio (L/R) or digital audio (coax or optical) cable

Set-top box/Satellite Video Out

Splitter In

1-to-2 splitter

Splitter Out

Audio In

Coaxial cable

Coaxial cable

TV In   IR Out

VCR Video In

MCE PC

VCR Video Out

Audio Out   TV Out

Coaxial cable

DVI or DVI-to-VGA adapter

Analog audio (L/R) cable or digital audio (coax or optical) cable via adapter

S-video or composite-video cable

Audio In

TV In   TV In

DVI or VGA cable

Receiver

Speakers

TV

PC Monitor

Figure 14: The MCE PC with two displays: the TV and the PC monitor.

Index

• G •

• H •

Notes

FOR DUMMIES®

The easy way to get more done and have more fun

PERSONAL FINANCE

0-7645-5231-7

0-7645-2431-3

0-7645-5331-3

Also available:

Estate Planning For Dummies
(0-7645-5501-4)

401(k)s For Dummies
(0-7645-5468-9)

Frugal Living For Dummies
(0-7645-5403-4)

Microsoft Money "X" For
Dummies
(0-7645-1689-2)

Mutual Funds For Dummies
(0-7645-5329-1)

Personal Bankruptcy For
Dummies
(0-7645-5498-0)

Quicken "X" For Dummies
(0-7645-1666-3)

Stock Investing For Dummies
(0-7645-5411-5)

Taxes For Dummies 2003
(0-7645-5475-1)

BUSINESS & CAREERS

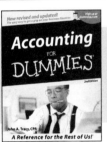

0-7645-5314-3

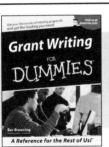

0-7645-5307-0

0-7645-5471-9

Also available:

Business Plans Kit For
Dummies
(0-7645-5365-8)

Consulting For Dummies
(0-7645-5034-9)

Cool Careers For Dummies
(0-7645-5345-3)

Human Resources Kit For
Dummies
(0-7645-5131-0)

Managing For Dummies
(1-5688-4858-7)

QuickBooks All-in-One Desk
Reference For Dummies
(0-7645-1963-8)

Selling For Dummies
(0-7645-5363-1)

Small Business Kit For
Dummies
(0-7645-5093-4)

Starting an eBay Business For
Dummies
(0-7645-1547-0)

HEALTH, SPORTS & FITNESS

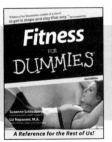

0-7645-5167-1

0-7645-5146-9

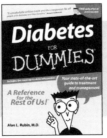

0-7645-5154-X

Also available:

Controlling Cholesterol For
Dummies
(0-7645-5440-9)

Dieting For Dummies
(0-7645-5126-4)

High Blood Pressure For
Dummies
(0-7645-5424-7)

Martial Arts For Dummies
(0-7645-5358-5)

Menopause For Dummies
(0-7645-5458-1)

Nutrition For Dummies
(0-7645-5180-9)

Power Yoga For Dummies
(0-7645-5342-9)

Thyroid For Dummies
(0-7645-5385-2)

Weight Training For Dummies
(0-7645-5168-X)

Yoga For Dummies
(0-7645-5117-5)

Available wherever books are sold.
Go to www.dummies.com or call 1-877-762-2974 to order direct.

FOR DUMMIES®

A world of resources to help you grow

HOME, GARDEN & HOBBIES

Feng Shui
0-7645-5295-3

Gardening
0-7645-5130-2

Guitar
0-7645-5106-X

Also available:

Auto Repair For Dummies
(0-7645-5089-6)

Chess For Dummies
(0-7645-5003-9)

Home Maintenance For
Dummies
(0-7645-5215-5)

Organizing For Dummies
(0-7645-5300-3)

Piano For Dummies
(0-7645-5105-1)

Poker For Dummies
(0-7645-5232-5)

Quilting For Dummies
(0-7645-5118-3)

Rock Guitar For Dummies
(0-7645-5356-9)

Roses For Dummies
(0-7645-5202-3)

Sewing For Dummies
(0-7645-5137-X)

FOOD & WINE

Cooking
0-7645-5250-3

Cookies
0-7645-5390-9

Wine
0-7645-5114-0

Also available:

Bartending For Dummies
(0-7645-5051-9)

Chinese Cooking For
Dummies
(0-7645-5247-3)

Christmas Cooking For
Dummies
(0-7645-5407-7)

Diabetes Cookbook For
Dummies
(0-7645-5230-9)

Grilling For Dummies
(0-7645-5076-4)

Low-Fat Cooking For
Dummies
(0-7645-5035-7)

Slow Cookers For Dummies
(0-7645-5240-6)

TRAVEL

Italy
0-7645-5453-0

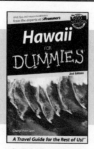

Hawaii
0-7645-5438-7

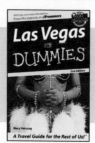

Las Vegas
0-7645-5448-4

Also available:

America's National Parks For
Dummies
(0-7645-6204-5)

Caribbean For Dummies
(0-7645-5445-X)

Cruise Vacations For
Dummies 2003
(0-7645-5459-X)

Europe For Dummies
(0-7645-5456-5)

Ireland For Dummies
(0-7645-6199-5)

France For Dummies
(0-7645-6292-4)

London For Dummies
(0-7645-5416-6)

Mexico's Beach Resorts For
Dummies
(0-7645-6262-2)

Paris For Dummies
(0-7645-5494-8)

RV Vacations For Dummies
(0-7645-5443-3)

Walt Disney World & Orlando
For Dummies
(0-7645-5444-1)

Available wherever books are sold. Go to www.dummies.com or call 1-877-762-2974 to order direct.

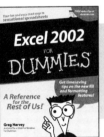

FOR DUMMIES®

Helping you expand your horizons and realize your potential

INTERNET

0-7645-0894-6

0-7645-1659-0

0-7645-1642-6

Also available:

America Online 7.0 For Dummies
(0-7645-1624-8)

Genealogy Online For Dummies
(0-7645-0807-5)

The Internet All-in-One Desk Reference For Dummies
(0-7645-1659-0)

Internet Explorer 6 For Dummies
(0-7645-1344-3)

The Internet For Dummies Quick Reference
(0-7645-1645-0)

Internet Privacy For Dummies
(0-7645-0846-6)

Researching Online For Dummies
(0-7645-0546-7)

Starting an Online Business For Dummies
(0-7645-1655-8)

DIGITAL MEDIA

0-7645-1664-7

0-7645-1675-2

0-7645-0806-7

Also available:

CD and DVD Recording For Dummies
(0-7645-1627-2)

Digital Photography All-in-One Desk Reference For Dummies
(0-7645-1800-3)

Digital Photography For Dummies Quick Reference
(0-7645-0750-8)

Home Recording for Musicians For Dummies
(0-7645-1634-5)

MP3 For Dummies
(0-7645-0858-X)

Paint Shop Pro "X" For Dummies
(0-7645-2440-2)

Photo Retouching & Restoration For Dummies
(0-7645-1662-0)

Scanners For Dummies
(0-7645-0783-4)

GRAPHICS

0-7645-0817-2

0-7645-1651-5

0-7645-0895-4

Also available:

Adobe Acrobat 5 PDF For Dummies
(0-7645-1652-3)

Fireworks 4 For Dummies
(0-7645-0804-0)

Illustrator 10 For Dummies
(0-7645-3636-2)

QuarkXPress 5 For Dummies
(0-7645-0643-9)

Visio 2000 For Dummies
(0-7645-0635-8)

Available wherever books are sold. Go to www.dummies.com or call 1-877-762-2974 to order direct.

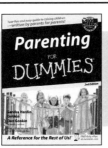
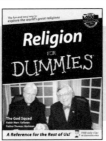